ASSASSINATIONS

ASSASSI

NATIONS

History's Most Shocking Moments of Murder, Betrayal, and Madness

R. G. Grant

With a foreword by James and Sarah Brady

Reader's Digest

The Reader's Digest Association, Inc.
Pleasantville, New York/Montreal

A READER'S DIGEST BOOK

This edition published by The Reader's Digest Association by arrangement with Toucan Books, Ltd.

FOR TOUCAN BOOKS
Design: Bradbury and Williams
Editor: Theresa Bebbington
Managing Editor: Ellen Dupont
Index: Marian Anderson
Picture Researcher: Christine Vincent
Proofreader: Constance Novis

FOR READER'S DIGEST
U.S. Project Editor: Robert L. Mills
Canadian Project Editor: Pamela Johnson
Project Designer: George McKeon
Executive Editor, Trade Publishing: Dolores York
Associate Publisher, Trade Publishing: Christopher T. Reggio
Vice President & Publisher, Trade Publishing: Harold Clarke

Front and back cover photographs:
Left to right, top to bottom: Hulton Getty, 1; John Frost Newspapers, 2, 5; Corbis/Hulton-Deutsch Collection, 3; Corbis, 4, 6; Corbis/Bettmann, 7; Topham/Picturepoint, 8.

Library of Congress Cataloging-in-Publication Data

Grant, R. G.
Assassinations: History's Most Shocking Moments of Murder, Betrayal, and Madness
p. cm.
Includes index.
ISBN 0-7621-0596-8
1. Assassination--Case Studies. I. Title

HV6278.G73 2005
364.152'4--dc22 2005046680

Address any comments about *Assassinations* to:
The Reader's Digest Association, Inc.
Adult Trade Publishing
Reader's Digest Road
Pleasantville, NY 10570-7000

For more Reader's Digest products and information, visit our websites:
www.rd.com (in the United States) www.readersdigest.ca (in Canada) www.readersdigest.com.au (in Australia)

Printed in China

1 3 5 7 9 10 8 6 4 2

"Assassination is the
extreme form of censorship."

GEORGE BERNARD SHAW (1856–1950)

CONTENTS

8 FOREWORD

10 INTRODUCTION

1

12 Moments in history

16 ABRAHAM LINCOLN

22 FRANZ FERDINAND

28 JOHN F. KENNEDY

2

36 Power struggles

40 PHILIP II OF MACEDON

42 JULIUS CAESAR

44 CALIGULA

46 THOMAS BECKET

48 LORD DARNLEY

50 PETER III

52 RASPUTIN

3

56 Revolutionary ferment

60 MARAT

62 ALEXANDER II

64 WILLIAM MCKINLEY

66 EMILIANO ZAPATA

68 MICHAEL COLLINS

70 ERNST RÖHM

72 LEON TROTSKY

76 ALDO MORO

4 78 Fighters for rights
82 MAHATMA GANDHI
86 MEDGAR EVERS
88 MALCOLM X
90 MARTIN LUTHER KING JR.
96 ARCHBISHOP ROMERO

5 98 In the name of God or nation
102 PRINCE ITO
104 COUNT FOLKE BERNADOTTE
106 ROBERT F. KENNEDY
110 LORD MOUNTBATTEN
112 ANWAR AL-SADAT
114 INDIRA GANDHI
116 YITZHAK RABIN

6 118 Secret service
122 REINHARD HEYDRICH
124 PATRICE LUMUMBA
126 NGO DINH DIEM
128 ZORAN DJINDJIC

7 130 Stalkers and lunatics
134 JAMES GARFIELD
136 HUEY LONG
138 OLOF PALME
140 ANNA LINDH

8 142 Assassination or murder?
146 THE ROMANOVS
150 STEPHEN BIKO
152 JOHN LENNON

9 154 Failed assassinations
158 QUEEN VICTORIA
160 VLADIMIR ILYICH LENIN
162 FRANKLIN D. ROOSEVELT
164 ADOLF HITLER
168 HARRY S. TRUMAN
170 CHARLES DE GAULLE
174 FIDEL CASTRO
176 GEORGE WALLACE
178 RONALD REAGAN
180 POPE JOHN PAUL II
182 MARGARET THATCHER

184 OTHER NOTABLE KILLINGS
190 INDEX
192 ACKNOWLEDGMENTS

"...assassinations have altered the presumed course of events, changing personal and public lives forever."

Foreword

In a split second, our lives were changed forever by an assassin's bullet...

When Jim entered his new office—the Office of the Press Secretary—at the White House on Inauguration Day, 1981, he found a gift waiting for him from Jody Powell, President Jimmy Carter's former press secretary. It was a bulletproof vest that had been handed down by previous press secretaries. Attached was a note that read: "It's not the bullets that will get you in this job, it's the gnats and the ants." We laughed—but just over 60 days later it would be a bullet that got Jim.

The Honorable James S. Brady *served as assistant to the president and as White House press secretary during Ronald Reagan's administration. Since that time, Mr. Brady and his wife, Sarah, have worked tirelessly lobbying to reduce gun violence through education, research, and legal advocacy. Mrs. Brady is the chair of the Brady Center to Prevent Violence and a leading spokesperson for the gun control movement.*

On March 30, 1981, John Hinckley Jr. shot President Ronald Reagan, Jim, Secret Service officer Tim McCarthy, and police officer Tom Delahanty, shattering all of our lives.

As with assassins before and after him, Hinckley altered many lives in far greater ways than he could ever have imagined. A stunned country followed our ordeal. But the pain was private: numerous life-threatening operations and years of agonizing rehabilitation. Jim lost his independence; our family lost its spontaneity; and our son, only two at the time, lost the daddy who could carry him to bed and take him for rides in his beloved yellow Jeep.

Several years later we decided we had to do everything in our power to help prevent tragedies such as ours from recurring. In 1993, after seven years of hard work, the U.S. Congress passed the Brady Bill—requiring background checks and a five-day waiting period for the purchase of firearms.

As you'll see throughout the pages of this book, assassinations inevitably have profound effects: Franz Ferdinand's assassination sparked a world war, while Martin Luther King Jr.'s murder mobilized the U.S. civil rights movement. From Julius Caesar to John Lennon, assassinations have altered the presumed course of events, changing personal and public lives forever.

In his eulogy for President John F. Kennedy, U.S. Supreme Court Chief Justice Earl Warren wrote, "It has been said that the only thing we learn from history is that we do not learn." While the chapters in *Assassinations* may at first suggest this to be true, we believe that learning about our darkest hours will lead to enlightenment, and that in turn will lead to action. It is this action that will make our world a safer, better place for us all.

Jim Brady   Sarah Brady

JAMES AND SARAH BRADY

Introduction

The word "assassin" comes from the name of a Shi'ite Muslim sect encountered by Crusader knights fighting in the Holy Land in the eleventh and twelfth centuries. The sect's first Grand Master, Hasan as-Sabah, built the impregnable citadel of Alamut, the "Eagle's Nest," in Iran, and from there sent out his followers on missions to kill leaders of the rival Sunni Muslims or, more rarely, of the Christian intruders. History books used to assert that "assassin" was derived from *hashishiyun,* and that it referred to the killers' use of a hallucinogenic drug to achieve a vision of the paradise that awaited them after death as a reward for their religious murders. Now, more prosaically, it is generally accepted to be simply an Arabic word for fundamentalist.

Assassination is defined as the killing of a prominent person, usually for a political motive and by surprise—although the term is often stretched to cover surprise killings without political motivation and politically motivated executions that lack the element of surprise. It was once primarily a feature of life at the courts of kings and emperors, where power struggles were often resolved by the violent elimination of a ruler or one of the ruler's rivals, with victim and assassin usually personally known to one another.

Approaching modern times, assassination, like other aspects of life, has been increasingly democratized. It has become the hallmark of ideologically motivated groups, inspired by fervent religious hatred, inflamed nationalism, or the revolutionary aspirations of socialism and anarchism. Their victims are more likely to be people the assassins have never met who symbolize hated power and authority.

Politically motivated assassins may be otherwise sane and well-balanced individuals who feel that cold-blooded killing is justified by their sacred cause. The classic American assassin, on the other hand, is an inadequate loner with a desperate thirst for recognition and status, haunted by a sense of meaninglessness that he or she feels can be resolved by a single violent act. The assassin may claim political motivation—as in the case of Leon Czolgosz, the killer of President William McKinley—without really seeming any different from other crazed lone assassins. When individual aspirations are much more important than political life, it is probably inevitable that assassination should become for some a path to self-fulfillment.

Conspiracy theories are popular in the United States—both at the time President Abraham Lincoln was shot and a century later when President John F. Kennedy was slain. Woven from the inevitable contradictions of ballistics evidence and eyewitness testimony, and sometimes inspired by a distrust of those in authority, conspiracy theories have become the necessary accompaniment for any assassination or attempted assassination in the United States. *Assassinations* takes the view that although some mysteries undoubtedly remain unresolved, the best available account of most assassinations is that referred to rather patronizingly by conspiracy theorists as the "official version."

The abiding impression left by a study of assassinations down the ages is inevitably one of sadness approaching despair. However altruistic some assassins may have been, their actions are always brutal and sordid. The person they set out to kill becomes for them a symbol of authority or a figment of their fantasy lives, not a human being of flesh and blood. The list of those struck down by assassins includes some of the finest individuals who ever lived. Assassination must never be condoned.

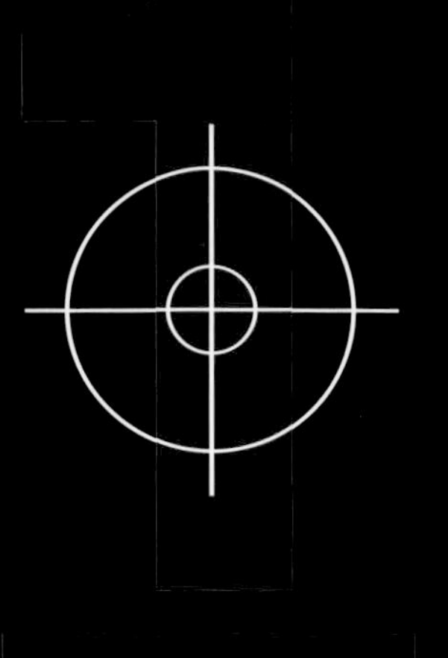

MOMENTS IN HISTORY

ABRAHAM LINCOLN · 1865

FRANZ FERDINAND · 1914

JOHN F. KENNEDY · 1963

Moments in history

The three assassinations covered in this chapter all stand out as watershed moments of history, although in different ways. The Archduke Franz Ferdinand, assassinated in Sarajevo in June 1914, was not a figure of any great stature. In fact, if he had not been assassinated, Franz Ferdinand would be an obscure figure.

The cases of Presidents Abraham Lincoln and John F. Kennedy are different. These were men who were struck down at a high point in their public careers. Although both were controversial in life, with almost as many enemies as admirers, their deaths gripped the emotions of their nation.

Death of an archduke

The importance of Franz Ferdinand's assassination lies entirely in its consequences. His death led directly to World War I, in which eight million soldiers died, as well as uncounted millions of civilians. In turn, World War I led to the Bolshevik Revolution in Russia, the rise of Hitler's Third Reich in Germany, and World War II. Without the shots fired in Sarajevo, there might have been no battle of the Somme, no Blitz, no Holocaust.

The emanicipator

In contrast to the archduke, President Abraham Lincoln's impact on American history was made in his life rather than his death. At the time of his assassination in April 1865, Lincoln had just led the North to victory in the Civil War, which preserved the Union. In his address at Gettysburg, he made a statement of principle as ringing as the Declaration of Independence, claiming Union soldiers had died "that government of the people, by the people, for the people, shall not perish from the earth." Through his rhetoric, he transformed a struggle involving conflicting interests and principles into an idealistic battle for democracy. The Civil War led to the abolition of slavery, which some see as Lincoln's greatest achievement.

Tribute to a president *A statue of Lincoln is housed in the Lincoln Memorial, Washington, D.C. The Gettysburg Address is inscribed on the south wall.*

The death of this honest, steadfast man at his moment of triumph has the true elements of tragedy, but its practical consequences are harder to gauge. Many historians believe that Lincoln would have succeeded in the postwar reconstruction of the South, reconciling southern whites to the loss of slavery while guaranteeing full rights to African Americans. His successors failed on both counts.

A young president

Kennedy's presidency had achieved only a few successful goals at the time of his assassination in Dallas in November 1963. JFK's impact was mostly a matter of image. Inaugurated at the age of 43, he was the youngest president ever elected. Referring to the 1960 election campaign between Kennedy and the Republican candidate, Richard Nixon, the author Norman Mailer stated that Americans chose "between glamor and ugliness." Kennedy's image was also enhanced by his stylish wife, Jacqueline.

To many Americans, Kennedy represented leadership in the dangerous world of the Cold War. Through the crisis of the building of the Berlin Wall in 1961 and the stationing of Soviet missiles in Cuba the following year, he steered a course that was resolute yet safe. His reputation, both as a man and as a president, has suffered since his killing. Yet many people who were alive at the time feel that, with his murder, hope and innocence fled the world.

The actual consequences of his assassination are even harder to assess than in the case of Lincoln. It has often been said that with Kennedy at the helm, America would have avoided the Vietnam War, but this idea should be approached with great caution. Kennedy had ordered a review of the Vietnam situation, but nothing in his past record suggested that he would have been unwilling to seek military solutions. His successor, Lyndon B. Johnson, continued with Kennedy's administration—the same individuals in key positions—and followed Kennedy's policy on Southeast Asia. In the civil rights arena, Johnson was more outspoken than Kennedy in his support for reform, especially for equal voting rights.

The change brought by Kennedy's death and its aftermath was subtler than shifts in government policy. The endlessly debated assassination contributed to a diminishment of American self-confidence and a widespread loss of faith in the basic honesty of government. It can also now be seen as the first in a sequence of killings, including Martin Luther King Jr. (see pp. 90–95) and Robert Kennedy (see pp. 106–9), that swept away the liberal leaders of 1960s America.

Mere coincidence?

Many people have been struck by coincidences between the assassinations of Presidents John F. Kennedy and Abraham Lincoln. Some are trivial but real, for example:

- both men were shot in the head
- both were shot on a Friday
- both were sitting next to their wives when they were shot
- both had vice presidents named Johnson
- both assassins were shot before their cases came to trial

Some are silly games with numbers, for example:

- Lincoln was elected to Congress in 1846 and president in 1860; Kennedy was elected to Congress in 1946 and president in 1960
- Andrew Johnson was born in 1808, Lyndon Johnson in 1908
- The names Lincoln and Kennedy both have seven letters; the full names of their respective assassins each have three words and 15 letters

Some are mindbendingly odd:

- Lincoln was shot in Ford's Theatre; Kennedy was shot in a Ford Lincoln automobile
- Lincoln's assassin ran from a theater to a warehouse, Kennedy's assassin ran from a warehouse to a (movie) theater
- Kennedy had a secretary named Lincoln; Lincoln had an aide named Kennedy

Killed by a rebel

In 1865, at the beginning of April, President Abraham Lincoln had a dream so striking that he recounted it not only to his wife and friends but also to senior politicians. In the dream, he saw a corpse lying on a catafalque in the White House. When he asked a guard whose body it was, the soldier told him it was the president, who had been assassinated.

Ford's Theatre *President Lincoln was shot as he sat with his wife in a box at this theater watching the play* Our American Cousin.

This apparently premonitory dream is perhaps not so remarkable if you think about how aware Lincoln must have been that his life was at mortal risk, considering the upheaval in the country at the time. After four years of Civil War, federal troops under Lincoln were about to finally defeat the Confederacy and force it back into the Union.

Confederate General Robert E. Lee surrendered to Union General Ulysses S. Grant at Appomattox on April 9. Given the circumstances, some desperate act against Lincoln by Confederate agents or sympathizers—either as revenge or to stave off final defeat—was to be expected. In fact, a Confederate plot to blow up the White House was foiled a day after General Lee's surrender.

Keeping up appearances

Although Lincoln knew his life was at risk, he stubbornly refused to abandon his usual public appearances and outings. On Good Friday, April 14, he was scheduled to visit Ford's Theatre, one of Washington's most fashionable places of entertainment. He and his wife were to be joined by General Grant and his wife to see an evening performance of a comedy, *Our American Cousin.*

Grant never saw *Our American Cousin.* He canceled the engagement, pleading that it clashed with other plans. However, the real reason for the cancellation was probably the uncomfortable relationship between his wife and First Lady Mary Todd Lincoln. Clara Harris, a senator's daughter, and her fiancé Major Henry Rathbone took the Grants' place.

Preparing for a killing

When the presidential party took their seats in the state box at the theater, about an hour after the start of the play, John Wilkes Booth, a well-known actor, was drinking whiskey in a bar next door. Since the early days of the Civil War, Booth had been operating undercover

as a Confederate agent. At around 10:00 P.M., Booth walked into Ford's Theatre. He was in familiar territory. No one who recognized him was surprised to see him there.

The final act

Booth made his way to the state box, outside which the president's coachman sat. According to the most reliable account, Booth told the coachman that he had a message for the president then entered the vestibule outside the box where the president's party was seated. Waiting for a crude comic moment to bring a loud laugh from the audience, Booth stepped into the box and fired a ball from his derringer pistol into the back of President Lincoln's head. The ball entered behind the president's left ear and lodged behind his right eye. He slumped forward, a dying man.

An actor to the core, Booth could not commit his crime without a dramatic gesture. Dropping his pistol, he addressed the audience, shouting the Latin phrase *"sic semper tyrannis"* ("thus always with tyrants"). This gave Major Rathbone time to react—he lunged at the assassin. Booth drew a hunting knife and slashed Rathbone's arm.

UNPROTECTED PRESIDENT

Considering the known risks that President Lincoln faced, he was surprisingly poorly protected at the time of the assassination. The president had asked for Major Thomas T. Eckert, a powerfully built officer, to accompany him to Ford's Theatre as a bodyguard, but the request was turned down by Secretary of War Edwin Stanton, who told the president—falsely—that Eckert had another assignment.

The man who did guard the president on the way to the theater was a member of the Washington police force, John F. Parker. He had a taste for strong liquor and a poor record for reliability. Accounts of Parker's role on the fatal evening differ. Some say that he was assigned to guard the presidential box but slipped away for a drink. Others claim that his task was only to escort the president to and from the event. Either way, there was no one guarding the entrance to the box during the performance.

The lack of protection for the president has been taken as evidence of a conspiracy, with Stanton the culprit. However, it would not have been unusual for a person to visit the president in his box at the theater. Consequently, it is unlikely that Booth would have been denied admission, whoever was at the door.

The killer's weapon *This intricately decorated single-shot derringer pistol was used to shoot President Lincoln. It was found on the floor in the state box where the president was shot.*

His final performance *John Wilkes Booth shot President Lincoln in the back of the head. Major Rathbone (far left) was also stabbed by the assassin.*

He then stepped onto the railing of the box and leaped down onto the stage. As he did so, one of the spurs on his boots caught a flag draped over the front of the box. This caused Booth to fall awkwardly, breaking his left shinbone. He hobbled off the stage and out of the theater into an alley, where a horse was waiting to take him away.

"Through the night...his life ebbed away. He was declared dead at 7:22 A.M...."

Lincoln was carried to a boardinghouse opposite the theater. Through the night that followed, his life ebbed away. He was declared dead at 7:22 A.M. on April 15. A national outpouring of grief began. Lincoln's body was carried by a funeral train to Springfield, Illinois, where he was buried.

JOHN WILKES BOOTH

Born in Baltimore in 1839, Lincoln's assassin was a successful actor, but not by the standards set by his own family. His father, Junius Brutus Booth, was one of the most famous actors in America in the first half of the 19th century. His brother Edwin Thomas Booth was at the height of his theatrical career at the time of the Civil War. Although John Wilkes Booth was a hit on the stage in Richmond, Virginia, he may well have been driven by the need for greater renown.

John Wilkes was the only member of his family to support the Confederacy in the Civil War, having become an advocate of slavery during his time in Virginia. As a touring actor, it was easy for his clandestine activities, such as smuggling medical supplies to the Confederate army, to go undetected. It was probably at a meeting with the Confederate Secret Service in Canada in 1864 that he undertook to kidnap President Lincoln, a plot that failed in March 1865. Whether he was then ordered to kill the president or undertook to do so on his own initiative is not known.

An actor's pose *This portrait of Booth was taken around 1860, five years before he killed Lincoln.*

Tracking down the assassins

Booth was tentatively identified as the assassin by several people in the theater. Within hours, Secretary of War Edwin M. Stanton, who took responsibility for coordinating the response to the assassination, ordered Booth's arrest. The authorities knew that Booth had not acted alone because Secretary of State William H. Seward had been stabbed at his Washington home at the same time that the president was assassinated.

Booth had already fled Washington by the time Stanton ordered his arrest. Although in great pain, he rode over the Navy Yard Bridge across the Potomac River and headed into southern Maryland, accompanied by coconspirator David Herold. They stopped at the home of Dr. Samuel Mudd, who set the broken bone, then crossed into Virginia several days later.

By checking on Booth's known friends and associates, the authorities were soon able to make arrests. A boardinghouse kept by Mary Surratt was identified as having been used by the conspirators. While the police were questioning Mrs. Surratt, Lewis Paine arrived at the door. Paine (whose real name was Lewis Thornton Powell) was the man who had knifed Secretary of State Seward.

On April 26, Booth and Herold were tracked by federal troops to a tobacco barn on a farm owned by Richard Garrett, outside Port Royal, Virginia. The troops surrounded the barn and ordered the two men to surrender. Herold gave himself up, however Booth chose to remain in the barn.

The troops set the building on fire. Booth was shot, but there is a debate over who fired the gun. One of the soldiers, Sergeant Boston

SURRAT. BOOTH. HAROLD.

War Department, Washington, April 20, 1865,

$100,000 REWARD!

THE MURDERER

Of our late beloved President, Abraham Lincoln,

IS STILL AT LARGE.

$50,000 REWARD

Will be paid by this Department for his apprehension, in addition to any reward offered by Municipal Authorities or State Executives.

$25,000 REWARD

Will be paid for the apprehension of JOHN H. SURRATT, one of Booth's Accomplices.

$25,000 REWARD

Will be paid for the apprehension of David C. Harold, another of Booth's accomplices.

LIBERAL REWARDS will be paid for any information that shall conduce to the arrest of either of the above-named criminals, or their accomplices.

All persons harboring or secreting the said persons, or either of them, or aiding or assisting their concealment or escape, will be treated as accomplices in the murder of the President and the attempted assassination of the Secretary of State, and shall be subject to trial before a Military Commission and the punishment of DEATH.

Let the stain of innocent blood be removed from the land by the arrest and punishment of the murderers.

All good citizens are exhorted to aid public justice on this occasion. Every man should consider his own conscience charged with this solemn duty, and rest neither night nor day until it be accomplished.

EDWIN M. STANTON, Secretary of War.

DESCRIPTIONS.—BOOTH is Five Feet 7 or 8 inches high, slender build, high forehead, black hair, black eyes, and wears a heavy black moustache.

JOHN H. SURRAT is about 5 feet, 9 inches. Hair rather thin and dark; eyes rather light; no beard. Would weigh 145 or 150 pounds. Complexion rather pale and clear, with color in his cheeks. Wore light clothes of fine quality. Shoulders square; cheek bones rather prominent; chin narrow; ears projecting at the top; forehead rather low and square, but broad. Parts his hair on the right side; neck rather long. His lips are firmly set. A slim man.

DAVID C. HAROLD is five feet six inches high, hair dark, eyes dark, eyebrows rather heavy, full face, nose short, hand short and fleshy, feet small, instep high, round bodied, naturally quick and active, slightly closes his eyes when looking at a person.

NOTICE.—In addition to the above, State and other authorities have offered rewards amounting to almost one hundred thousand dollars, making an aggregate of about TWO HUNDRED THOUSAND DOLLARS.

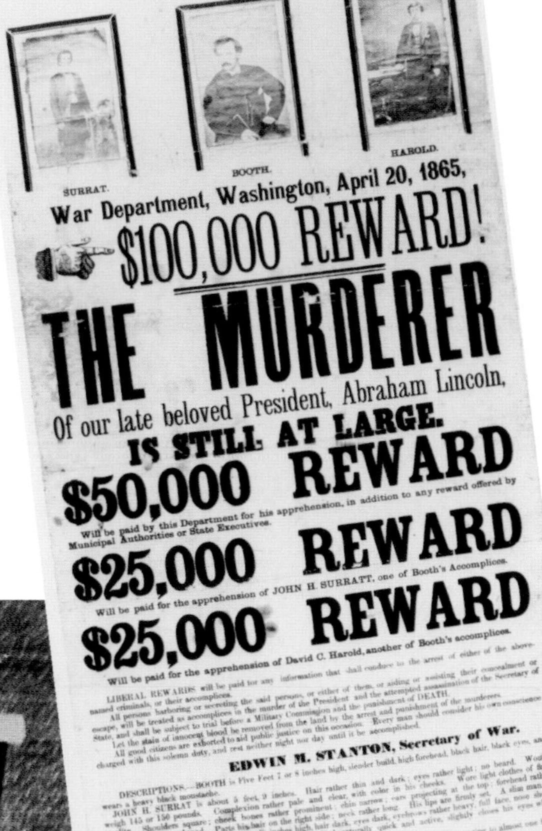

Wanted! *Rewards are offered for the capture of John Wilkes Booth and two of his coconspirators.*

Corbett, may have found an opportunity to shoot the assassin in the back by firing through a crack in the barn. Other versions of the story suggest that Booth turned his gun on himself. Either way, he was dragged from the barn and died two hours later.

The conspirators' fate *Four of the conspirators, including Mrs. Surratt (left), were hanged.*

Summary justice

Four of Booth's coconspirators were sentenced to death by hanging in what was no doubt a

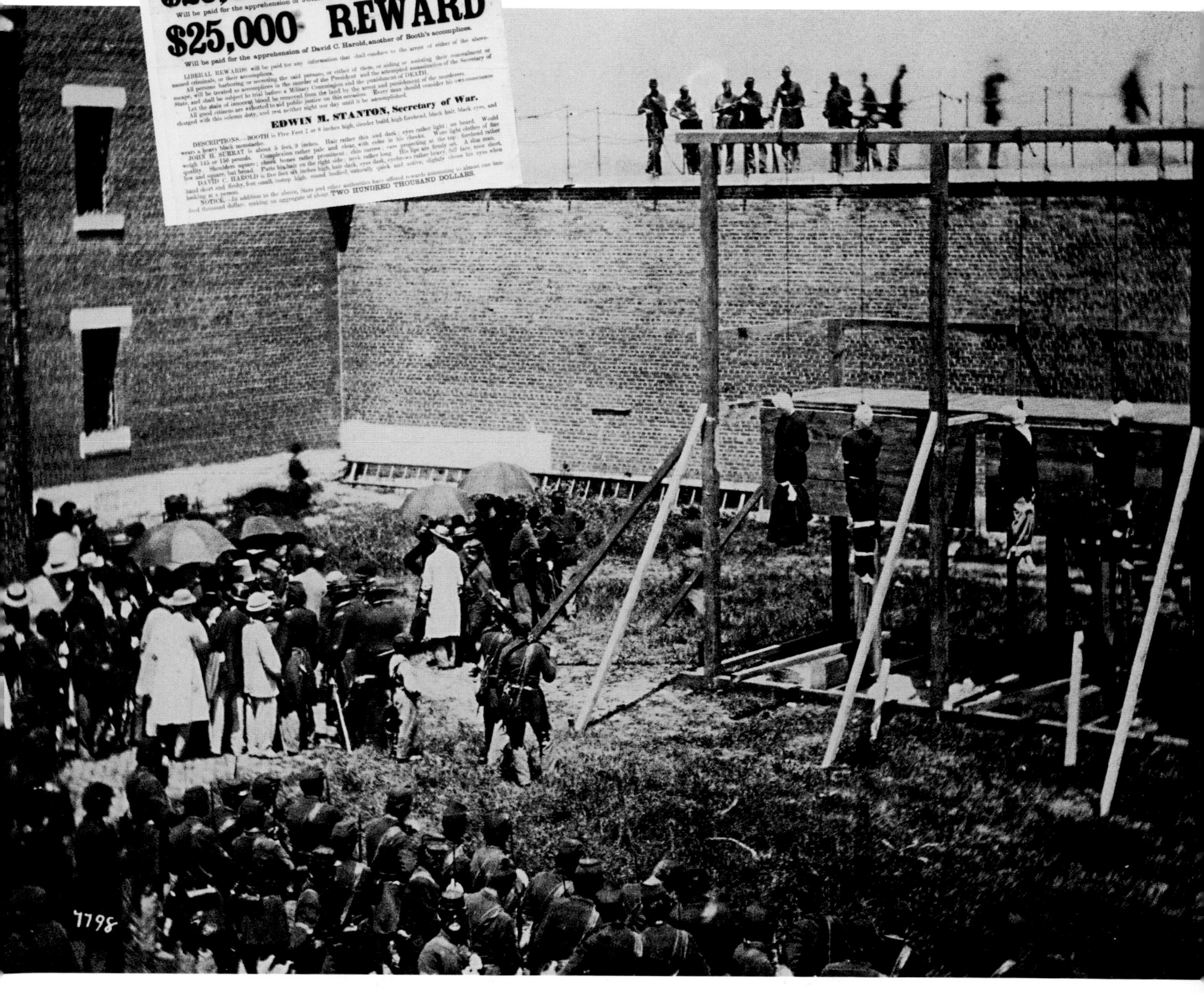

KEY DATES

1809 Born near Hodgenville, Kentucky, on February 12

1830 His family moves to Illinois

1834 Elected to Illinois state legislature

1837 Begins practicing law in Springfield, Illinois

1842 Marries Mary Todd

1846 Elected to House of Representatives

1856 Joins the Republican Party

1860 Elected president, although without a majority of the popular vote

1861 Civil War begins

1863 In January, issues Emancipation Proclamation, declaring slaves free in Confederate states; in November, delivers Gettysburg Address

1864 Reelected president

1865 Assassinated on April 14 while attending a play in Ford's Theatre, Washington

rush to judgment. A nine-man military commission was established to try eight conspirators: Lewis Paine, George Atzerodt, Mary Surratt, David Herold, Dr. Samuel Mudd, and three other associates of Booth—Michael O'Laughlen, Edman Spangler, and Samuel Arnold. Mary Surratt's son John would also have been tried, but he managed to escape abroad. The only other person accused was the Confederate President Jefferson Davis, by then already a prisoner.

"There was never any doubt that Lincoln had been the victim of a conspiracy."

He was charged because the government believed that the Confederate leaders had sent the assassins to do their work.

In the intense emotional atmosphere that followed the assassination, the trial fell short of the best standards of justice. Although the defendants had lawyers, key evidence known to the prosecution was not revealed in court—notably, the existence of Booth's diary, which was found on his body at Garrett's farm. Much of the testimony given by witnesses is now known to have been perjured.

Guilty verdicts were reached on July 6. Paine, Herold, and Atzerodt were sentenced to be hanged. More surprisingly, Mary Surratt, whose supposed connection with the conspiracy depended on highly unreliable testimony, was also sentenced to hang. She was the first woman to be executed in the United States.

The other conspirators were imprisoned, although none served long sentences. O'Laughlen died in prison. All the rest were pardoned in 1869.

A Confederate conspiracy

There was never any doubt that President Lincoln had been the victim of a conspiracy. It could not have been a coincidence that while Booth was shooting the president in the theater, in another part of Washington one of his associates, Lewis Paine, was carrying out a savage knife attack on Secretary of State William H. Seward. Although he caused severe wounds to Seward's face and neck, Paine failed to kill him. Apparently, there was also a plot to assassinate Vice President Andrew Johnson, but the would-be assassin, George Atzerodt, lost his nerve and got drunk instead.

The story of the assassination, as it emerged from the official investigation, was relatively clear-cut. Booth and his accomplices had been working clandestinely for the Confederacy. Originally, they had become involved in a plot to kidnap Lincoln on March 17, 1865; however, the plot was foiled by a sudden change in the president's plans that day. Several members of the group had gone on to carry out the assassination.

Whether the Confederate government had ordered the Lincoln assassination was less clear. The Civil War had generated such bitterness between Confederates and the Union that any action against leaders on either side would have seemed justified. Lincoln himself had authorized a raid on the Confederate capital in Richmond, Virginia, which included among its objectives the killing of Confederate President Davis. It is possible that Davis or his Secretary of State Judah Benjamin might have authorized the assassination of Lincoln.

However, Booth's diary seemed to show that he had masterminded the assassination alone and on short notice, acting on his own initiative. His motives were personal hatred for Lincoln and his antislavery policies, and a desire to avenge the defeated South.

A plotting vice president

Soon after the assassination, rumors began to circulate that there had been an official cover-up, hiding the identity of those really responsible for the killing. In particular, the finger of suspicion pointed at Andrew Johnson, who became president as a result of President Lincoln's death.

Johnson was a controversial figure. He had disgraced himself on Lincoln's inauguration day in 1865 by getting drunk and making a shockingly incoherent speech. He was later nearly impeached—the Senate voted against impeachment by a single vote. Referring to him as "that miserable inebriate," Mrs. Lincoln wrote in a letter to her friend Sally Orne that "As sure as you and I live, Johnson had some hand in all this." Many people agreed with her. In 1866, Johnson's political opponents in Congress set up an Assassination Committee to investigate his possible role in Lincoln's death.

The most embarrassing evidence, from Johnson's point of view, was that about seven hours before the assassination Booth had left a card at the hotel where the vice president was staying. The card carried the message, "Don't wish to disturb you. Are you at home? J. Wilkes Booth." Johnson had almost certainly run into Booth in the past, but no explanation for the note being left on such a momentous day could be found. The Assassination Committee did not discover any further evidence to link Johnson with Lincoln's death, and none has emerged since. However, this did not stop rumors from circulating on the subject for years afterward.

A case of mistaken identity?

Another popular rumor in the aftermath of the assassination was that Booth had not died at Garrett's farm and that the person killed there had been another man. This rumor persisted, although the body was handed over to the Booth family in 1869 and identified by family members, as well as by the family dentist. Subsequently, many people claimed to have seen Booth, who was rumored to be still alive and living under an assumed name.

In 1903, in Enid, Oklahoma, a man known as David E. George stated on his deathbed that he was John Wilkes Booth. An enterprising mortician mummified George's corpse, and it was exhibited for many years in circus sideshows as the body of President Lincoln's assassin.

Speculation about the president's assassination has never ceased—even international bankers and Catholic extremists have been blamed for his death. However, most historians believe that the official story is correct. President Lincoln was one of the last victims of the Civil War.

THE STANTON THEORY

In 1937, Otto Eisenschiml published *Why was Lincoln Murdered?*. Among several theories, he suggested that Secretary of War Edwin Stanton was behind Lincoln's assassination. Stanton had opposed Lincoln's moderate policy for Reconstruction of the South after the Civil War, favoring a more punitive postwar policy. This allegedly motivated him to plot to kill the president. According to Eisenschiml's theory, Stanton left Lincoln unprotected at the theater, allowed Booth to escape, then covered his tracks by arranging for Booth to be killed and tearing out 18 pages of incriminating material from Booth's diary.

Eisenschiml's theory remained popular for decades. However, more recently, historians have refuted it. Stanton's refusal to supply Major Eckert as a bodyguard, for example, was actually part of an attempt to dissuade Lincoln from attending the theater, which Stanton regarded as dangerous. Stanton's failure to telegraph a message ordering guards to apprehend Booth on the road to Maryland is explained by the simple fact that no telegraph facilities existed along that road. The diary from which pages were torn was used by Booth as a notepad—he often tore sheets from it to hand to people.

Catalyst for war

It was 9:50 A.M. on a sunny Sunday morning, June 28, 1914, when Archduke Franz Ferdinand, heir to the throne of the Hapsburg Empire of Austria–Hungary, and his wife, Sophie, stepped off the train that had brought them to Sarajevo, Bosnia.

Franz Ferdinand was visiting Sarajevo in his capacity as inspector general of the Austro–Hungarian Army, and his first duty of the day was to review troops drawn up in glittering ranks on the Philipovic parade ground. In reality, the archduke had not wanted to visit Sarajevo at all. According to his private secretary, Paul Nikitsch, "the whole trip appalled him from the beginning."

The possibility of assassination had made Franz Ferdinand reluctant to undertake the visit to Sarajevo, but Emperor Franz Joseph had persuaded him to go by giving permission for his wife, Sophie, to accompany him. This was significant since Sophie had been banned from accompanying her husband at official functions (see box, opposite).

At the time, members of European royal families were fearful of assassination by anarchists, who used guns and bombs to try to overthrow the establishment. In particular, the Hapsburgs—as rulers of an archaic empire—were seen as symbols of oppression by these revolutionary rebels.

Simmering resentment

The province of Bosnia was a hotbed of agitation against Hapsburg rule. Along with neighboring Herzegovina, it had been administered by Austria–Hungary since 1878 and had been annexed in 1908. Serbia, a rising power in the Balkans, had resented the annexation. Serbian nationalists wanted to create a Greater Serbia, which would include Bosnia within its borders.

Bosnia was populated by a mixture of Serbs, Croats, and Muslims. Hostility toward Austrian rule was widespread among Bosnian Serbs, and there had been many assassination attempts on Austrian officials. Many Serbs considered a visit by one of the Hapsburg

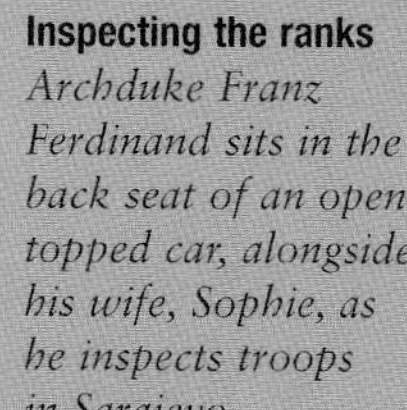

Inspecting the ranks *Archduke Franz Ferdinand sits in the back seat of an open-topped car, alongside his wife, Sophie, as he inspects troops in Sarajevo.*

A happy family *The Archduke Franz Ferdinand and his wife, Sophie, pose with their three children: Sophie, Maximilian, and Ernst.*

FRANZ FERDINAND AND SOPHIE

Archduke Franz Ferdinand was a controversial figure who was usually at odds with Emperor Franz Joseph and much of the rest of the Hapsburg establishment. The archduke had become heir to the throne because of a tragedy that had shocked the Hapsburg monarchy—the suicide of Crown Prince Rupert and his lover, Mary Vetsera, in a hunting lodge at Mayerling, Austria, in 1889. Franz Ferdinand became heir to the throne in 1896, following his father's death.

The emperor and the archduke had a bitter conflict over Franz Ferdinand's choice of a wife. In 1894, at the age of 31, he fell in love with a 26-year-old Czech countess, Sophie Chotek. However, her blood was not considered pure enough to be mixed with that of the Hapsburgs, a proud and punctilious dynasty that traced its origins back at least 800 years. Because Franz Ferdinand refused to give up Sophie and marry a daughter of a European ruling family, the emperor forced him to renounce the throne for his offspring. In a humiliating court ceremony, Franz Ferdinand had to swear not only that his children would have no claim to the Hapsburg inheritance, but also that his wife would neither bear a royal title nor be treated as a royal personage. The date of this oath was June 28, 1900—the trip to Sarajevo was taken exactly 14 years later.

Franz Ferdinand was a devoted husband and adored his children. However, the circumstances of his marriage were a constant humiliation to him. The Hapsburg establishment was ruthless in enforcing rules that excluded Sophie from imperial status. She never set foot in a palace or took part in a ceremonial event—except at Sarajevo in 1914.

VICTIM

Empress Elizabeth

In September 1898, the 61-year-old Empress Elizabeth, wife of Hapsburg Emperor Franz Joseph and aunt of Archduke Franz Ferdinand, was an ailing woman, plagued by anemia, insomnia, and heart trouble. She had been instructed by her doctors to spend time in the healthy Swiss mountain air.

With her lady-in-waiting Countess Sztaray, the empress traveled to Geneva, Switzerland. On September 10, 1898, the two women left to board a lake steamer to carry them to the health resort. As they crossed the deserted quay toward the boat, an Italian anarchist named Luigi Luccheni rushed toward them, slashed at the empress with a metal file, and then ran off.

At first the empress appeared ruffled but unhurt. The countess helped her onto the steamer, supporting her with an arm around the waist. Once on the boat, the empress suddenly complained of a pain in her chest and crumpled to the deck. Doctors found a stab wound under her breast. She died some hours later.

On hearing the news of his wife's death, Emperor Franz Joseph is reported to have hidden his face, crying, "Am I to be spared nothing in this world?"

dynasty to Sarajevo on June 28 as particularly provocative. This date was the anniversary of the Battle of Kosovo in 1389, in which a defeat by the Turks had cost Serbia its independence.

Considering the known risks, the security for Franz Ferdinand's visit to Sarajevo was astonishingly lax. The archduke and his wife were protected by only 120 local police officers, and the route and schedule for the visit had been widely publicized and even pasted onto walls all across the city.

There were six cars in the procession that headed through Sarajevo from the parade ground to City Hall. Franz Ferdinand and Sophie sat in the back of the second car. Their route took them along a wide avenue called Appel Quay. It was here that seven would-be assassins were waiting, mingling with the rest of the crowd.

"I come to Sarajevo to visit and I have bombs thrown at me. It's outrageous!"

A narrow ecape from death

Six members of the assassination group—Gavrilo Princip, Nedjilko Cabrinovic, Trifko Grabez, Danilo Ilic, Vaso Cubrilovic, and Cvijetko Popovic—were Bosnian Serbs. The other member, Muhamed Mehmedbasic, was a Bosnian Muslim, apparently selected to give the operation a more "Bosnian" and less exclusively "Serbian" air. They had four Serbian army pistols and six bombs. They also carried cyanide capsules to swallow in case they were captured.

The seven assassins were spread out along Appel Quay. Mehmedbasic was first in line, but he did nothing as the cars passed—he later claimed that there had been a policeman too close to him. The second conspirator, Cabrinovic, threw a bomb straight at the royal couple as the archduke's car drew level with him. Catching sight of the black object flying toward his wife, Franz Ferdinand thrust out an arm and deflected it away from her onto the hood of the car. From there it dropped onto the ground and exploded. An officer in the car behind was wounded and a dozen onlookers were also injured in the blast.

After throwing the bomb, the assassin swallowed the cyanide capsule, then jumped into the river. However, the water was too shallow to drown him, and the cyanide was not a lethal dose. Cabrinovic was seized and handed over to the police. No other attempts were made as the procession continued to its destination.

Finally, Franz Ferdinand arrived at City Hall. As the mayor began giving a welcome speech, the archduke interrupted, shouting: "What is the use of your speeches? I come to Sarajevo on a visit and I have bombs thrown at me. It's outrageous!" However, Franz Ferdinand calmed down, the mayor finished his speech, and the visit to City Hall proceeded as planned.

A fatal mistake

Despite making remarks about the probability that someone else would take a shot at him, Franz Ferdinand was determined to continue

Bloody uniform *The jacket of the uniform worn by Archduke Franz Ferdinand on the day he was murdered has been preserved, blood stains and all.*

KEY DATES

1863 Born in Austrian provincial town of Graz, December 18

1889 Crown Prince Rupert kills himself, making Franz Ferdinand next in line to succeed Emperor Franz Josef after his father

1894 Meets Countess Sophie Chotek in Prague, Czechoslovakia

1896 Archduke Karl Ludwig, Franz Ferdinand's father, dies; Franz Ferdinand recognized as heir apparent to the Austrian throne

1898 Empress Elizabeth, his aunt, assassinated on September 10

1900 Marries Countess Sophie Chotek and renounces his future children's right to the Austrian throne

1908 Bosnia–Herzegovina is annexed by Austria

1913 Becomes inspector general of the Austro–Hungarian Army

1914 Assassinated along with his wife in Sarajevo by Gavrilo Princip, June 28; Austria–Hungary declares war on Serbia, precipitating World War I, July 29

1918 Assassin Gavrilo Princip dies of tuberculosis in prison; armistice declared, ending World War I, on November 11

with his schedule. First he decided to visit the officer injured in the attack who had been taken to the hospital.

The line of cars headed back down Appel Quay. Then came a moment of confusion. The chauffeur of the leading car stuck to the original route rather than heading for the hospital. General Potoriek, who was responsible for the safety of the archduke and his wife, accompanied the royal couple in the second car. He spotted the error and had the driver of their car brake and put the car into reverse.

Death by chance

By this time, the would-be assassins had given up for the day. As Gavrilo Princip stood talking to an acquaintance on the sidewalk in Franz Joseph Street, the archduke's car stopped almost beside him. Princip looked up to see the archduke less than five feet (1.5 m) away from him.

With remarkable presence of mind, Princip immediately grasped the situation and pulled out his gun. There was no one between the assassin and the royal couple. Princip fired twice, hitting the

Second attempt *A postcard depicts the second assassination attempt of the day. This time Gavrilo Princip's bullets killed Archduke Franz Ferdinand and his wife, Sophie.*

archduke in the neck and Sophie in the abdomen. General Potoriek immediately ordered the chauffeur to drive quickly to the governor's residence.

At first, the archduke seemed to be the more gravely wounded of the couple; however, his wife rapidly turned pale and soon lost consciousness. His mouth full of blood, the archduke mumbled, "Sophie, Sophie, don't die! Stay alive for our children!" She was dead by the time they reached the governor's residence. Franz Ferdinand died about 10 minutes later.

Meanwhile, Princip swallowed his cyanide capsule and attempted to shoot himself, but onlookers stopped him. They grabbed hold of him and would probably have lynched him if the police had not intervened. Princip was led away into custody—the cyanide had succeeded only in making him violently sick.

An idealist on trial

At his trial, Princip stated, "The idea arose in our own minds and we ourselves executed it. We have loved the people. I have nothing to say in my defense." He was only spared the death penalty because he was under the age of 20. Instead, he was jailed in the fortress at Theresienstadt, where he died of tuberculosis a few years later in 1918.

Under arrest *The assassin Gavrilo Princip, second from right, is taken into police custody.*

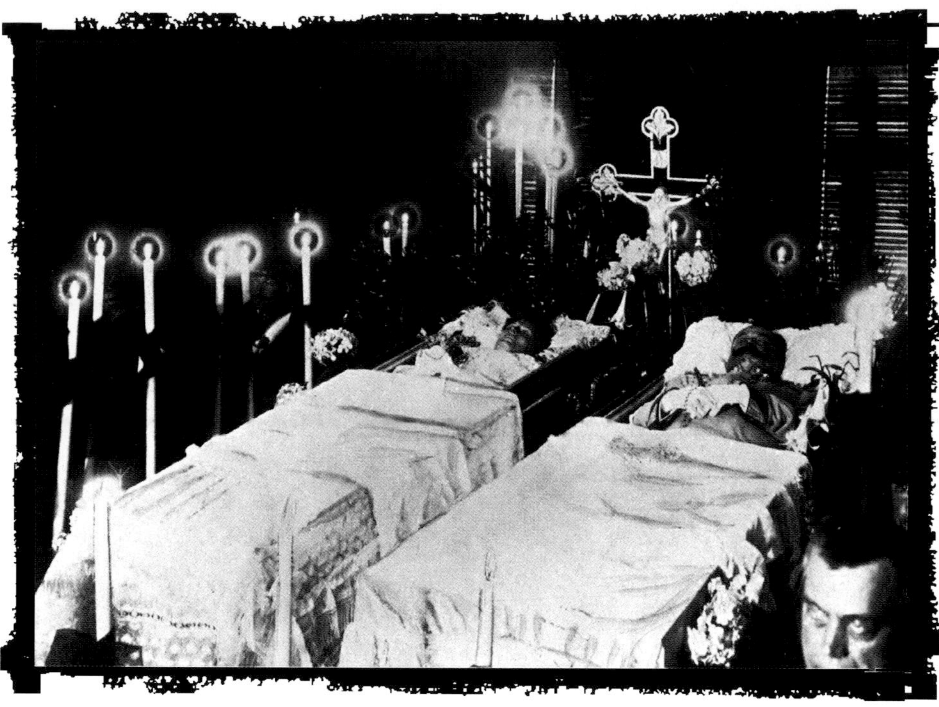

Final rest *Sophie, the duchess of Hohenberg, lies alongside her husband, the Archduke Franz Ferdinand.*

A muted reaction

The news of the death of the archduke and his wife did not bring much mourning to the Hapsburg court. The 84-year-old emperor said, "A higher power has restored that order which I could unfortunately not maintain." Those in charge of court protocol did their utmost to limit the official mourning. There was no state funeral for the slain couple.

Franz Ferdinand had foreseen that Sophie would be denied burial in the Hapsburg family tomb, so he had instructed in his will that he was not to be buried there either. The couple were interred side by side in a private crypt at Artstetten in the valley of the Danube River.

An excuse for war

Whatever their indifference, in public the Austro–Hungarian leaders were indignant about the assassination, using it as an opportunity to take a stance against Serbia. Many powerful figures wanted war, believing that a swift victory over the Serbs would enhance imperial prestige and add territory to the empire. They had the support of Germany, their powerful ally. The German ruler Kaiser Wilhelm wrote on June 30, "The Serbs must be disposed of and that right soon!"

A secret inquiry into the assassination revealed no links between the conspirators and the Serbian government, but on July 23 Austria–Hungary declared Serbia responsible for the outrage. It issued an ultimatum, making 15 demands that the Serbian government had to comply with to avoid war. The Serbs did not reject the ultimatum but accepted every demand except one. However, this one rejection was enough for Austria–Hungary to justify a declaration of war on Serbia on July 29, 1914.

Descent into Armageddon

From this point onward, Europe plunged rapidly into Armageddon. Serbia's ally, Russia, mobilized its troops as a threat to Austria–Hungary. Germany responded by declaring war on Russia on August 1, then on Russia's ally France on August 4—the same day on which Britain declared war on Germany.

During the following four years, the war sparked by the Sarajevo assassination caused the deaths of over eight million combatants and countless civilians—it also brought about the destruction of the Hapsburg Empire.

PLOT AND COUNTERPLOT

It is now known that the assassination of Archduke Franz Ferdinand was organized by the Serbian army's senior intelligence officer, Colonel Dragutin Dimitrijevic, who was also a leading figure in a secret society known as the Black Hand. Whether the Serbian government knew about the plot is not known. After a rigged trial in front of a military tribunal, four Black Hand members, including Dimitrijevic, were sentenced to death in March 1917. There is speculation that these men may have been killed so that they could not tell the truth about Serbian government complicity in the killing.

Alternatively, the Hapsburg establishment may have sent the archduke to Sarajevo in hopes he'd be killed—his assassination would give them an excuse to attack Serbia and rid them of a problematic heir to the throne. Emperor Franz Joseph and others at the Hapsburg court considered Franz Ferdinand irresponsible and unstable and feared that if he became emperor, he would create a new federal "United States of Austria." A Hapsburg plot would explain why the provocative date of June 28 was chosen; why a warning of an assassination attempt given by the Serbians to Austria was ignored; why security was so lax; indeed, why the archduke was even sent to Sarajevo.

Conversely, pigheadedness and complacency remain more obvious explanations. The Hapsburgs viewed Bosnia as a happy province in a contented empire. To change a date out of concern for Serb sentiment or to provide extra police or guards would have meant admitting that all was not well—a step they were not prepared to take.

Camelot ends

On the morning of November 22, 1963, President John F. Kennedy awoke in his suite at the Hotel Texas in Fort Worth. His two-day visit to Texas had been arranged with the following year's presidential election in mind. The Dallas motorcade was an event that just might sway a few voters gratified by a close-up view of the young president and his attractive wife, cruising slowly by in the custom-built Lincoln.

Debarkment *President Kennedy and his wife, Jackie, walk down the ramp of* Air Force One.

A supporting role

Jacqueline Kennedy had not gone with her husband on campaign trips before, but, because of the level of political hostility to him in Texas, and especially in Dallas, her presence was needed. The city was known as a center for extreme right-wing views. One of the city's newspapers had described the Kennedy administration as being composed of "subversives, perverts, and miscellaneous security risks." The day before the presidential visit, handbills with Kennedy's image in full face and profile had been distributed in the city with the words "wanted for treason" printed below. JFK's campaign staff hoped that Jackie's glamour would generate enthusiasm with the Dallas crowd, even with those who were apathetic or even hostile to her husband.

It had been raining that morning, but by the time Kennedy and his entourage landed at Love Field in Dallas, after the short hop from Fort Worth, the sun was shining. It was 11:25 A.M. when the Kennedys stepped down from the aircraft, the president wearing a blue-gray suit and blue tie, and Jackie dressed in a pink suit, pillbox hat, and white gloves.

By motorcade through Dallas

Thirty minutes later the motorcade left the airport. In the presidential Lincoln were driver Bill Greer; alongside him, secret service bodyguard Roy Kellerman; in the middle seats, Texas Governor John B. Connally and his wife, Nellie; and in the back, the Kennedys.

At first, the motorcade progressed through residential suburbs and light industrial zones, where only a scattering of people lined the sidewalks, but toward the center of Dallas, the crowd thickened. By the time the cars reached Main Street, it seemed that fears over the visit had been unfounded. The people of Dallas—many of them office workers on their lunch break—lined the sidewalk in a cheering, waving mass. The president and Jackie smiled and waved back.

The motorcade turned right off Main Street onto Houston at Dealey Plaza, heading for the Dallas Trade Mart, where Kennedy planned to make a lunchtime speech. The crowds were thinner there, but the reception just as warm. Mrs. Connally turned to the president and remarked, "You sure can't say Dallas doesn't love you, Mr. President."

The next turn was a left, onto Elm Street. The turn was sharp, slowing the motorcade to a crawl. The president's limousine was advancing at 11.2 mph (18 kph). Kennedy raised his hand to wave to a young child who was being held up above the crowd.

Crowd pleaser *The president greets people in a crowd in Fort Worth, Texas, on the morning of his assassination.*

KEY DATES

1917 John F. Kennedy born on May 29 in Brookline, Massachusetts

1941 Joins the Navy, becoming commander of a torpedo boat

1946 Elected to Congress as a Democratic Representative from Massachusetts

1952 Elected to the U.S. Senate

1953 Marries Jacqueline Lee Bouvier

1960 Wins the presidential election

1962 Leads the United States through the Cuban Missile Crisis

1963 Assassinated on November 22 in Dallas, Texas

1964 Warren Commission presents official opinion of a lone assassin

1978 House Select Committee states that Lee Harvey Oswald probably did not act alone

The president is shot
Jackie Kennedy scrambles on the back of the car as a Secret Service man climbs aboard in the seconds after President Kennedy was shot.

The sound of a shot rang out through the sunny afternoon.

Fatal shots

Millions later witnessed the shocking events of the next few seconds, thanks to dress manufacturer Abraham Zapruder's 8-mm home-movie camera. Yet exactly what happened in those seconds has never been settled to most people's satisfaction. We know that the president was hit by two shots, one wounding him in the neck and back, the other blowing off the side of his head. We know that Governor Connally was wounded in the back and wrist and fell against his wife, crying, "My God, they're trying to kill us all." We know that Jackie Kennedy crawled over the back of the car, screaming, "They've killed Jack, they've killed my husband." However, exactly how many shots were fired, from what direction, and by whom, have remained matters of passionate controversy ever since.

Rapid reactions

After the shooting, the president's limousine sped off to Parkland Hospital, where he was pronounced dead at 1:00 P.M. Overriding the protests of Parkland doctors, who wanted to do an autopsy right away, Secret Service agents took the body to the presidential

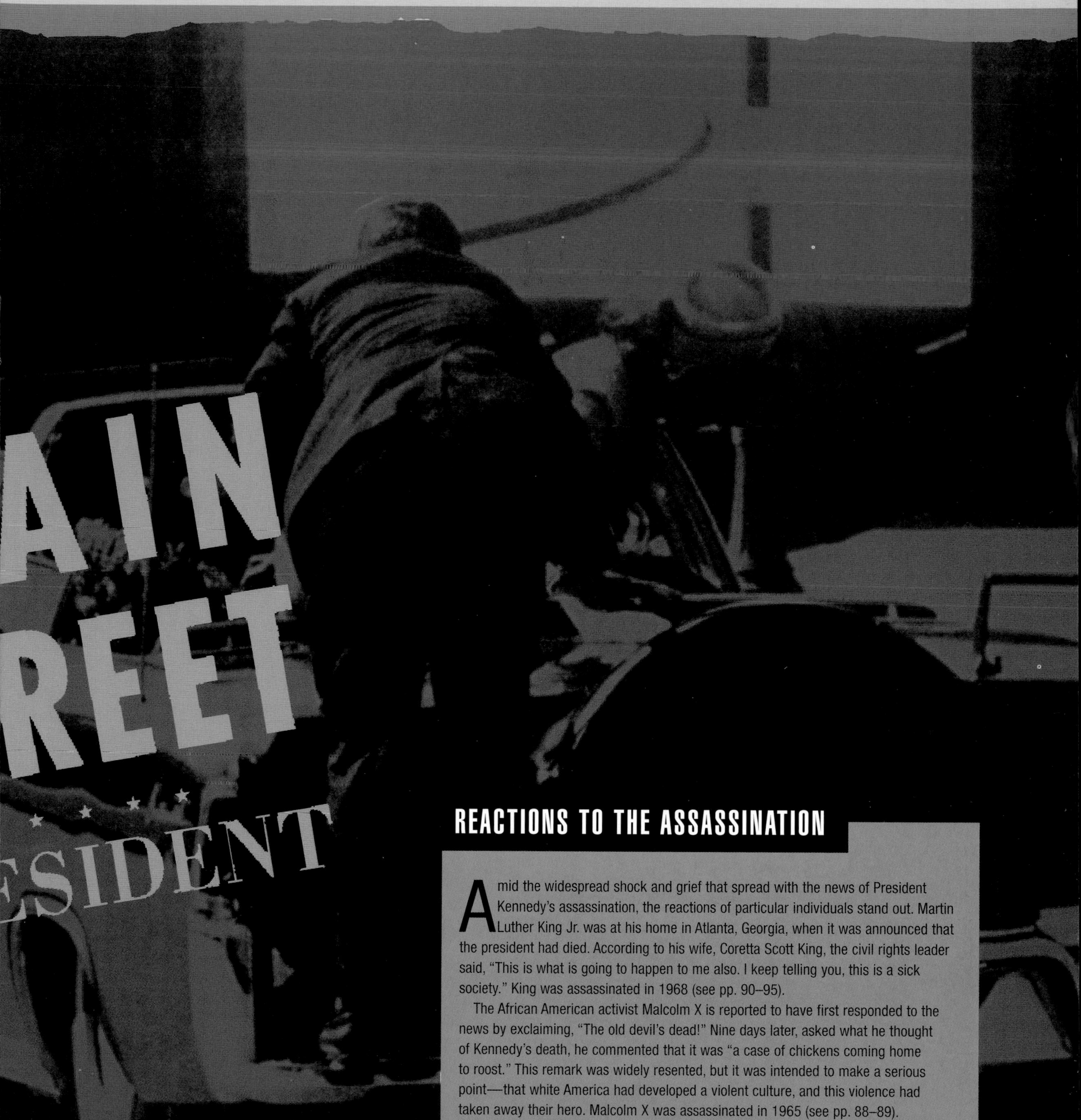

AIN
REET
ESIDENT

REACTIONS TO THE ASSASSINATION

Amid the widespread shock and grief that spread with the news of President Kennedy's assassination, the reactions of particular individuals stand out. Martin Luther King Jr. was at his home in Atlanta, Georgia, when it was announced that the president had died. According to his wife, Coretta Scott King, the civil rights leader said, "This is what is going to happen to me also. I keep telling you, this is a sick society." King was assassinated in 1968 (see pp. 90–95).

The African American activist Malcolm X is reported to have first responded to the news by exclaiming, "The old devil's dead!" Nine days later, asked what he thought of Kennedy's death, he commented that it was "a case of chickens coming home to roost." This remark was widely resented, but it was intended to make a serious point—that white America had developed a violent culture, and this violence had taken away their hero. Malcolm X was assassinated in 1965 (see pp. 88–89).

One man who didn't seem saddened by Kennedy's death was FBI Chief J. Edgar Hoover. It was Hoover who transmitted the news—by telephone—to the president's brother Bobby. He did so without any expression of sympathy or formal condolences.

A new president *Lyndon B. Johnson takes the oath of office aboard* Air Force One, *with the widowed Jackie Kennedy standing to his right. Johnson's wife, Lady Bird, is to his left.*

aircraft, *Air Force One*. On board the plane, Lyndon B. Johnson was sworn in as president, with Jackie Kennedy standing alongside him, still in her bloodstained suit.

As they flew back to Washington, a shock wave of grief swept across the United States. People wept in the streets. There was panic in the high echelons of government.

"...the commission was appointed to restore public confidence."

One early reaction was that President Kennedy's assassination might be the first stage of a nuclear strike against the United States by the Soviet Union. The armed forces were put on alert, and security was tightened around all government buildings.

The hunt for the killer

In Dallas, it appeared that the mystery of the assassination was being rapidly unraveled. Although opinions differed, many of those present when the assassination took place thought that the shots had been fired from the Texas School Book Depository Building. Police sealed the building and checked all of the employees present. They found a bolt-action rifle behind some boxes on the sixth floor. The gun was traced through its serial number to "A. Hidell," a name used by Lee Harvey Oswald.

Meanwhile, 45 minutes after the president had been shot, there was another killing in Dallas. A patrolman, J. D. Tippit, was shot by a pedestrian using a .38 revolver. The hunt for Tippit's killer focused on a cinema, the Texas Theater, where police overpowered a man with a revolver who turned out to be Lee Harvey Oswald. He was first charged with the murder of Tippit, then with killing the president. Oswald denied both murders.

On Sunday, November 24, Oswald was silenced for good. While being transferred to the county jail, he was shot at point-blank range by nightclub owner Jack Ruby in the underground parking lot of Dallas police headquarters. With terrible irony, Oswald, like Kennedy, also died in Parkland Hospital (as did Ruby, of cancer, four years later).

The search for the truth

The question of how and why the president was assassinated had to be answered quickly, and in a way that maintained the stability of the administration and its global policies. In a bid to quell speculation that there had been a conspiracy to kill the president, President Johnson announced the establishment of the Warren Commission. Chaired by the Chief Justice of the Supreme Court, Earl Warren, and packed with senior political figures, the commission was appointed to restore public confidence. After five months of hearings and testimony from over 500 witnesses, the commission reported in September 1964 that Oswald had acted alone in the assassination.

In subsequent years, however, it became apparent that the Warren Commission had failed to uncover all the relevant facts linked to the Kennedy assassination. In truth, for many individuals and groups, the Kennedy assassination threatened to open a can of worms. President Johnson, for example, was convinced that the assassination had been the work of Castro or the Kremlin, but to declare this would have obliged the United States to make a punitive response involving the risk of nuclear war. Hence, little significance was attributed to Oswald's left-wing political views, his defection to the Soviet Union, and his public show of support for Castro.

Both the CIA and the FBI held back information from the Warren Commission. The CIA did not want its plots to assassinate Castro, which also involved the Mafia, to become known. FBI Chief J. Edgar Hoover did not reveal evidence of Mafia bosses' desire

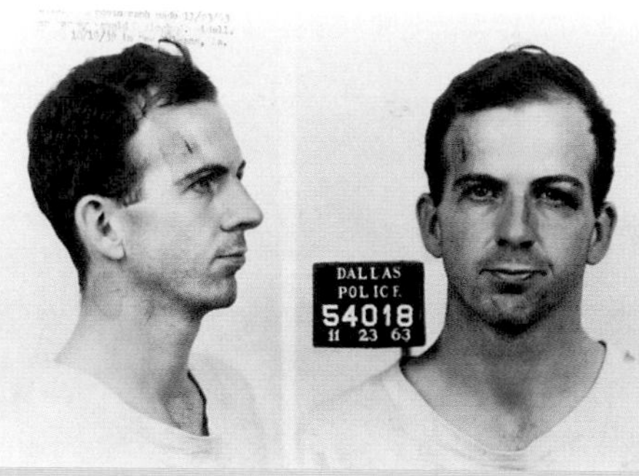

LEE HARVEY OSWALD

Lee Harvey Oswald joined the Marines at the age of 17. He had had an unhappy childhood, but life in the Marines was no better. He then decided to become a Marxist and defect to the Soviet Union in 1959, where he hoped to be welcomed in return for secrets he had acquired as a former Marine.

In 1962, tired of a marginalized life in Moscow, Oswald returned to the United States with a Russian wife, Marina, and two children. In April 1963, Oswald allegedly decided to express his political views and gain fame by shooting the right-wing General Edwin Walker. The assassination attempt failed, but Oswald continued his left-wing political activity, achieving local notoriety by campaigning in New Orleans in behalf of the Fair Play for Cuba Committee.

In 1963, Oswald visited the Soviet and Cuban embassies in Mexico. Defectors from the Soviet KGB denied that he was a Soviet agent, but the Cubans might have persuaded him to kill Kennedy. However, it is more likely that if he had indeed been the killer, that his motives were personal.

A killer assassinated
Lee Harvey Oswald (right), while surrounded by security guards, gasps in pain as Jack Ruby, a Dallas nightclub owner (center), shoots him in the basement of the Dallas police headquarters.

to see Kennedy killed, probably because he wanted to conceal the extent of the FBI's bugging of the Mafia and because questions might have been raised about the FBI's failings in its duty to protect the president.

More surprisingly, Attorney General Robert Kennedy made no serious effort to investigate the killing, and he kept some relevant facts to himself, possibly because he wanted to avoid damaging the reputation of the president and the Kennedy family.

Conspiracy theories abound

Two years after the Warren Commission delivered its report, Mark Lane's *Rush to Judgment* appeared, the first of several books ridiculing the commission's conclusions. In 1978, a U.S. House of Representatives Select Committee on Assassinations examined the killings of John F. Kennedy and Martin Luther King Jr. and issued a report stating that in all probability neither was the work of a lone assassin.

Amid the proliferation of conspiracy theories about the Kennedy assassination, two key allegations stand out. One was that Oswald could not have carried out the assassination on his own because four shots, not three, were fired. Some people present at the time, including Mrs. Connally, heard four shots. According to this theory, a second gunman, positioned on the "grassy knoll" in front and to the right of the presidential car,

Family tragedy *Jackie Kennedy, holding the hands of John Jr. and Caroline, with Bobby Kennedy and other members of the Kennedy clan behind her, leave the White House to attend the funeral of her slain husband.*

THE ASSASSINATION WEAPON

The weapon with which Lee Harvey Oswald allegedly killed the president was a 1938 Mannlicher-Carcano bolt-action rifle, which was bought by mail order for $21.45. The Mannlicher-Carcano is a modified form of the German Mauser, which explains why the weapon was first identified as a Mauser by Dallas police.

The Mannlicher-Carcano rifle was standard issue for Italian infantry in World War II and has been called "the weapon that lost Italy the war." However, fitted with a telescopic sight, the gun could certainly have hit a man at a distance of 100 yards (90 m). The rifle can be fired three times in just over five seconds, fast enough to satisfy the official version of the Kennedy assassination, but it would have taken great skill to keep the weapon trained on its moving target during this rapid fire.

allegedly fired the shot that hit the president's head. The other key allegation was that Dallas nightclub owner Jack Ruby would not have killed Oswald out of anger at the president's death. Ruby's Mafia connections meant that he would have killed only if ordered to do so.

The "second gunman" theory turned into a technical debate about ballistics, exit and entry wounds, sniping technique, and sound analysis. According to the official version, one bullet passed through Kennedy's head and neck, wounded Connally, and was found on a stretcher in the hospital. Analysis of the path taken by the bullet has proved inconclusive.

The only solid evidence of a fourth shot comes from the sound recorded from a police motorcycle radio in Dealey Plaza. When this recording was analyzed, the House Select Committee became convinced that there had been a conspiracy. Yet the policeman involved maintained that he was not in the position relative to the presidential vehicle attributed to him by the sound analysis experts, and reconstruction of the event using computer modeling confirms this.

A lone gunman or a conspiracy to kill?

Conspiracy theories still flourish half a century after Kennedy's death because no solid evidence has emerged to pin the killing on anyone except Oswald. If only three shots were fired, Oswald could have carried out the assassination alone. According to his Marine records, he was a proficient shot, and he had the personality profile of an assassin. Oswald was also given the opportunity to shoot the president when his motorcade passed near the building where he worked. However, Ruby's shooting of Oswald remains the chief block to accepting the "lone assassin" theory. Was he the kind of man who might shoot a person on impulse? Was he in the Mafia? No final conclusion has been reached.

For millions, the burial of John F. Kennedy in Arlington National Cemetery on November 25 provided release. The heartrending sight of the president's two children with the black-veiled Jackie brought many tears. But in high levels of government, a search for closure of another kind was under way. Questions surrounding the assassination of the president had to be answered.

WHO WANTED KENNEDY KILLED?

Kennedy was a man who excited strong emotions in a country divided by political conflict. The most prominent national issue at the time was civil rights. Defenders of white supremacy regarded Kennedy as a supporter of civil rights agitation and a dangerous subversive, a view that was widely held in Dallas.

Cuba was another source of dispute. Kennedy had authorized the invasion of Cuba by Cuban exiles in 1961, but he refused to provide military support when they faced Castro's forces at the Bay of Pigs. In 1962, in the Cuban Missile Crisis, Kennedy forced the Soviet Union to abandon plans to put nuclear missiles in Cuba. Because Kennedy had not used military force, he was denounced by anti-Communists and reviled by Cuban exiles and their CIA contacts for his "betrayal." In 1963, Castro accused U.S. leaders of plotting against him and warned, "They themselves would not be safe."

Kennedy had also earned the hatred of leading figures in organized crime. Sam Giancana, a Chicago Mafia boss, had helped Kennedy come to power in the closely contested 1960 election, only to face an anti-Mafia crackdown led by the president's brother, Attorney General Robert Kennedy. Another embittered Mafia boss was Carlos Marcello of New Orleans, who was deported only months after Kennedy came to office.

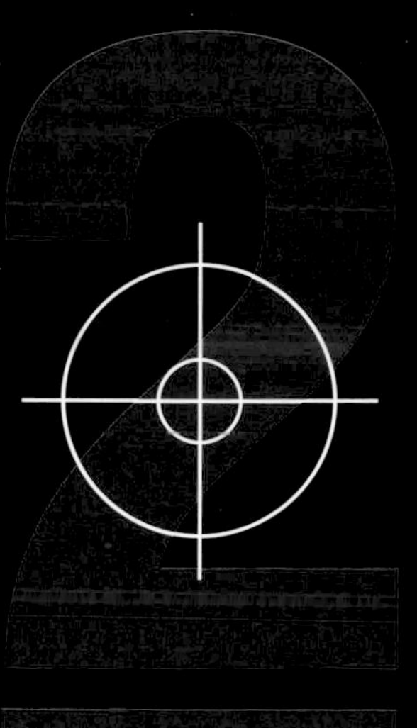

POWER STRUGGLES

PHILIP II OF MACEDON · 336 B.C.
JULIUS CAESAR · 44 B.C.
CALIGULA · A.D. 41
THOMAS BECKET · 1170
LORD DARNLEY · 1567
PETER III · 1762
RASPUTIN · 1916

Power struggles

Before modern times, the courts of the monarchs and emperors who wielded dictatorial power were dangerous places. Disputes occurred over who should inherit the throne and conflicts between rival factions were common. More often than not, these disagreements were resolved by poison, the dagger, or the sword.

The victim might be the incumbent of the all-powerful throne, or someone who threatened the ruler's authority. In either case, the killing was often seen as a personal affair—the assassins and their victims were known to one another, probably close relatives, or friends who had fallen out. At the core of these assassinations was either naked ambition or the clashing interests of powerful individuals or institutions.

Greek and Roman leaders

Probably the two most famous political and military leaders in ancient Greece and ancient Rome were directly or indirectly involved in assassinations. Alexander the Great (356–323 B.C.), whose conquests carried Greek civilization into the heart of Asia, owed his throne to the assassination of his father, Philip of Macedon. He may, in turn, have been assassinated himself.

The Roman general Julius Caesar was stabbed to death in what was intended—by at least some of the large group of assassins—to be a principled defense of the Roman Republic against his growing dictatorship. However, Caesar's murder turned out to be the first step in a power struggle to determine who would succeed to the empire that he had created.

Nothing illustrates better the danger of living as a powerful person than the first century of the Roman Empire (see box, opposite). Of the first eleven Roman emperors, only one is known to have died of natural causes; the others were probably killed. Only two were unquestionably assassinated—the most famous being Caligula.

European court life

Court life in medieval and early modern Europe also offers many examples of the murderous battle for power in action. In England during the 13th century, the "murder in the cathedral," when Archbishop

GIVLIO CESARE

Julius Caesar *The dictatorial ruler of Rome was stabbed to death by senators who were resentful of his power.*

Thomas Becket was killed at Canterbury on the orders of King Henry II, was the result of a conflict between the power of the Church and the State. It was also a personal struggle between two former friends. King Henry II was hot-tempered and therefore a dangerous man to anger, while Becket was stubborn and may even have sought martyrdom.

In Scotland in the 16th century, Mary, the "Queen of Scots," was at the center of a violent power struggle, leading to the assassination of her secretary David Rizzio, followed by the murder of her husband, Lord Darnley. Mary tried to prevent the first assassination but was far from playing a passive role in the murder of her husband.

Russian rule

By the 18th century, assassination had ceased to be a feature of court life in most of Europe, but the Russian court of the czars was different. The ruler Catherine the Great owed her throne to the assassination of her husband, Czar Peter III, in 1762, while Catherine's grandson Alexander I inherited the throne when his father Paul was assassinated in the early 19th century.

Death in Imperial Rome

The first eleven Roman emperors died as follows:

Augustus, died A.D. 14	Possibly poisoned by his wife, Livia
Tiberius, died A.D. 37	Thought to have been poisoned by Caligula
Caligula, died A.D. 41	Assassinated by the Imperial Guard
Claudius, died A.D. 54	Possibly poisoned by his wife, Agrippina
Nero, died A.D. 68	Committed suicide to avoid execution
Galba, died A.D. 68	Killed by enemies in civil war
Otho, died A.D. 69	Committed suicide when defeated in civil war
Vitellius, died A.D. 69	Killed when defeated in civil war
Vespasian, died A.D. 79	Natural death
Titus, died A.D. 81	Possibly poisoned by his successor, Domitian
Domitian, died A.D. 96	Assassinated by a servant

As late as December 1916, the strange, unkempt "holy man" Grigorii Rasputin, who had become an influential and powerful figure at the court of Czar Nicholas II, was assassinated by conspirators close to the throne. Only two months later revolution swept away the czarist regime. Life at the court of Russia's new Communist rulers would be far more dangerous than in ancient Rome or medieval Europe—but that is another story (see pp. 72–75 and pp. 160–61).

POWER SUFFOCATES

In the Turkish Ottoman Empire, which ruled most of the Middle East and parts of Europe from the 15th century to the early 20th century, assassination was a normal part of government. When a new sultan came to the throne, all of his close male relatives were killed to prevent a power struggle from breaking out. The Ottomans' chosen method for these killings was strangulation with a bowstring. The bowstring was looped around the victim's neck and tightened until he suffocated.

Death by bowstring was also favored for executing any important servant of the sultan who failed in a mission. For example, in 1683, Kara Mustafa, the Grand Vizier of Sultan Mehmed IV, commanded an Ottoman army that besieged the Austrian capital, Vienna. The army was driven out by a Christian counterattack and forced to retreat to Belgrade, Serbia. The Grand Vizier was a man of immense power, who carried with him the symbols of political, religious, and military authority: the imperial seal, the key to the Kaaba (the holiest place of Islam), and the holy banner. But once he had suffered such a humiliating defeat, nothing could save him.

At the end of December 1683, two senior officials of the Sultan's court arrived in Belgrade as Kara Mustafa was at midday prayers. They ordered him, in the name of the Sultan, to hand over the seal, key, and banner, and to "entrust his soul to Allah, the ever Merciful." Kara Mustafa completed his prayers and took off his turban. A bowstring was then tightened around his neck until he died.

Fallen warrior

In the spring of 336 B.C., Philip II, the warrior king of Macedonia, was ready to embark on a major campaign that would crown a career already rich with military triumphs. He planned to lead his subservient Greek allies in an invasion of Persian-ruled Asia. Like any ruler of his day, Philip asked the Delphic oracle for a prophecy. The message was less than explicit: "Wreathed is the bull; the end is near, the sacrificer is at hand." Philip was satisfied, sure that he was the sacrificer and the Persians the bull to be sacrificed. However, the prophecy was open to a more ominous interpretation—what if Philip were the bull dressed for sacrifice?

KEY DATES

382 B.C. Born in Pella, Macedonia

359 B.C. Becomes regent after death of Macedonian King Perdiccas

356 B.C. Assumes the throne in place of Perdiccas's infant son, Amyntas

343 B.C. Greek philosopher Aristotle goes to Macedonia as tutor to Philip's son Alexander

338 B.C. Conquers the Greek city-states and declares he will lead them against the Persians

336 B.C. Assassinated in the spring; succeeded by Alexander III (the Great)

Invitation to a wedding

The following summer was a time of public festivity at the Macedonian court. King Philip invited the rulers of the Greek states to celebrate the wedding of one of his daughters to the Greek king of Epirus. The Greeks viewed Macedonia as an uncivilized place—a barbaric northern kingdom that dominated them through brute military power. Philip intended to surprise them with a range of civilized entertainments, such as banquets, poetic recitations, and athletic games.

There was much to be said for the Greeks' view of Macedonia. Philip himself was a fighting man, bearded, scarred, and one-eyed after 20 years of campaigning. His court was riven by jealousy and rivalries.

Warring wives

At the age of 46, Philip had seven wives. Until recently, Olympias had been the favorite among them—and she was the mother of his most able son, 20-year-old Alexander. However, Philip's seventh wife, Eurydice, had supplanted Olympias as the king's favorite. After Eurydice gave birth to a son for the king, Olympias fled the court and Alexander's chances of inheriting the throne seemed to be at risk.

Great leader *This profile of Philip II of Macedon shows him when he was in his prime.*

Ambitious son *Philip's son Alexander wears the dress of a warrior as he rides into battle.*

ALEXANDER THE GREAT

Whether or not Philip's son Alexander had any part in his father's assassination, he certainly took full advantage of the opportunity. After crushing his opponents in the Macedonian court, he began a campaign of conquest that took him as far as northern India, where he destroyed the Achaemenid Persian Empire.

Alexander was 33 years old when he died in Babylon, in what is now Iraq. According to some accounts, he was assassinated by having poison slipped into his wine during a banquet. This was allegedly the work of some of his generals, who were disgruntled at Alexander's adoption of Persian customs and wanted to end the relentless campaign that carried them farther from home. Today, most historians believe that Alexander died of natural causes, probably of a fever.

A spectacular entrance

Foreign leaders gathered for the festivities; wine flowed freely; the whole event went smoothly. The following day was to be given over to the games. To start the proceedings, at dawn images of the gods were carried in stately procession into the arena, which was packed with foreign visitors and Macedonian nobility. Among the images was one of the king himself—a bid for superhuman status that spoke volumes for Philip's pride and ambition.

Philip planned to enter the theater at the rear of the procession. He had dismissed his bodyguards, whose armed presence around him would have marred the impression of civilized authority he wanted to project. Instead, wrapped in a white cloak, he advanced, flanked only by his son Alexander and his new son-in-law, the king of Epirus.

Philip never made it into the theater. Pausanias, one of his bodyguards, stood waiting at the entrance. As Philip drew near, Pausanias leaped forward, caught hold of the king with one hand, and with the other drove a dagger up under his ribs. The king fell dying while the assassin ran off, quickly pursued. Pausanias had a horse waiting by the city gates and might have escaped had he reached it. However, he tripped on a vine and was overpowered. Dragged back to the arena, he was clamped by the neck, arms, and legs, and was left to die a lingering death by starvation.

"...what if **Philip** were the **bull** dressed for **sacrifice?**"

Scandal at court

According to an account written by the philosopher Aristotle, who was tutor to Philip's son Alexander at the time, the roots of the killing lay in a homosexual relationship. Allegedly, Pausanias was one of Philip's ex-lovers—the king satisfied his desires with both sexes. Already upset over losing the king's attentions, Pausanias was further embittered when Philip refused to take action against one of Eurydice's relatives, who had sexually abused Pausanias.

This official version satisfied few of Philip's contemporaries. Rumor had it that the assassination had been plotted by Olympias, desperate to give her son Alexander a chance to seize the Macedonian throne while Eurydice's son was still an infant. It was whispered that on the night of the assassination, Olympias returned to the court and placed a golden crown on Pausanias's head as he hung in public agony.

The suggestion that he might have been complicit in his father's death cast an early shadow over the career of the young man who would later be known as Alexander the Great.

Et tu, Brute?

On the night before March 15, 44 B.C., Julius Caesar, the 56-year-old dictator of the Roman Republic, did not sleep well. The following morning he was due to attend a meeting of the Roman Senate, but when he woke his wife pleaded with him not to go—she had seen him lying dead in a dream. Being susceptible to omens, Caesar hesitated.

Elsewhere in Rome that night, prominent Roman citizens were planning to kill Caesar at the Senate meeting hall. The leaders, Cassius Longinus and Marcus Brutus, had induced up to 60 senators to join their conspiracy.

Dictator for life

Caesar had made himself powerful through his military successes as a general. He had used his legions not only to expand the area under Roman rule but also to dominate Rome itself, defying the authority of the Senate and crushing Pompey, his fellow Roman general, in a brief civil war. In February of 44 B.C., Caesar had declared himself "dictator for life." He had his head displayed on coins—an unprecedented step in Rome—and adopted the title of "imperator." Roman senators, the city's aristocracy, resented Caesar's power.

Although Cassius and Brutus had both sided with Pompey in the civil war, Caesar kept them in office after Pompey's defeat. Cassius continued to feel slighted. Brutus had a more principled opposition to Caesar; he wanted to defend the republic that Caesar seemed about to destroy. He also had private reasons for resenting Caesar. It was rumored that he might be Caesar's illegitimate son.

KEY DATES

***c.* 100 B.C.** Born in July

60 B.C. Establishes a ruling triumvirate with Pompey and Crassus

58 B.C. Begins series of campaigns, the Gallic Wars

55 B.C. Invades Britain

52 B.C. Defeats revolt of the Gauls

50 B.C. Refuses the Senate order to disband his army

49 B.C. Starts a Roman civil war

48 B.C. Defeats rival General Pompey in civil war

47 B.C. Has a son, Caesarion, by Queen Cleopatra.

46 B.C. Institutes the Julian calendar, with a 365-day year and an extra day every fourth year

44 B.C. Made dictator for life; killed March 15

The Ides of March

The assassination plot was precipitated by the announcement of Caesar's departure from Rome, set for March 18. On the morning of March 15, Brutus left home with a dagger concealed beneath his toga. A crowd of other conspirators met at Cassius's house, using the pretext that Cassius's son was to assume the toga of manhood, a coming-of-age event to be celebrated. They proceeded to the hall carrying daggers in their stylus cases (the stylus was used for writing on clay tablets).

The senate was meeting in a hall where a statue of the defeated General Pompey had been erected. When Caesar failed to appear, Decimus Brutus, one of Caesar's most trusted officers, was sent to Caesar's home. Caesar told him that he was not feeling well, but Decimus persuaded him that the Senate would be offended if he did not attend the meeting.

According to some accounts, as he was carried through Rome in his litter, Caesar was approached by a soothsayer, who warned, "Beware the Ides of March." Near the meeting hall, Caesar was given a more precise warning. A Greek teacher, Artemidorus of Cnidus, gave him a note with details of the plot. Caesar was holding it, unread, as he entered the hall.

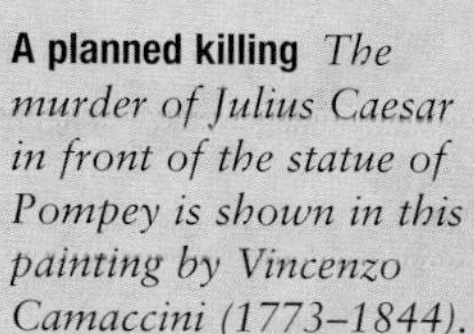

A planned killing *The murder of Julius Caesar in front of the statue of Pompey is shown in this painting by Vincenzo Camaccini (1773–1844).*

Fatally wounded

Mark Antony, one of Caesar's most loyal supporters, was kept from going into the hall by one of the conspirators, who began a conversation with him. Inside the hall, as soon as Caesar sat on a seat under Pompey's statue, Tillius Cimber took hold of Caesar's toga and pulled it off his shoulders. Another assassin, Casca, struck the first blow, stabbing Caesar's neck. Caesar struck back, ramming his sharp stylus into Casca's arm. According to the historian Plutarch, the conspirators then "all bared their daggers and hemmed Caesar in on every side. Whichever way he turned, he met the blows of daggers...for it had been agreed that they must all take part in this sacrifice and all flesh themselves with his blood."

Still Caesar did not succumb. Then Brutus stepped forward to deliver his blow. According to Latin author Suetonius, Caesar cried out in Greek: "You, too, my child?" (not the Latin *"Et tu, Brute?"* that appears in Shakespeare). He then slumped to the ground below the statue and died.

The hall quickly emptied as senators fled the scene. A weeping crowd gathered in the streets to see Caesar's body carried to his house on a litter. Instead of hailing the assassins as liberators, the Roman people were hostile. Mark Antony took control of Rome. In two years, Brutus and Cassius were dead.

VICTIM

Pompey

Roman General Pompey (Gnaeus Pompeius Magnus) was Caesar's greatest rival. After the defeat of his army by Caesar's forces in Greece in 48 B.C., Pompey became a fugitive. Pompey headed by sea to Egypt, his best hope for a safe refuge. Anchoring off shore, he sent a messenger to King Ptolemy XII, seeking protection. Ptolemy's advisers wanted to avoid Caesar's wrath, but they feared Pompey's anger if his request was refused. They decided their best course was to kill Pompey. Caesar would then be appeased and Pompey need no longer be feared.

An Egyptian known as Achillas and two Roman soldiers who had once served under Pompey were sent in a small boat to bring Pompey to shore. As they approached the shore, the three men stabbed Pompey in the back. Once ashore, they cut off his head as evidence of their act.

Death of a tyrant

On January 24, A.D. 41, the Roman emperor Gaius, known by his childhood nickname Caligula ("little boots"), was enjoying himself in style at the Palatine Games held in a temporary theater next to his palace. The 28-year-old emperor may have inspired fear and disgust in all who knew him, but he had never stinted on popular entertainments.

Caligula arrived at the theater in good spirits, an important point for those around him, because the emperor had been known to kill people on a whim when in a bad mood. Caligula was not a man to blanch at a little blood—or even a lot of it. In his four years as emperor, he had installed a reign of terror.

"Caligula was not a man to blanch at a little blood—or even a lot of it."

He began the day with the sacrifice of a flamingo—the killing of exotic birds was a trademark of his peculiar religious practices, which centered on the worship of himself. As the bird was killed, blood spurted over the emperor and some of the spectators. This set the tone for the day's entertainment. Next, there was a performance of *Laureolus*, a melodrama in which the leading actor coughs blood over the stage.

His victims unite

Cassius Chaerea, who held the rank of tribune in the Praetorian Guard—an elite military force—had to see the emperor each morning to be told the password for the day. Because Chaerea had a high-pitched voice, Caligula referred to him as "girl" and chose passwords with lewd connotations. In response to this humiliating behavior, Chaerea plotted the emperor's murder, together with another tribune of the Guard, Cornelius Sabinus, and with various senators who had also been victims of Caligula's cruel pranks.

Chaerea and his coconspirators planned to lie in wait for the emperor when he left the theater for lunch. They would attack as he walked through narrow passageways, where they could strike without interference from Caligula's German bodyguards. The assassins were frustrated as the emperor first delayed leaving the theater, then stopped backstage to talk to some young Asian actors who were preparing for an afternoon performance. At last the conspirators found the right moment.

The brutal attack

Chaerea struck first, slicing between Caligula's neck and shoulder with his sword. Sabinus gave a blow that toppled the emperor to his knees, then came a savage flurry of blows as the group of conspirators attacked, stabbing Caligula until he was a heap on the floor.

At first only two litter bearers attempted to defend the emperor. Then the German guards arrived, in time to send a few heads

KEY DATES

A.D. 12 Born August 31 in Anzio, Italy

A.D. 31 Summoned to join the Emperor Tiberius at his villa on Capri

A.D. 37 Becomes emperor on the death of Tiberius

A.D. 38 His favorite sister Drusilla dies

A.D. 40 Attempts to invade Britain

A.D. 41 Assassinated on January 24

spinning with savage blows of their swords. The Praetorian Guard, running amok in the imperial palace, found Caligula's wife, Caesonia, with her small daughter Drusilla. The mother was cut down with a single blow of a sword. One of the soldiers swung the child against a wall, crushing her skull.

Rumors spread around Rome that Caligula was not really dead—that the assassination was one of his jokes, designed to find out who would rejoice, after which he would take his vengeance. Slowly a sense of relief took the place of panic. Caligula had, in the words of Roman historian Dio Cassius, "learned by actual experience that he was not a god."

THE WARPED EMPEROR

Ancient Roman authors elaborated upon the vices and follies of Caligula's rule. He used his power to indulge both his sexual fantasies and a dark sense of humor. The list of those the bisexual emperor enjoyed sexually was long. He committed incest with all of his sisters and had his favorite sister Drusilla elevated to the status of a goddess. Caligula also wanted to be worshipped as a god and planned to have a statue of himself erected in the Temple at Jerusalem, causing the Jews to threaten a revolt.

Caligula invited his favorite horse, Incitatus, to dinner and was intending to appoint the horse to the office of consul. The emperor's disregard for human life was legendary. He once sparred with a gladiator armed with a wooden sword, then stabbed him to death with a real dagger. Many modern historians have thrown doubt on stories of Caligula's excesses, yet no firm evidence has come to light disproving the writings of those who lived at that time.

Blood sport *Gladiators fought one another to the death for the amusement of the Roman public—and the emperor.*

Unholy murder

In 1155, England's King Henry II appointed Thomas Becket, one of his closest friends, as chancellor of the kingdom. The two men had been companions in hunting, drinking, and high-spirited games. As chancellor, Becket enjoyed the king's fullest trust, governing England while Henry spent much of his time expanding his domains in France.

The Archbishopric of Canterbury, the highest ecclesiastical post in England, became vacant in 1162. Henry insisted that Becket take the job—it was within the king's power to place whomever he wanted in charge. However, Becket was reluctant to take the position, warning the king that "our friendship will turn to hate." Still the king insisted. He wanted a friend as archbishop because he intended to shift the balance of power between Church and State, encroaching on previous church prerogatives.

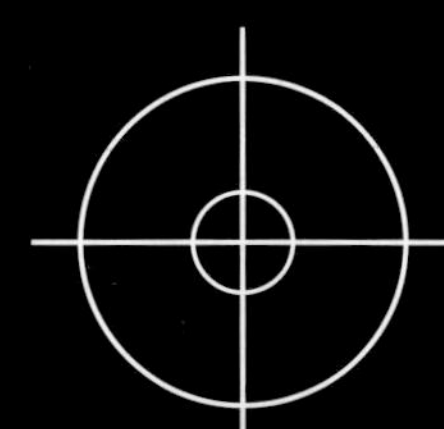

A reformed man

Henry had not anticipated that Becket would take his new role seriously, but he did. Living with the Canterbury monks, the pleasure-loving chancellor was transformed into an ascetic churchman who wore a hair shirt under his fine robes, slept on the floor, and lived off bread and water. Becket also stood up for the interests of the Church against Henry's reforms. Making Henry angry was a dangerous thing to do—he was noted for his violent outbursts of temper. After a confrontation with the king in 1164, Becket fled abroad to escape royal vengeance.

Pope Alexander III reinstated Becket as Archbishop of Canterbury and threatened to excommunicate Henry. Becket returned to Canterbury in 1170 after long negotiations.

Relations between the two men did not improve, and Becket soon asked the pope to excommunicate the Archbishop of York, who was more amenable to the king's wishes. On hearing news of this, Henry flew into a rage and shouted, "Will no one rid me of this troublesome priest?" Henry afterward claimed that this was no more than a rhetorical question shouted in the heat of the moment. However, four of his knights took it seriously.

An eyewitness account

Reginald FitzUrse, William de Tracey, Hugh de Morville, and Richard le Breton set off for Canterbury. They arrived at the archbishop's palace on December 29, 1170. The events of that day are known through an

KEY DATES

1118 Born in London, son of a wealthy merchant

1155 Appointed chancellor, Henry II's top government official

1162 Appointed Archbishop of Canterbury

1164 Flees to France after conflict with the king

1170 Returns to Canterbury; assassinated December 29

1173 Canonized as a saint

1174 King Henry does public penance at his tomb

MURDER'S AFTERMATH

The assassination of Archbishop Thomas Becket was a political disaster for Henry II. Faced with widespread condemnation, he was forced to beg forgiveness of the pope and to perform public penance. Thus, in 1174, the proud ruler of England walked barefoot to the place of the assassination and knelt there in prayer while Canterbury monks whipped his bare back.

The four knights responsible for the killing took refuge in the remote northern county of Yorkshire. They were not punished but were eventually compelled to do penance in the form of a journey to distant Jerusalem. None of the assassins survived the pilgrimage to the holy city.

account given by Becket's crossbearer, Edward Gryme. The knights demanded to see Becket. They accused him of having "broken the peace" and ordered him to leave England. Becket refused, saying, "I am not moved by threats, nor are your swords more ready to strike than is my soul for martyrdom."

The knights left, only to return as daylight faded. Armed with swords and axes, they broke in by force. The archbishop's servants and clerks scattered—as Gryme wrote, "like sheep before the wolf"—but Becket made no move to save himself. Some monks forcibly bundled him from his palace, propelling him through the cloisters to the cathedral.

A killing in the cathedral

Vespers were being sung in the dimly lit cathedral as the archbishop entered, closely pursued by the knights with swords drawn. One of them cried, "Where is Thomas Becket, traitor to the king and realm?" Becket stepped out from the shadows and said firmly, "I am here, no traitor to the king, but a priest."

The knights tried to drag Becket out of the church to reduce the sacrilegious nature of their act, but he clung to a pillar. Addressing FitzUrse, he said, "Touch me not, Reginald. You owe me fealty and subjection." FitzUrse replied, "No faith nor fealty do I owe you against my fealty to my lord the king." With that, he swung his sword and cut into Becket's head, at the same time almost severing Gryme's arm as he tried to shelter the archbishop. Two more blows brought Becket to the ground. As he lay on the floor, a final sword stroke sliced off the crown of his head. Gryme wrote, "The blood white with the brain and the brain red with blood dyed the surface of the virgin mother church with the life and death of the confessor and the martyr."

The hallowing of Becket as a martyr began immediately, as people in the church took pieces of his bloody clothing as holy relics. He was canonized three years later and his tomb in Canterbury Cathedral has become England's most famous place of pilgrimage.

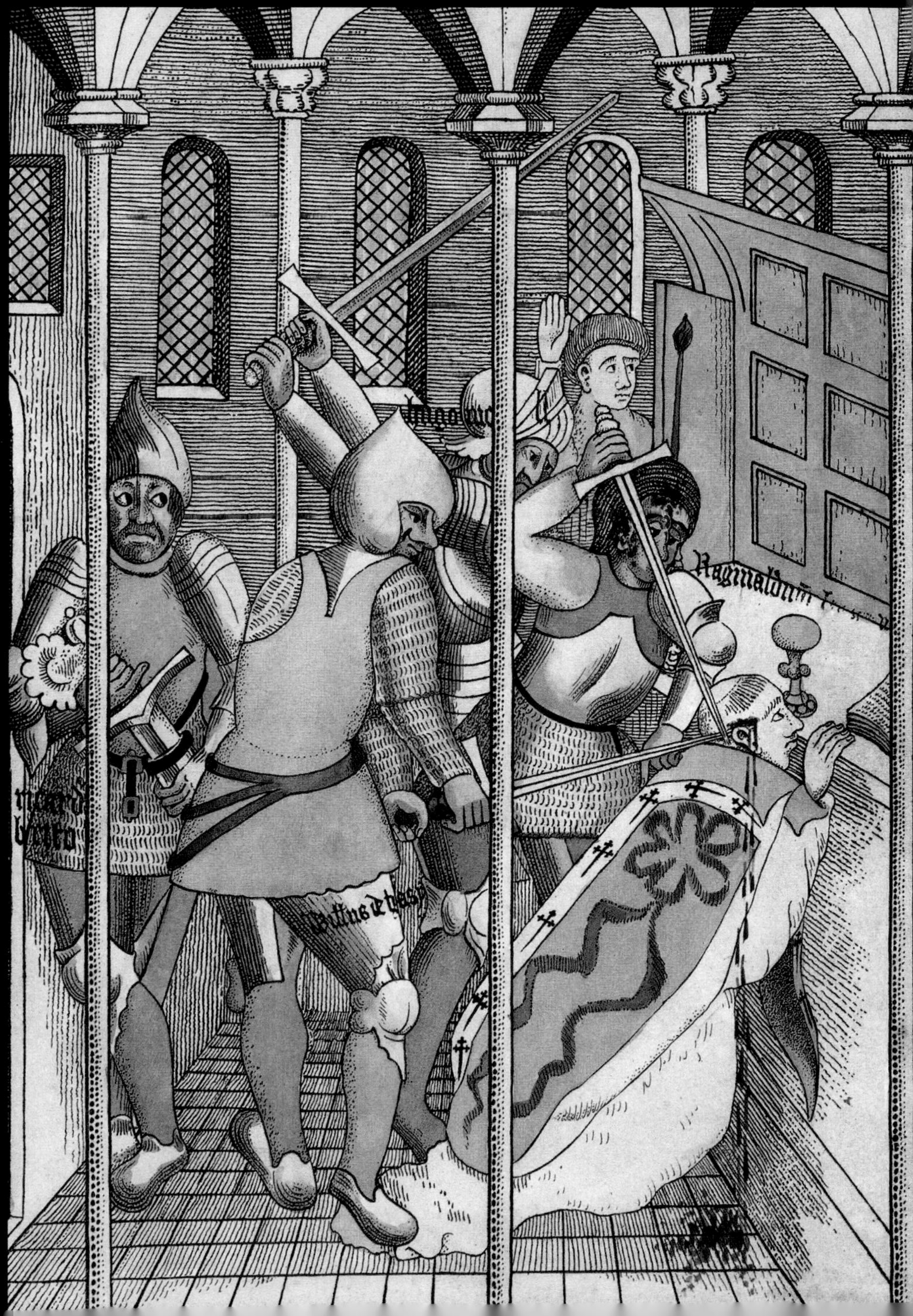

Struck down *Blows rain down on the kneeling archbishop in this 19th-century print depicting the murder, based on a fresco in Stratford-upon-Avon, England.*

Royal murder

On the evening of February 9, 1567, Mary Stuart, queen of Scotland, left the house in Edinburgh, where her husband of two years, Lord Darnley, lay ill, to attend a masque at Holyrood Palace. She had not yet returned when, at 2:00 A.M., a trail of gunpowder was lit in the basement of the house. An explosion demolished the building, but Darnley was not inside it. His body, along with that of one of his servants, was found in the garden. Realizing what was happening, the two had climbed down a rope from a window, only to be killed by the force of the explosion or, according to other accounts, had been strangled and stabbed as they tried to escape in their nightclothes.

"Cursed be this poxy fellow that troubleth me this much!"

The roots of Darnley's assassination lay hidden in political and romantic intrigue. When Mary arrived from France to assume the Scottish throne in 1561, Scotland was divided by religious conflict. Mary was a Catholic, but Scotland was mainly Protestant. Protestant preachers railed against her from their pulpits, and there were riots when she attended a Catholic mass.

Mary formed a close friendship with James Hepburn, the earl of Bothwell. However, she could not stop the Protestant lords, led by her illegitimate half-brother, the Earl of Moray, from exiling Bothwell in 1562.

Marriage of convenience

Mary needed supporters to give her power in the Scottish court. Marriage provided the answer. In 1565, Mary married her cousin Henry Stuart, Lord Darnley—the son of the earl of Lennox and an English Catholic mother. After the wedding, Bothwell returned to Scotland and, fighting alongside Lennox, defeated Moray and other Protestant lords who had opposed the marriage.

Soon Mary became pregnant. However, her marriage was not happy.

The scene of the crime
Holyrood Palace is where Darnley married Mary, and where he later had Rizzio murdered.

Instead of ruling as a king, Darnley was marginalized, with government in the hands of Bothwell and a largely Catholic council. He saw little of the queen, who preferred to spend her time with Bothwell and her Italian secretary, David Rizzio.

Jealousy—a motive for murder

In Darnley's discontent, the Protestant lords saw their opportunity. They persuaded him to help them kill Rizzio (see box, below). After the murder, Mary persuaded Darnley that the Protestant lords had been using him—as indeed they had. By the time Mary gave birth to the future King James I of England in June, she and Darnley had joined up with Bothwell again and put Rizzio's murderers to flight.

Bothwell then allowed Moray and the exiled Protestant lords back from exile and invited all the factions to a conference at Craigmillar Castle. The nobles agreed with Bothwell that Darnley had to go. Mary refused to divorce him because this would have made her son illegitimate. So Bothwell induced the nobles to agree to Darnley's assassination. Mary certainly knew of the plot. In a secret letter to Bothwell, she wrote of her husband: "Cursed be this poxy fellow that troubleth me this much!" On February 1, Mary brought Darnley to Edinburgh, where the plotters planned to kill him. Then she carefully absented herself on the night of the killing.

For Bothwell and Mary, the assassination led to catastrophe. Moray blamed the killing on them. Faced with public outrage, Bothwell staged an abduction of the queen and soon married his willing captive. It was political suicide. Their supporters evaporated. Bothwell fled to Norway, while Mary was taken prisoner by Moray and forced to abdicate.

Mary and Bothwell spent the rest of their lives in captivity: she in England, he in Scandinavia, where he died in prison in 1578. Queen Elizabeth I of England (who was Mary's cousin) had Mary executed in 1587.

KEY DATES

1542 Mary is born on December 8; succeeds to the Scottish throne six days later

1545 Lord Darnley is born on December 7

1559 Mary weds King Francis II

1560 Francis II dies

1561 Mary returns to Scotland to take the throne

1565 Mary weds Darnley

1566 David Rizzio is assassinated on March 9

1567 Lord Darnley is killed on February 9; Mary marries Bothwell, abdicates throne

1568 Mary is held captive

1587 Mary is executed on February 8

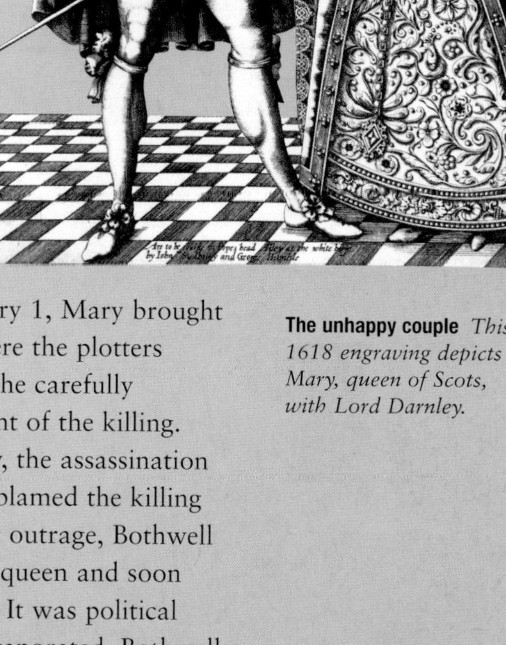

The unhappy couple *This 1618 engraving depicts Mary, queen of Scots, with Lord Darnley.*

VICTIM

David Rizzio

On March 9, 1566, Mary was dining in her private apartments at Holyrood Palace, Edinburgh. Those at the table included Italian musician David Rizzio who was her secretary and close friend. Mary's husband Lord Darnley burst into the room, followed by a group of Protestant lords. With daggers drawn, they told the queen they had come for Rizzio, who they claimed was enjoying her sexual favors.

Mary stood in front of the Italian. After a scuffle, Darnley held his wife while Rizzio was dragged into the next room. There he was killed, his body stabbed more than 50 times. The killers had also intended to murder the queen's closest confidant, the earl of Bothwell, but he escaped through a window. Afterward, Mary plotted with Bothwell to cause her husband's downfall.

The Jealousy of Darnley *Giovanni Battista Cipriani (1727–85) captures a jealous stare from Darnley (left) toward Rizzio (right).*

A bloody crown

In 1742, Empress Elizabeth of Russia declared her 14-year-old nephew the heir presumptive to her throne. She then chose a minor German royal, Sophia Augusta von Anhalt-Zerbst, as his wife. The two teenagers were married in 1745. The groom was the future Czar Peter III, but his bride was also destined to rule Russia, as the Empress Catherine the Great.

Impotence and lust

The first duty of the couple, from a dynastic viewpoint, was to produce a son to carry on the Romanov line. This they singularly failed to do. It was rumored that Peter was impotent. Catherine, a woman of strong desires, soon began to take lovers. When she gave birth to a son in 1754, her lover, not her husband, was believed to be the father.

As long as Elizabeth lived, Catherine was safe in the Empress's favor, but once her husband acceded to the throne as Peter III in December 1761, her position was in danger.

An unpopular czar *This portrait of Peter III, Czar of Russia, was painted in 1760.*

KEY DATES

1728 Born February 10, son of duke of Holstein Gottorp and Czar Peter I's daughter Anna

1742 Declared heir presumptive

1744 Marries his cousin Sophia Augusta von Anhalt-Zerbst (Catherine the Great)

1761 Succeeds to the throne on the death of Empress Elizabeth

1762 Assassinated on July 7

Peter now had the power to dismiss her from the court or to send her into exile.

The czar's politics

As czar, Peter's foreign policy quickly alienated the Russian establishment. Russia was at war with Prussia and about to win, but Peter, who admired the Prussians, hastened to make peace with them on generous terms. The Russians were outraged. The czar's enemies circulated stories that he was insane or had the mentality of a child. It was said that he spent his days playing with toy soldiers.

Catherine did not hesitate to put herself forward as ruler. As the mother of a son who—at least officially—was of Romanov blood, she was a valid successor in the royal line. Her current lover, Count Grigorii Orlov, was an officer of the elite imperial guard, as were his two brothers. She exploited this connection to win military backing. On June 28, 1762, while Peter was away, leaders of the nobility and church in St. Petersburg declared Catherine empress. Peter was arrested and imprisoned.

A ruthless wife

If he had stayed alive, Peter would have been a constant embarrassment and threat to Catherine. He had to be killed. A week after the arrest, Count Grigorii Orlov, his brother Alexei, and other guard officers rode to the castle. Count Alexei Orlov was entrusted with carrying out the assassination. He apparently sat drinking with Peter until the former czar had relaxed, then strangled him. The next September Catherine was crowned empress.

Catherine saw to it that the Orlovs were rewarded for the assassination, although Grigorii had been supplanted as her lover. The murder did Catherine's reputation no harm. She was lauded by Russian patriots for her ruthless expansion of the country's territory and likewise by sophisticated Europeans.

The empress *Catherine the Great became known for her exquisite style and extravagent spending.*

The grieving son

The only person to remember Peter with regret was Catherine's son, Paul. Despite the rumors, he believed that Peter was his father and hated his mother for her role in the murder. Catherine despised Paul, whom she regarded as only good for breeding heirs—he fathered 10 children during his marriage.

"...Peter would have been a constant embarrassment and threat..."

Toward the end of her long reign, Catherine planned for the throne to pass at her death to her grandson Alexander, bypassing Paul. But she failed to make the arrangements in time, and her son succeeded her as Czar Paul I.

VICTIM

Paul I

Catherine the Great's son, Paul, was also assassinated. As czar he made powerful enemies by attacking certain privileges of the nobility and trying to alleviate the sufferings of the serfs. His enemies claimed he was insane and unfit to rule.

Among the losers when Paul came to power was Catherine's last lover, Count Platon Zubov. Along with the Russian Police Chief Count Peter von Pahlen, he plotted Paul's assassination. On the night of March 12, 1801, Pahlen, Zubov, and others broke into the czar's bedchamber. Some say Paul was hiding behind a screen, others that he defended himself as the assassins attacked him with swords, until he was subdued, then strangled.

His son, who succeeded him as Alexander I, presumably approved the plot to kill his father since none of the assassins was ever punished for their crime.

RASPUTIN · 1916

Hard to kill

On December 18, 1916, workmen crossing the River Neva in St. Petersburg noticed bloodstains on the parapet of the Petrovsky Bridge. Police were called and began searching the ice-covered river.

They found a bloodstained body, its hands and feet bound with cords. It had been in the river since the night of December 16. The upper half of the bearded corpse was clad in a blue satin blouse, embroidered with cornflowers by Czarina Alexandra, wife of the ruler of the Russian Empire. The body was that of her favorite companion, the "Mad Monk" Grigorii Rasputin.

Sinner turned holy man

Rasputin was born to peasants in the village of Pokrovskoye, Siberia, probably in 1869. He was a lecherous and drunken youth—in fact, Rasputin is a nickname derived from the Russian for "dissolute."

In his early life, Rasputin turned to a religious sect known as the Khlysty, who indulged in wild rites involving group nudity and flagellation, on the principle that sin was

Holy men
Rasputin (left) poses with a Russian Orthodox archbishop and a priest.

the first step to redemption. Rasputin then became a wandering holy man.

High society

In 1903, Rasputin arrived in St. Petersburg, the capital of the Russian Empire. At that time, the Russian upper class pursued all types of alternative beliefs, including spiritualist séances. They also made a cult of the supposed wisdom of the Russian peasant. Rasputin was filthy and smelly. He had greasy shoulder-length hair and pieces of food stuck to his beard. He could barely read or write, and his manners were crude and insulting.

With his piercing eyes and rough manners, the self-styled holy man soon had the wives of the aristocracy swooning at his feet. The more he humiliated them, the more they craved his company. His debauchery was legendary. Some said his disciples lay naked with him to foster their spiritual and physical healing.

Rasputin gained entrance to the palaces of the richest, most powerful figures in Russia, including the court of Czar Nicholas II. The mystically inclined German-born Czarina Alexandra was emotionally dependent on him, based partly on his apparent ability to heal her son's hemophilia (see box, right).

A powerful figure at court

Through his unassailable position at court, Rasputin also gained political power. He was handing out a government post one moment, excusing someone from military service the next. His power and favoritism brought the monarchy into discredit, but Czar Nicholas would do nothing about it. He insisted that Rasputin was "just a good, religious, simple-minded Russian." Nicholas also valued the calming effect of the holy man on the Czarina. "Better one Rasputin than 10 fits of hysterics a day," he once remarked.

In 1914, Russia went to war with Germany and Austria–Hungary. As defeats accumulated and food became scarce, discontent with the Romanov dynasty grew. Alexandra and Rasputin were suspected of pro-German sympathies, and wild rumors spread. People believed that Alexandra was having a lesbian affair with her companion Anna Vyrubova and that the two women had had orgies with Rasputin.

Rescuing the regime

If Rasputin was hated by enemies of the czar, he was loathed even more by those who supported the Czarist regime. By 1916, the war was going badly and revolution was being preached on the streets. Major figures at court and politicians decided to take action and restore the credibility of the czar and save the regime. To do so, they planned to kill Rasputin and have Alexandra declared insane.

The leader of the plot was 29-year-old Prince Felix Yusupov, who was married to the czar's niece, Grand Duchess Irina Alexandrovna. Other conspirators included the czar's nephew Grand Duke Dmitri

"...they planned to kill Rasputin and have Alexandra declared insane."

THE SPALA MIRACLE

The heir to the Russian throne, Czarevich Alexis, suffered from hemophilia, a hereditary disease passed down from his mother. The slightest mishap could cause fatal internal bleeding. Rasputin's presence could calm the boy and apparently stop any bleeding. How this was achieved is not known, although Rasputin may have used hypnosis.

The strangest demonstration of Rasputin's apparent powers came in October 1912. The czar's family were at Spala in eastern Poland, when Alexis began to bleed. Alexandra telegraphed the news to Rasputin, who was visiting his home village of Pokrovskoye, Siberia. Rasputin wired back, "God has seen your tears and heard your prayers. Do not grieve. The little one will not die." Within hours, Alexis had made a recovery.

Rasputin's hold over Alexandra was stronger than ever. The czarevich's illness was kept secret from the Russian people, so they were unaware of the reason for the czarina's close relationship with Rasputin.

The last czarevich *Alexis was killed along with the rest of his family during the Russian Revolution* *(see pp. 146–49).*

KEY DATES

c. 1869 Born in the village of Pokrovskoye, western Siberia

1880s Associated with the Khlysty sect

1890s Becomes a wandering holy man

1903 First appears in St. Petersburg

1905 Introduced to the court of Czar Nicholas II

1912 Apparently heals the Czarevich at long distance in the so-called Spala miracle

1914 World War I begins

1916 Assassinated on December 16

Pavlovich; Grand Duke Nikolai Mikhailovich; right-wing politician Vladimir Purishkevich; and a medical doctor, Stanislaus Lazovert.

Conspiracy to kill

The conspirators planned to kill Rasputin at night in Yusupov's riverside palace, then dump his body in the river so that he would simply disappear. To lure the holy man to the palace, Yusupov offered him a bait he could not resist—he told him that the glamorous Duchess Irina wanted to meet him. The plotters were hopeless at maintaining secrecy, and Rasputin was advised to turn down Yusupov's invitation—but he accepted.

Late on the night of December 16, Dr. Lazovert, wearing a chauffeur's coat, drove Yusupov to pick up Rasputin from his apartment. At the palace, Yusupov led Rasputin to a basement room, while the others played a gramophone upstairs to simulate a party in progress. Telling Rasputin that Irina would be down shortly, he offered him cakes and wine that had been laced with a supposedly lethal dose of cyanide.

Impossible to kill?

The poison had no effect. An hour passed, and, after a panicky debate with his coconspirators upstairs, Yusupov grabbed a Browning pistol from Grand Duke Dmitri and shot Rasputin in the chest. The holy man fell to the floor with a scream.

The Russian mystic
This photograph of an unkempt Rasputin was taken in about 1909.

Half-an-hour later, when Yusupov was alone with the body, Rasputin opened his eyes and tried to grab the prince, who fled from the room. Rasputin staggered out of the palace into a courtyard, with Purishkevich pursuing him. As Rasputin approached a gate to the river embankment, Purishkevich pulled out a Sauvage pistol and fired four shots. The first two missed, but the third hit Rasputin in the shoulder and the fourth in the head. The conspirators kicked and beat the fallen monk.

Disposing of the body

The conspirators tied the body hand and foot, wrapped it in a curtain, loaded it in their car and drove to a bridge to dispose of the corpse. They heaved it over the parapet, forgetting to add weights to sink the body to the bottom of the river. When the body was discovered two days later, there was water in the lungs—Rasputin had apparently survived all attempts to kill him and had finally died of drowning.

Most of the Russian court and society were relieved at Rasputin's death. However, Alexandra was grief-stricken. The killing had none of the effect its perpetrators had desired. Czar Nicholas drew even closer to his wife and, if it were possible, even more out of touch with his people. In February 1917, the long-expected revolution came and overthrew the Czarist regime.

THE FATE OF THE ASSASSINS

Some of Rasputin's assassins were victims of the revolution they had failed to avert. Grand Duke Nikolai Mikhailovich was executed by Bolshevik revolutionaries in January 1919—for being a grand duke. The politician Purishkevich died of typhus while fighting against the Bolsheviks in the civil war that followed the revolution.

Count Yusupov (right) fled Russia. He sued MGM for its portrayal of him in the 1932 film *Rasputin and the Empress.* He died in France in 1967.

Czarina Alexandra had Grand Duke Dmitri Pavlovich exiled to Persia. By the 1930s, he was selling champagne in Florida. He died in Switzerland in 1941.

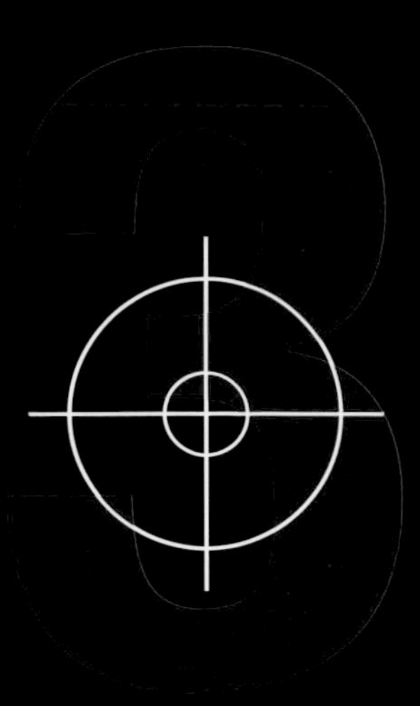

REVOLUTIONARY FERMENT

MARAT · 1793
ALEXANDER II · 1881
WILLIAM MCKINLEY · 1901
EMILIANO ZAPATA · 1919
MICHAEL COLLINS · 1922
ERNST RÖHM · 1934
LEON TROTSKY · 1940
ALDO MORO · 1978

Revolutionary ferment

Revolutions and revolutionary movements have given rise to assassinations in two ways: as part of the violent struggle for power between revolutionary factions and as a terrorist technique designed to undermine society and the state.

The assassination of revolutionary leaders has often been seen, at least by the assassin, as a principled act. Charlotte Corday assassinated revolutionary activist Jean-Paul Marat because she was filled with an idealistic dream of maintaining the purity of the French Revolution of 1789. Irish republican leader Michael Collins died because some of his erstwhile IRA colleagues felt his policy of compromise had betrayed the cause for which they had fought.

In contrast, Emiliano Zapata's enemies killed him because he wanted to make fundamental changes in order to benefit Mexico's peasants. Others, however, believed the Mexican Revolution was over. His death was also an episode in a long-running armed struggle between revolutionary warlords with private armies, of which Zapata was one.

Attacking the opposition

Once in power, the rulers of revolutionary states have used assassination with total cynicism. Soviet dictator Josef Stalin was indifferent to his former Bolshevik colleague Leon Trotsky's arguments for a "permanent revolution." He had Trotsky killed because he could not tolerate any opposition, although Trotsky, living in exile in Mexico, no longer posed any threat to his dictatorship.

German dictator Adolf Hitler—who also came to power through a revolution, if of a very different kind—had one of his oldest colleagues, Ernst

Revolutionary soldier *The Red Army, established by Trotsky after the 1917 Bolshevik Revolution, was notoriously violent.*

THE COMBAT ORGANIZATION

The Socialist Revolutionary (SR) Party, established in 1902, was responsible for political assassination in czarist Russia in the early 20th century. The party was publicly committed to peaceful political action, but it had set up a small autonomous clandestine group, known as the Combat Organization, to carry out terrorist operations in support of the party's aims. The Combat Organization assassinated Russian Minister of the Interior Vyacheslav Plehve in a bomb attack on his carriage in July 1904, and also Grand Duke Sergei, who was murdered in a similar manner in February 1905.

The man who headed the Combat Organization during this period, Yevno Asev, was also acting as a police spy. He had been recruited by the secret police, the Okhrana, in 1893, and reported to them regularly—without giving them information that might inhibit the assassination plots that he masterminded. Asev's double-dealing was discovered by the SRs in 1909 and he fled Russia. He died of natural causes in Berlin, Germany, nine years later.

The SRs continued their terrorist activities after the 1917 Russian Revolution, striking against their revolutionary rivals, the country's new Bolshevik rulers. One SR member, Fanya Kaplan, seriously wounded Bolshevik leader Vladimir Ilyich Lenin in 1918 (see pp. 160–61), and the Combat Organization also plotted to assassinate Leon Trotsky during the same period. The Bolsheviks, however, were more thorough and ruthless in suppressing revolutionary terrorism than the czar's regime had been, and SR activity was soon stamped out.

Röhm, killed not because Röhm had wanted to take the Nazi revolution further, but because the German officer corps was threatened by his power.

Anarchy and terrorists

The use of assassination as a form of revolutionary action, designed to overthrow the existing society or punish those who uphold it or benefit from it, was first developed in Russia in the 19th century. The People's Will *(Narodnya Volya),* the clandestine group that assassinated Czar Alexander II in 1879, can be regarded as the first modern terrorist organization. The group had successors in Russia until 1914, but none managed to kill a czar.

The basis for assassination as a form of revolutionary politics was provided by the Russian anarchist Mikhael Bakunin. One of his disciples wrote in 1869, "The revolutionary is a dedicated man.... He knows but one science, that of destruction." Some anarchists rejected violence, but others embraced the idea of killing powerful people as a way of undermining governmental authority, breaking the will of the ruling class, and advertising social injustice. Assassination became what Italian anarchist Enrico Malatesta called "propaganda by the deed." Among victims of anarchist assassins were French President Sidi Carnot (1894), Spanish Prime Minister Canovas del Castillo (1897), the empress of Austria (1898), Italian King Umberto I (1900), and U.S. President William McKinley (1901).

The anticapitalists

Most anarchist assassinations were carried out by individuals acting alone or by small amateurish groups. However, the would-be revolutionaries who formed anticapitalist terrorist groups in the 1960s and 1970s, such as the Baader Meinhof gang in Germany and the Red Brigades in Italy, had more in common with the pre-1914 Russian tradition. These radicals formed sophisticated clandestine organizations and preferred spectacular acts of "popular justice," attacking politicians, judges, police, and businessmen. Leading Italian politician Aldo Moro was the most prominent victim of these "urban guerrillas."

Assassinations carried out by anarchists and terrorists have failed to advance the workers' revolution or bring capitalism to its knees. Their main effect has been to stimulate and justify measures of repression by the state.

Killed in the bath

On the evening of July 13, 1793, a young woman with striking gray eyes stood outside the home of the revolutionary Jean-Paul Marat. She wore a stylish black hat with green ribbons that she had purchased that morning. At the same time, she'd bought a kitchen knife that was hidden in her dress.

The convent-educated daughter of a poor provincial nobleman, Charlotte Corday had seen little of the world outside her home town of Caen in Normandy. However, she had avidly followed reports of the revolution that had broken out in Paris in 1789. Her imagination had been stirred by reading stories about ancient Greece and Rome. When France became a Republic after Louis XVI was deposed in 1792, she imagined that a new equivalent of the Roman Republic was being born—a republic of heroic virtue.

KEY DATES

1743 Born May 24 near Neuchâtel, Switzerland

1759 Begins to study medicine in France

1765 Begins to practice medicine in England; while there, publishes scientific and philosophical books

1777 Returns to France, working as a doctor in the service of the Comte d'Artois

1789 After the start of the French Revolution, begins publishing his radical paper *L'Ami du Peuple*

1792 Elected to the National Convention

1793 Arrested on the orders of the Girondins in April, but is acquitted; assists in their downfall in June; assassinated on July 13

The Jacobin
Jean-Paul Marat was a revolutionary who considered himself the people's friend and the enemy of the rich.

Paris in turmoil

In reality, factions battled for power. The king was guillotined and agitators demanded the spilling of more blood. Jean-Paul Marat was in the forefront of those demanding the death of anyone labeled a traitor to the republic.

Marat was a revolutionary journalist with a gift for rhetoric. His denunciations of the so-called enemies of the revolution and demands for vengeance against the rich had made his newspaper, *L'Ami du Peuple (The People's Friend)*, very powerful. A member of France's parliament, the National Convention, he was prominent in the political clubs that incited and organized popular agitation.

In June 1793, the Jacobins—the political group to which Marat belonged—seized power from the Girondins, the faction that had dominated the Republican government. The Girondin leaders were put under house arrest. Some fled to raise a revolt in the provinces. In Caen, Corday talked with their leaders. She had probably already identified Marat as a hate figure—the man responsible for ruining the republic of her dreams.

Ready for murder

In July, Corday went to Paris. One of her heroes was Brutus, the assassin of Julius Caesar. She planned to assassinate Marat in the National Convention, as Brutus had killed Caesar in front of the senate. However, Marat was ill. Suffering from a skin disease—most likely psoriasis—Marat rarely left the bath that provided relief from his pain.

Corday went to Marat's home in the morning but was turned away—he was too sick to receive visitors. She sent him a message saying that she had important information from Caen and would return that evening. This she did, carrying a new message that ended on a note designed to appeal to Marat: "I am unhappy; this itself is sufficient to give me a claim on your protection."

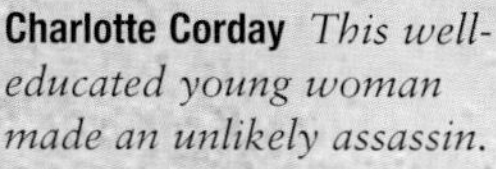

Charlotte Corday *This well-educated young woman made an unlikely assassin.*

Corday managed to slip inside. Marat's lover Simonne Evrard intercepted her on the stairs, but Marat called out for her to enter. The bath where he sat was covered with a rug and a board supporting his writing materials.

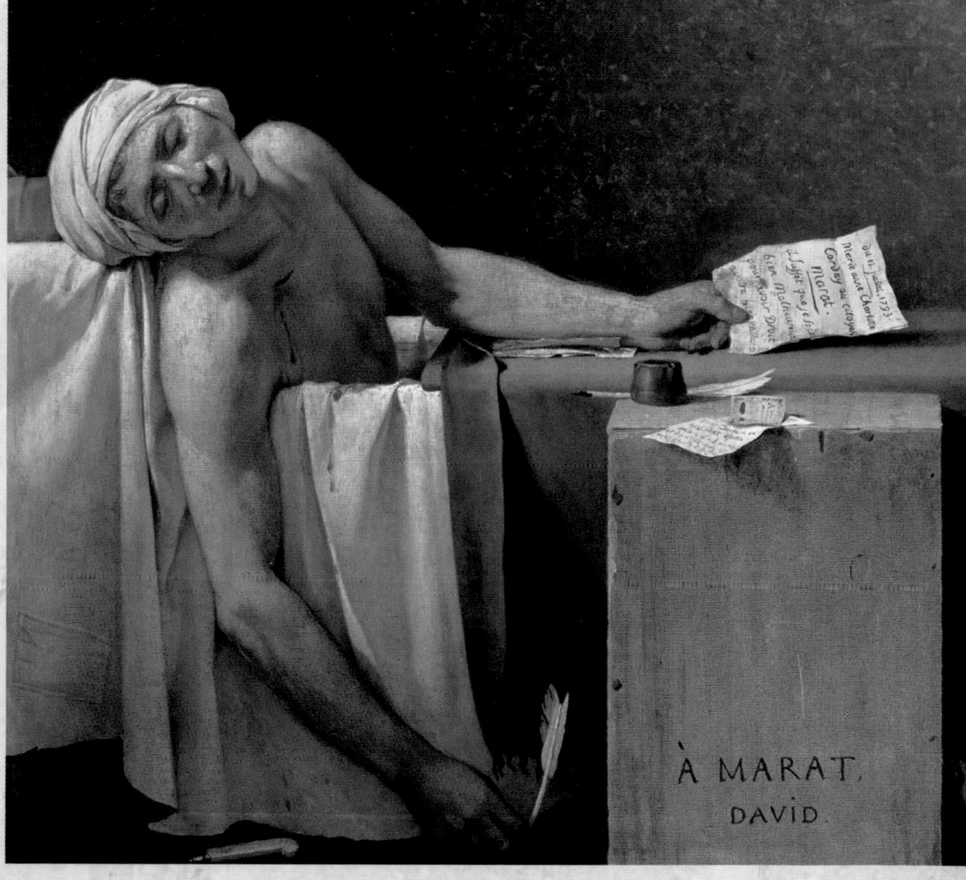

The Death of Marat *The painter Jacques-Louis David was Marat's friend. His sensitive depiction of the murdered man in this painting, rendered shortly after the assassination, shows the affection he felt for his friend.*

Sitting on a chair near the bath, Corday recited the names of leading Girondins in Caen; Marat said it would not be long before they were guillotined. Evrard left the room. Instantly, Corday pulled the knife from under her dress and plunged it into Marat's side, piercing a lung and a major artery. Hearing him cry out, Evrard and others rushed in and seized Corday. All efforts to save Marat failed.

No regrets

Corday denied being in collusion with the Girondins and claimed that she "killed one man to save a hundred thousand." Awaiting death, she wrote that she expected "to enjoy the repose of the Elysian Fields with Brutus and the ancients." Four days after the murder, a hostile crowd watched her ride to the guillotine. As the executioner held up her severed head, he struck it with his fist.

The assassination did not have the effect Corday had hoped. Marat's associates executed the Girondin leaders and imposed a reign of terror that cost thousands of lives.

BURIED IN STATE

Marat's funeral was an occasion of intense public mourning. His bath and bloodstained shirt were carried behind the coffin like holy relics. He was likened to Jesus in speeches by Parisian radicals. Marat's friend and fellow revolutionary Jacques-Louis David portrayed him as a martyred saint in his painting *The Death of Marat.*

In 1794, the National Convention escorted Marat's remains to the Panthéon, resting place of the heroes of the Republic. Afterward, opinion turned against the revolutionaries. In 1795, his body was removed from the Panthéon and buried in an ordinary cemetery.

Blown to pieces

Racing home *The dying czar is transported by a sleigh to the Winter Palace after the attack.*

In the 1870s, a generation of young Russians with socialist ideas wanted to overthrow the autocratic czarist government and end poverty and inequality in Russia. Repressed by the czarist police, the young revolutionaries turned to violence. In 1879, one group formed a secret organization called the "People's Will" *(Narodnya Volya)*. Among its leaders were Andrei Zhelyabov, the son of a serf, and his lover, Sophia Perovskaya, the daughter of the governor general of St. Petersburg. The People's Will chose the czar himself as their prime target.

The Liberator

Early in his reign, Czar Alexander II had freed the Russian peasants from the semislavery of serfdom—he is sometimes known as the Liberator. However, his reforms did not grant a constitution or representational government. By the 1870s, "progressive" Russians regarded him as an oppressor. The czar survived two assassination attempts: A student named Dmitri Karakosov had shot at him in 1866, and Alexander Solovev had done the same in 1879.

The People's Will

The campaign of the People's Will was well organized and unrelenting. They used nitroglycerine, a new invention. In November 1879, assassins tried twice to blow up the czar as he returned by train from a vacation in the Crimea. In one case, their mine did not go off; in the other, it blew up the wrong train.

For their next attack, terrorist Stephen Khalturin got a job in the czar's Winter Palace. On February 5, 1880, he blew up the dining room. Alexander should have been at the table, but he had been delayed. The blast killed 11 soldiers and wounded 56.

KEY DATES

1818 Born April 17, in St. Petersburg, son of Czar Nicholas I

1841 Marries Princess Marie of Hesse-Darmstadt (Maria Alexandrovna)

1855 Becomes czar on the death of his father

1861 Decrees emancipation of the serfs

1863 Severely represses a nationalist revolt in Poland

1866 First attempt on the czar's life

1881 Assassinated in St. Petersburg on March 1

The czar no longer felt safe. He slept in a different bed each night, feared poison in his food, and traveled in anonymous trains.

Success at last

After two further attempts failed, the People's Will leadership planned one last major attack in St. Petersburg. On Sundays, it was the czar's custom to go to a riding academy. The terrorists rented a cheese shop along his route and dug a tunnel under the road, which they packed with explosives. "Throwers" armed with nitroglycerin bombs would also be positioned to close in on the czar's carriage.

The terrorists were in a race against time. Two of their leaders had been arrested: Alexander Mikhailov in October 1880, Zhelyabov in February 1881. The remaining terrorists decided to strike immediately, even though preparations were not complete. Their explosives expert, N. I. Kibalchich, worked through the night to have bombs ready for the morning of March 1.

There was a last-minute change to the czar's route that day. Perovskaya, who was in charge of the throwers, ordered them to wait along the Catherine Canal, where the czar was expected to pass on his way back from the riding academy. She took up position on the other side of the canal to give a signal as the czar approached. The waiting throwers, Nikolai Rysakov and Ignatai Grinevitsky, strolled about with explosives under their arms. At 2:15 P.M., the czar's carriage, flanked by his cossack escort, drew near.

Rysakov threw his bomb first, but it fell behind the carriage, exploding amid the cossack riders. Two of the cossacks and a passerby were killed. The czar climbed down from his damaged carriage and waited for another one to arrive. As he climbed into the new carriage, Grinevitsky ran up to the czar and dropped his bomb. It was a suicide attack. Both the assassin and his victim were torn apart by the explosions. Each was carried off to die: the czar to the Winter Palace, the assassin to prison.

Rysakov was arrested at the scene of the bombing; Perovskaya and Kibalchich were picked up soon after. Along with Zhelyabov and Mikhailov, they were hanged on April 3.

> "Grinevitsky **ran** up to the **czar** and dropped his **bomb**. It was a **suicide attack**."

LENIN'S INSPIRATION

In 1887, a group of Russian students, inspired by the example of the People's Will terrorists, plotted to kill the oppressive Czar Alexander III. The plot was foiled and the students were arrested. Among those hanged for their part in this assassination attempt was 19-year-old Alexander Ulyanov.

The event had a profound impact on Ulyanov's admiring younger brother Vladimir, who was to dedicate his whole life to the revolutionary cause—and would later, as leader of the Bolsheviks, call himself Lenin (see pp. 160–61) and rule Russia.

Site of carnage *The Alexander II Memorial Church was built at the scene of the czar's murder.*

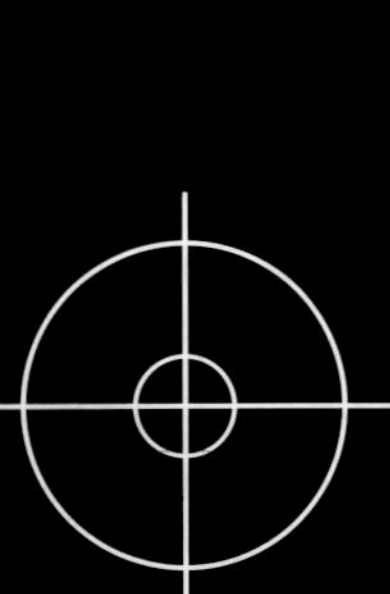

An anarchist act

In September 1901, President William McKinley, in the first year of his second term at the White House, visited the Pan-American Exposition in Buffalo, New York—a lavish display of technological progress and culture. Shortly after 4:00 P.M. on September 6, the president stood in the Temple of Music, shaking hands with a line of visitors to the exposition. The line was moving in a chaotic manner and the president's Secret Service guards were busy trying to keep people moving along.

Shot at close range

McKinley found himself face to face with a slim young man who had a handkerchief tied around his right hand. Before the president could decide whether to shake hands normally or to proffer his left hand, the young man fired two shots from a .32 caliber short-barreled revolver hidden by the handkerchief.

In the pandemonium that followed, the man who had fired the shots was knocked to the ground and beaten. He might have been killed but the president, who was lying gravely wounded with blood staining his white shirt, said softly but firmly, "Go easy on him, boys." The news of the attack spread among visitors to the exposition, and rioting broke out as the angry crowd demanded vengeance. Soldiers had to be deployed to restore order.

A healthy 58-year-old, McKinley might have survived since one bullet had only caused a flesh wound, while the other had perforated his stomach. However, the surgeon available at the exposition was inexperienced. When he explored the president's stomach wound, he could not find the bullet and left it inside when he sewed the patient up. The president's condition temporarily improved, but he developed an infection and died eight days later of gangrene. Ironically, one of the first X-ray machines was on display as an exhibit at the exposition. Had the doctor thought to use it, he might have saved McKinley's life.

The lonely anarchist

The interrogation of the president's assassin revealed that he was Leon Czolgosz, a 28-year-old Polish American born in Detroit. His parents had arrived in the United States shortly before his birth and struggled to bring up a family of eight in their new homeland. They moved to a farm near Cleveland, where Leon became a factory worker at 16. He gave up his Catholic faith and came into contact with the ideas of socialists and anarchists, who were challenging the power of governments and factory bosses alike.

In 1898, Czolgosz seems to have had some kind of mental breakdown. He gave up his job at a wire mill and returned to the family farm, where he spent his time reading about violent acts by anarchists and the brutality of the authorities in crushing workers' protests. His life drifted until May 1901, when he heard the anarchist Emma

KEY DATES

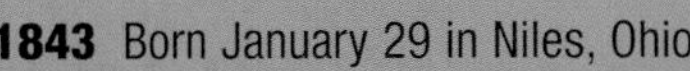

1843 Born January 29 in Niles, Ohio

1861 Joins the Union Army in the Civil War

1876 Elected to Congress

1890 Introduces the McKinley Bill, which imposed high tariffs on imports

1892 Elected governor of Ohio

1896 Elected president

1898 Leads the United States into war with Spain over Cuba

1900 Reelected president

1901 Assassinated on September 6; died September 14; succeeded by his vice president, Theodore Roosevelt.

The anarchist *Leon Czolgosz assassinated President McKinley.*

The assassination *Czolgosz hides a gun under a handkerchief as he's about to shoot President McKinley.*

Goldman make a speech at the Federal Liberal Club in Cleveland. Goldman became his new obsession. He followed her to Chicago and began to mix in anarchist circles, but he was not welcome. His desperation to meet with anarchist leaders and his tendency to make unbalanced, violent statements aroused suspicion. He was denounced in *Free Society*, an anarchist publication, as a probable police spy. The assassination of the president may in part have been a reaction to his rejection by the anarchists whom he wanted to serve.

WICE SHOT, BUT LIVES.

The aftermath

Czolgosz's trial opened only nine days after the president's death. He insisted that he had acted alone. "No one else told me to do it, and no one paid me to do it." After a plea of insanity had been brushed aside, the death sentence was a formality. As Czolgosz was strapped into the electric chair on October 29, 1901, he cried out, "I killed the president because he was the enemy of the good people! I did it for the help of the good people, the working men of all countries!" A switch was thrown and 1,700 volts shot through his body. The electric chair was then still a novel form of execution. Thomas Edison released a movie purporting to show the execution in detail—however, it was a re-creation.

The assassination was a disaster for the anarchists. Goldman was harassed by the police and enraged members of the public. Yet she refused to condemn Czolgosz, stating, "He committed the act for no personal reason or gain. He did it for what is his ideal…that is why my sympathies are with him."

VICTIM

King Umberto I

The spark that ignited Leon Czolgosz's desire to become an assassin may have been a killing that took place in Italy on July 29, 1900. Italian King Umberto I was attending a gymnastic performance at Monza, near Milan, when he was shot at close range. He died almost immediately.

His assassin was Gaetano Bresci, an Italian silk weaver who had emigrated to the United States, where he lived with his wife and seven-year-old daughter in Paterson, New Jersey. Bresci had a deep hatred of the monarchy, and he returned to Italy to join an anarchist group in Milan. They drew lots to decide which of them should shoot the king.

Czolgosz identified with Bresci, collecting press clippings about his crime. The killing focused his interest on the anarchist movement and prepared the way for his own plan to kill the president.

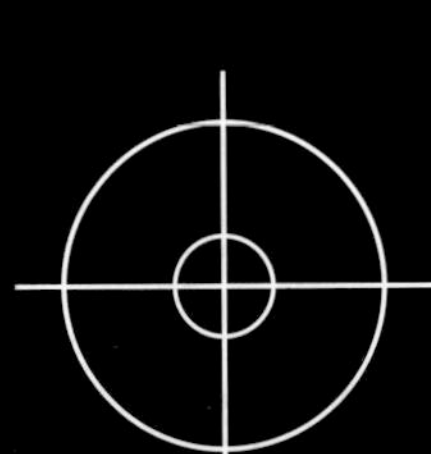

Betrayed

The life of Mexican revolutionary leader Emiliano Zapata was devoted to winning the land that Indian peasant farmers of Mexico believed belonged to them. Zapata grew up in the village of Anenecuilco in the state of Morelos, south of Mexico City, where his family struggled to live off a small plot of land. By the age of 30, he was a recognized leader in his village.

A national figure

Zapata was transformed from a local agitator into a personality of national importance by the outbreak of the Mexican Revolution in 1910. The decision of defeated presidential candidate Francisco Madero to start a revolt against the long-established dictatorship of Porfirio Diaz initiated more than a decade of complex military conflict and political power play. Zapata mobilized a peasant army in the state of Morelos that helped overthrow Diaz and exercised a major influence over the course of the revolution that followed.

Zapata's was only one of several guerrilla armies during the revolution—another famous band of fighters was led by Pancho Villa in the north. However, Zapata had the clearest political program. Known as the Plan of Ayala, it called for land to be taken from the

KEY DATES

1879 Born August 8 in Anenecuilco, Morelos, Mexico
1909 Seizes land for distribution among the peasants
1911 Leads guerrilla forces in Morelos against President Diaz
1913 Opposes General Huerta after President Madero is killed
1914 His guerrillas occupy Mexico City
1915 Loses control of Morelos to Carranza's forces
1919 Assassinated on April 10

The peasants' leader
Emiliano Zapata, a local spokesman for the rights of the peasants, became a national hero.

haciendas, or large estates, and distributed to the peasants, with compensation if estates' owners cooperated, without if they did not.

The Zapatista's downfall

Although the Zapatistas occupied Mexico City in 1914—surprising the terrified city dwellers by politely requesting money and food rather than seizing it—Zapata was never strong enough to lead a Mexican government. In Morelos, he oversaw land seizures and the destruction of haciendas, but at the national level he was too naive and incorruptible.

After 1915, both Zapata and Villa were put on the defensive as Venustiano Carranza, a conservative revolutionary, rose to power. Commanded by General Pablo Gonzalez, Carranza's forces rampaged through Morelos, destroying villages and terrorizing peasants. The Zapatistas held out in the hills, raiding government-held towns and haciendas. Gonzalez realized that to subdue the guerrillas, he would have to eradicate their leader.

Setting a trap

In the spring of 1919, Gonzalez found an opportunity to lure Zapata into a trap. Colonel Jesus Guajardo, one of Gonzalez's officers, had quarreled with him and was suspected of being in sympathy with the guerrilla cause. Zapata sent the colonel a message inviting him to join him, but the message was intercepted and passed to Gonzalez. The general presented Guajardo with a choice: Play a part in a plot to assassinate Zapata or be shot as a traitor.

Guajardo responded to Zapata's message, offering to join him and to bring forces to increase the guerrillas' ranks. Zapata and Guajardo met for the first time on April 9. The colonel gave Zapata a fine stallion and the two men decided to continue their talks the next day at the hacienda of Chinameca.

Zapata was riding the stallion when he turned up at the hacienda at 2:00 P.M. on April 10. Although he arrived with 150 armed men, only a handful rode into the hacienda with him. Guajardo's soldiers were drawn up like a guard of honor to welcome Zapata. At a signal sounded by a bugler, the soldiers opened fire. Riddled with bullets, Zapata and his companions fell from their horses.

Zapata's body was carried into the town of Cuautla for burial. Gonzalez had the corpse photographed to prove that the leader was dead. Despite this, and the fact that the body lay on display for two days before burial, the peasants of Morelos believe to this day that Zapata never died. His memory still inspires those struggling against poverty in Mexico.

VICTIMS

Murdered Leaders

Violent death was not unusual for leading players in the Mexican revolution. Revolutionary leader Francisco Madero was shot in 1913 after being overthrown in an American-backed coup led by General Huerta. President Venustiano Carranza was gunned down in 1920 when rebels seized power. Pancho Villa was assassinated in 1923, ambushed by gunmen in the service of Jesus Salas Barranzas, a congressman loyal to President Obregón. In 1928, President Obregón himself was assassinated by José de León Toral, a newspaper cartoonist, because of his anti-Catholic policies.

Zapata's men *Headed by Emiliano Zapata (dressed in black, with a cross on his hat), Zapatistas gather in the streets of Mexico City in 1915.*

A shoot-out

The Big Fellow *Michael Collins, one of the heroes of the Irish independence struggle, was prepared to die to unify his country.*

On August 22, 1922, Michael Collins, commander in chief of the army of the new Irish Free State, was driving in county Cork in southwestern Ireland, preceded by two automobiles and a scout car and followed by an armored car. Ireland was in a civil war in which Free State soldiers were opposed by Republican Irregulars. Collins knew that he was a prime target for the Irregulars.

The burly 32-year-old Collins, known as the Big Fellow, was the most charismatic hero of the Irish struggle for independence from Britain. He had fought in the failed Easter Rising, staged by a small band of Irish Republicans in Dublin in 1916, and had led the guerrilla warfare and terrorism conducted by the Irish Republican Army (IRA) against the British forces in Ireland and the Royal Irish Constabulary from 1919 to 1921.

Collins adopted assassination, saying, "To paralyze the British machine it was necessary to strike at individuals." In one of the most famous incidents of the campaign, on November 21, 1920, he organized the killing of 14 British officers operating

KEY DATES

1890 Born October 16 near Clonakilty, West Cork

1916 Takes part in the Easter Rising in Dublin and is captured by the British

1917 Elected to the Sinn Fein Executive, the governing branch of the Irish republican political movement

1918 Helps to form an Irish parliament, the Dáil

1919 Becomes commander of the IRA

1920 Orders the killing of British officers, an event that was dubbed Bloody Sunday

1921 Signs the Anglo-Irish Treaty

1922 Killed in an ambush on August 22

undercover in Dublin. His agents struck at 9:00 A.M. at different locations around the city. (In retaliation, the British soldiers fired a machine gun into an Irish soccer crowd.)

Peace talks

When the future of Ireland became a subject for talks instead of bullets, Collins was a realist. In December 1921, he was part of an Irish Republican delegation that signed an Anglo-Irish Treaty. The British accepted the right of Collins and his colleagues to rule in Dublin in return for two concessions: The Dublin government would not control the six counties of Northern Ireland, and southern Ireland would be a self-governing dominion within the British Empire, not a republic. Collins argued for the treaty, saying it brought "the freedom to achieve freedom." However, many Republican politicians and a substantial part of the IRA rejected the treaty. Collins commented that in signing the treaty, he had signed his own death warrant. So it proved.

Return to violence

In June 1922, disagreement over the treaty turned to civil war. Anti-treaty Republicans occupied prominent buildings in Dublin, including the Four Courts. Under pressure from the British to restore order, Collins ordered a full-scale military assault. Within a week all of Dublin was under Free State control, but much of the rest of Ireland was in the hands of anti-treaty Irregulars.

At about 8:00 P.M. on August 22, Collins's convoy was ambushed. As firing broke out from all sides, Collins returned fire. The gunfight went on until a shot blew off the back of Collins's head. No one else was killed.

Collins's body was shipped to Dublin, where he lay in state for three days. Hundreds of thousands lined the streets to see his coffin carried to Glasnevin Cemetery for burial.

VICTIM

Sir Henry Wilson

Part of the background to Collins's death was the assassination of one of his arch-enemies, Field Marshal Sir Henry Wilson, who was responsible for the ruthless measures taken against the Irish rebels during their struggle for independence. He was also an outspoken supporter of the Northern Ireland Protestants in their battle against the IRA.

On June 22, 1922, two Irish ex-servicemen, Reggie Dunne and Joseph O'Sullivan, shot Wilson in London. They said they acted on impulse after drinking in a pub, a claim given some credibility when they jumped into a taxi to escape, only to fall out the other side. However, Collins was suspected of ordering the killing. The British government, outraged by Wilson's murder, pressured Collins to act against the rebels at the Four Courts in Dublin; his action may have motivated those who killed him.

Final farewell *Thousands of mourners watched Michael Collins being taken one last time down the streets of Dublin.*

Nazi killing

The SA on display *Ernst Röhm (center, wearing a swastika armband) inspects a SA troop in Berlin in 1933.*

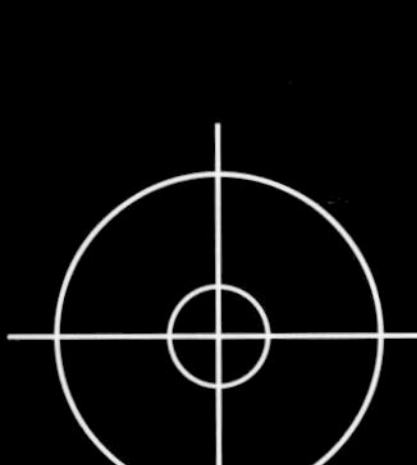

German Chancellor Adolf Hitler sent a message to one of his oldest associates at the end of 1933, the year in which Hitler and his National Socialist (Nazi) Party took control of the German state. "I thank you my dearest Ernst Röhm, for the services which you have given to the National Socialist Movement and the German people...." Röhm had created and led the brown-shirted Stormtroopers (*Sturmabteilung*, or SA), who provided the muscle to back Hitler's rise to power. However, the friendly tone of Hitler's message was deceptive—Röhm and the SA were already becoming a problem that needed to be resolved.

KEY DATES

1887 Born November 28 in Germany

1921 Plays leading role in the creation of the SA Stormtroopers

1924 Tried alongside Hitler for treason; found guilty but not sentenced

1925 Leaves Germany to become an adviser to the Bolivian army

1931 Returns to Germany and is appointed chief of staff of the SA

1933 Appointed state commissar in Bavaria

1934 Assassinated on July 1 on Hitler's orders

Army of street fighters

The Stormtroopers had been recruited from unemployed youth in the depression-struck Germany of the early 1930s. They were tough street fighters who specialized in beating up Jews and smashing windows. Hitler, who wanted to persuade bourgeois Germany that his government represented order and security, became embarrassed by their unruly behavior. The SA were equally discontented with Hitler. They had benefited little from Hitler's power.

Röhm was a coarsely spoken homosexual soldier who reveled in the male bonding of military life. His ambition was to see the SA become Germany's national army. Röhm had begun to speak of a "Second Revolution" to plunder the wealth of Germany's capitalists and middle classes. The German officer corps made it clear to Hitler that if Röhm and the SA were not dealt with soon, the Nazi government would lose their support.

Time for a change

By the summer of 1934, rumors were circulating that Röhm was plotting to use the SA to overthrow Hitler and seize power. It is not known if Hitler feared an SA uprising or if he or other Nazi leaders had spread the rumors to justify an attack on the SA. If Röhm had come up with a plot, it never came to fruition. Instead, Hitler struck ruthlessly against those who had helped him to power.

"If I am to be killed, let Adolf do it himself."

The leaders of the SA were called to a conference at the end of June at Bad Wiessee, near Munich. Röhm and his colleagues gathered at the Hanselbauer Hotel for a dissolute evening of drunken carousing. Meanwhile, the SS and gestapo drew up plans for a blow against the SA leadership and other individuals who had angered the Nazis. Hitler hesitated until June 29, when Stormtroopers in Munich staged demonstrations against the regime. That was the trigger for the killing to begin.

Hitler flew into Munich early in the morning of June 30; then a convoy of cars raced toward Bad Wiessee. Hitler and his SS men reached the Hanselbauer Hotel at 6:30 A.M. Carrying a whip, Hitler burst into the bedroom where Röhm was sleeping off a night of heavy drinking. Two SS men with pistols walked in behind him. Hitler shouted, "Röhm, you're under arrest!" In another room, Edmund Heines, the SA Obergruppenführer for Silesia, was in bed with a boy. According to some accounts, Heines was shot outside. Others say that, along with Röhm and the other hotel occupants, he was driven to Munich's Stadelheim prison.

A terrible choice

By the time Hitler arrived back in Berlin, many of those listed to be killed had died in front of SS firing squads or been shot where they were found, but Röhm was still alive. During a garden party the next afternoon, Hitler ordered his old colleague's death. A revolver was left in his prison cell so that he could kill himself, but Röhm refused: "If I am to be killed, let Adolf do it himself." Two SS officers then stripped him to the waist and fired into his bare chest at point-blank range.

A NIGHT OF KILLINGS

Along with Röhm, an estimated 150–400 people were massacred by the SS on the "Night of the Long Knives." Former German Chancellor General Kurt von Schleicher was gunned down in his home. General Ferdinand von Bredow was shot as he answered his front door. SA Gruppenführer Karl Ernst was boarding a ship at Bremen for a honeymoon trip when the SS picked him up—he thought it was a practical joke until he was shot. A music critic, Dr. Willi Schmid, was shot because the SS confused him with SA Gruppenführer Wilhelm Schmidt.

Mass adulation *The "Night of the Long Knives" confirmed Hitler's grip on power. Many admired him for cracking down on unruly elements in the party.*

Stalin's orders

In the summer of 1940, exiled Russian revolutionary Leon Trotsky was a hunted man. He had been placed under sentence of death by his former revolutionary colleague, Soviet dictator Josef Stalin. Since being expelled from the Soviet Union in 1929, Trotsky had incessantly attacked the Stalinist dictatorship as a brutal perversion of the revolution he had helped to create. Stalin wanted his dissenting voice silenced.

Mexican haven

For many years, Trotsky had led a nomadic existence, regarded as persona non grata by some countries (such as the United States) because he was a revolutionary, and by others because they feared the wrath of the Soviet Union if they gave him asylum. In 1937, he found a haven in Mexico, whose government was sufficiently left-wing to welcome an old Bolshevik, yet owed no allegiance to Stalin. With his wife, Natalia Ivanovna Sedova, he found shelter in a house on a quiet tree-

Revolutionary hero *Leon Trotsky spoke out against his old colleague Stalin, who had him expelled from the Soviet Union.*

Inspecting the troops *Trotsky, creator of the Red Army, reviews his troops in Moscow in 1919.*

lined street in Coyoacán, on the outskirts of Mexico City.

Trotsky had no illusions that even that far from Moscow he would be beyond Stalin's reach. He therefore turned the house into a small fortress. It was surrounded by high stone walls overlooked by a watchtower, and it had a permanent police guard stationed outside. Inside, Trotsky occupied a small villa surrounded by a garden, where he kept rabbits and tended plants. In a way, it was an oasis of calm in a war-torn world—this was the time of Nazi Germany's invasion of France and the Battle of Britain—but Trotsky knew that Stalin's assassins would one day find him.

LENIN, TROTSKY, AND STALIN

Lenin and Trotsky (shown below, Lenin speaking, Trotsky near the podium) fought together to bring about the Bolshevik Revolution in 1917 and win the ensuing civil war. On Lenin's death in 1924, Stalin won a power struggle between himself and Trotsky. Although Stalin and Trotsky fought on the same side in the revolution and civil war, they were different in personality and background. Stalin was raised in poverty and had little education. Trotsky was born into a well-off, cultured Jewish family. A formidable intellectual, he shone both as an orator and an author. He was arrogant and individualistic. Stalin hated Trotsky for being an intellectual and, being himself a confirmed anti-Semite, he also hated him for being Jewish.

Both men were ruthless revolutionaries. Trotsky had the blood of massacres on his hands. When he disagreed with Stalin, it was often due to Stalin's conservatism rather than his revolutionary excesses. However, as Stalin grew more ruthless in the 1930s, Trotsky's brave opposition to the dictator and his secret police earned the respect of even the liberals who rejected the beliefs of Trotskyism.

An attack with machine guns

The first attempt on Trotsky's life was made on May 24, 1940. In the early hours of the morning, a group of armed men wearing police uniforms attacked the house. Two women sent in ahead of them had used their seductive charms to lead away some of the Mexican police stationed outside. The remaining police guards were swiftly and silently overcome and tied up. The telephone lines from the house were cut, and the alarm linked to the local police station was disabled. A young American, Bob Sheldon Harte, was in control of the security system at the door that night. Either he was part of the plot and let the attackers in or, more probably, they found some other way into the house and overpowered him from behind.

Once inside, the attackers ran into the courtyard garden and began shooting with machine guns, firing through the windows and doors of the bedrooms where Trotsky, his wife, and his grandson Seva Volkov were sleeping. Trotsky and Natalia crouched on the floor in a corner of their room as bullets penetrated their bed. They could hear Seva's screams and saw flames leap up as a closet caught fire in the child's bedroom. Then the attackers disappeared as suddenly as they had come. There was, in Natalia's words, "a deathly silence, a total unbearable silence that petrified us." Remarkably, they had all survived. Only Seva was injured—he had been shot in the toe. The steel shutters on the windows had deflected some of the fire, but 76 bullets were found embedded in the walls and floors of the rooms. An unexploded bomb was also discovered; had it gone off, it would have destroyed the entire building.

"Mornard pulled the ice pick from inside his coat and forcefully struck Trotsky's skull."

Trail of evidence

The Stalinist Communists claimed that Trotsky had faked the incident to win publicity or sympathy. However, Mexican detectives found a trail of evidence that led them to David Alfaro Siqueiros, a painter. He was also a founding member of the Mexican Communist Party and a supporter of Stalin. He and his coconspirators were arrested. The young American Sheldon Harte disappeared on the night of the attack; his body was later found in a pit of lime at a house that had been rented by some of David Siqueiros's relatives.

KEY DATES

1879 Born October 26 in Ukraine; named Lev Davidovich Bronstein

1898 Arrested by the czarist police; exiled to Siberia

1902 Escapes and joins Lenin in London; takes the name Trotsky

1905 Leads the St. Petersburg workers' soviet (council) during the failed Russian Revolution of 1905

1907 Sentenced to Siberian exile; escapes

1917 Plays a role in the Bolshevik Revolution

1918 Creates the Red Army; wins Russian civil war

1924 Engages in power struggle with Josef Stalin

1928 Exiled to Alma Ata in Central Asia

1929 Expelled from the Soviet Union; lives in Turkey

1936 Arrives in Mexico from Norway

1940 Assassinated on August 20; dies August 21

After this attack, Trotsky had no illusions about the likelihood of his surviving for much longer. "I know I am condemned," he told an associate. "I am alone with a few friends and almost no resources against a powerful killing machine...."

Work began right away on strengthening the fortress that had proved such a fallible defense. But while more barbed wire, watchtowers, and alarm systems were put in place, and more police sent to patrol outside the walls, one of Stalin's secret agents was about to be invited inside the gates.

Friendly foe

Only four days after the attack, a suave young man calling himself Jacson Mornard appeared at Trotsky's house, giving Natalia and two of Trotsky's friends a lift in his car. Mornard was the lover of Russian-born American leftist Sylvia Agelof, and he had recently arrived with her in Mexico. Trotsky became friendly with Agelof. She was invited to tea on August 8 and Mornard went with her. They visited twice more in the following days, becoming familiar figures to the guards.

Natalia later remembered that on the fatal day, August 20, Trotsky slept well—a relief since his health was poor. As usual, he fed the rabbits and tended the plants in the garden, then spent the rest of the day at his desk writing, still committed to the revolutionary struggle that had consumed his life.

Mornard parked in front of the house just after 5:00 P.M. Most of Trotsky's guards were occupied with installing a siren in one of the watchtowers. None of those who let Mornard in thought it strange that he was carrying a raincoat on a fine evening, or noticed that the coat was bulky. He was established in their eyes as a friend of the family.

The attacker strikes

Natalia saw Mornard standing with Trotsky by the rabbit hutches. He wanted Trotsky to read an article that he had written, so the two men walked to Trotsky's study. Trotsky sat down behind his desk. Mornard would have to act decisively because there was a loaded pistol in one of the desk drawers, another pistol on top of the desk, and under the desk was a buzzer for a security alarm bell.

As Trotsky bent forward to read the article, Mornard put his raincoat down on the desk. Inside the lining of the coat were an ice pick, a dagger, and a pistol. Perching on the edge of the desk, Mornard pulled the ice pick from inside his coat and forcefully struck Trotsky's skull. He must have intended to strike with the point of the pick on the crown of the head—a blow that would have caused instant death—but, panicking, he used the blunt end of the pick head and struck the side of Trotsky's head. The blow still drove about 2¾ inches (7 cm) into Trotsky's brain, but it was not enough to kill him instantly. Instead, Trotsky rose and fought with his assassin. His screams brought people running from around the fortress. When Natalia reached the study, Trotsky was standing on his feet with blood streaming down his face. He then fell to the floor.

THE ASSASSIN UNMASKED

The true identity of Trotsky's assassin remained a mystery for many years. He was known to his girlfriend as Jacson Mornard, but he claimed after his arrest to be Jacques Mornard Vandendreschd, the son of a Belgian diplomat. The police soon realized that this, too, was a false name. In 1950, an investigator discovered his real name by asking Spanish police to check his fingerprints against their files. They matched those of Jaime Ramon Mercader del Rio, a Spanish Communist, who had been arrested in Barcelona in 1935.

Ramon Mercader was born in 1913 and spent his early life in France. He was recruited by the Soviet secret police (OGPU), probably because his Cuban-born mother was having an affair with an OGPU officer. Mercader was told to form a relationship with Sylvia Agelof so that he could get her to introduce him to Trotsky.

A Mexican court sentenced the assassin to prison in 1943. When he was released from prison in 1960, Mercader flew to the Soviet Union and was given the Order of Lenin. He reportedly died of cancer in Havana.

In his will, Trotsky wrote, "Life is beautiful. May the future generations cleanse it of all evil, oppression, and violence, and enjoy it to the full." It was this generosity of spirit that made even those who disagreed with his revolutionary politics see Trotsky's death as a tragedy.

Last words

As some of the guards tackled the assassin, Trotsky lay waiting for an ambulance to arrive, his mind still lucid. At one point he whispered, "It's the end.... This time... they've succeeded." He was right. An operation failed to save him, and he died in the hospital on the evening of the following day.

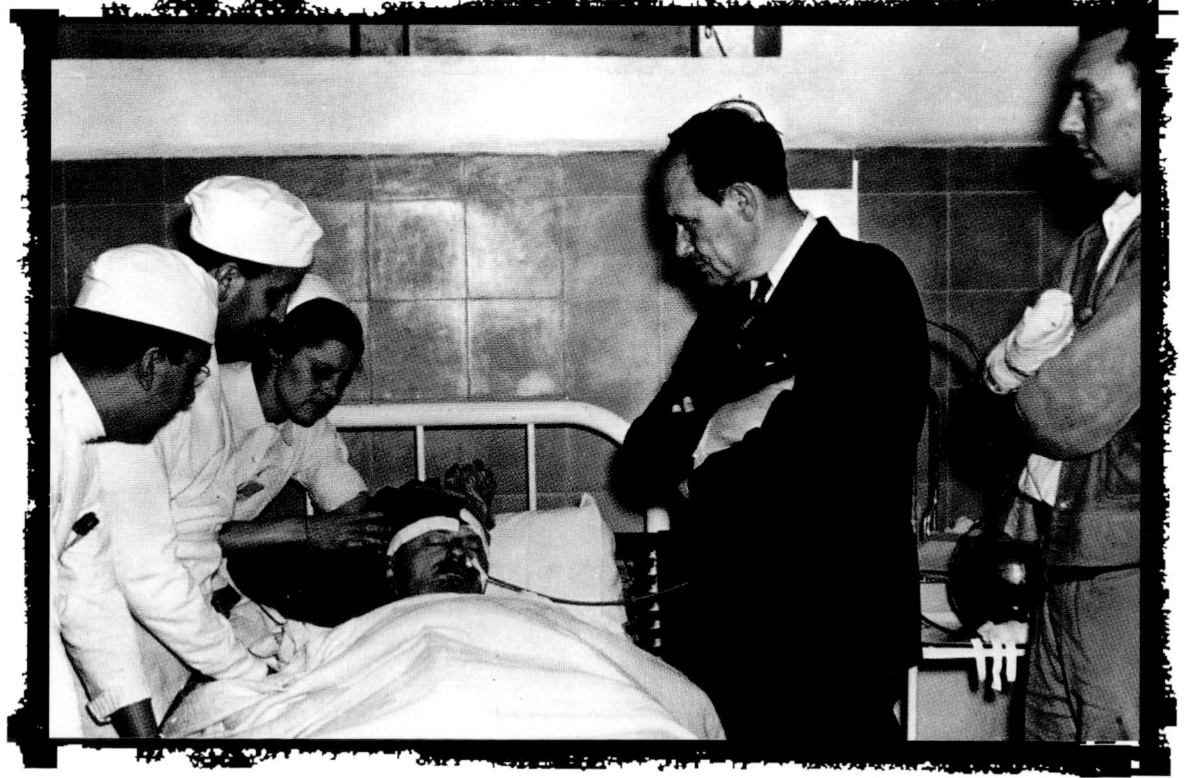

Deathbed *Trotsky died slowly after being fatally struck in the head with an ice pick.*

Kidnapped

Aldo Moro, president of the Christian Democrats, the largest political party in Italy, left his Rome apartment on March 16, 1978, to drive to his church for morning prayers. Later that day he was to inaugurate a new coalition government that would include the Italian Communist Party for the first time. Moro had worked hard to allow the Communists—who had the support of almost one-third of the Italian electorate—a share of responsibility for government. It was a move to help stabilize Italy's democracy during a period of economic crisis and to reduce terrorist activities—nationwide, there had been more than 100 incidents each month.

Kidnapped in broad daylight

Moro left for church sitting in the back seat of his car, with his driver and a bodyguard in front. Another car with two more bodyguards and its driver followed. As they traveled down a street named Via Fani, a Fiat 128 reversed from a side road in front of them. Moro's car braked quickly and the car with the two bodyguards ran into the back of it. A man and a woman jumped out of the Fiat and shot the driver and bodyguard in Moro's car. At the same time, four men wearing airline pilots' uniforms, who had been standing on the sidewalk outside a bar, also pulled out guns, ran forward, and sprayed the second car with bullets, fatally wounding all inside.

Moro was seized, bundled into a getaway car, and driven a short distance to a side street where a van was parked. The kidnappers put him in a trunk,

Calling card *This photo of Moro in front of a Red Brigades flag was found in a phone booth. It revealed the identity of his captors.*

loaded him into the van, and drove to a specially constructed prison inside an apartment on Via Montalcini.

The Red Brigades

Two days later, the police learned that Moro was being held by the Brigate Rosse, or the Red Brigades—Italy's notorious left-wing terrorist group. The Red Brigades opposed the entry of the Communist Party into a coalition government. In their opinion, Communists should not help run a capitalist country.

The terrorists demanded the release of 14 of their members on trial in Turin. The Italian government responded by adopting a stance of no negotiation. More than 20,000 police and troops hunted for the "people's prison," where Moro was being held.

The government's stance was controversial and was rejected by Moro himself. His captors allowed him to write letters to his family, newspapers, and public figures. He wrote of his "profound bitterness and shock" at the attitude adopted by his Christian Democrat colleagues. "I face the solitary fate of the political prisoner condemned to death," he wrote. According to Mario Moretti, the Red Brigades terrorist who had planned and led the kidnapping, a bond developed between Moro and his captors, united in their disgust at the refusal of the authorities to negotiate. On April 15, the terrorists announced that Moro had been condemned to death by a "people's court," but death threats did not change the government's position.

KEY DATES

1916 Born September 23 in Puglia, southern Italy

1940 Becomes a university professor at the age of 24

1948 Elected to the Italian parliament as a Christian Democrat

1959 Becomes political secretary of the Christian Democrat Party

1963 Becomes leader of a series of coalition governments with the socialists

1974 Becomes prime minister for the second time

1976 As president of the Christian Democrat Party, advocates relations with the Italian Communist Party

1978 Kidnapped by Red Brigades terrorists on March 16; assassinated May 9

Executed

The Red Brigades were split over what to do with their captive. Some wanted to let him go, but the majority decided he must be killed. "To free him without getting anything in return," Moretti later said, "would have meant admitting that our strategy was condemned to failure." Moro was shot repeatedly until dead.

Even supports of the extreme left were horrified by the cold-blooded execution of Moro. In its aftermath, terrorism declined. Most of the kidnappers were arrested and received long prison sentences. The Red Brigades still exist, carrying out occasional terrorist acts, including assassinations.

The body *The Red Brigades left Moro's body in the back of a car parked midway between the Rome headquarters of the Christian Democrat and Communist parties.*

RUMORS OF CONSPIRACY

Since 1978, there has been doubt that the official story of the assassination of Aldo Moro is correct. Of various conspiracy theories, the most plausible is that the kidnapping was planned by the Italian secret service and, behind them, the CIA. Allegedly, the CIA regarded Moro as dangerously "soft on Communism" and was unhappy with his plan to introduce the Communist Party into government.

According to some former Red Brigades members, Moretti, the man who directed the kidnapping and carried out the assassination, was a Secret Service agent who had infiltrated the terrorist organization. The other members of the Red Brigades cell were presumably his innocent dupes. However, several commissions of inquiry have examined the Moro assassination since 1978, without finding any evidence of the involvement of anyone but the Red Brigades.

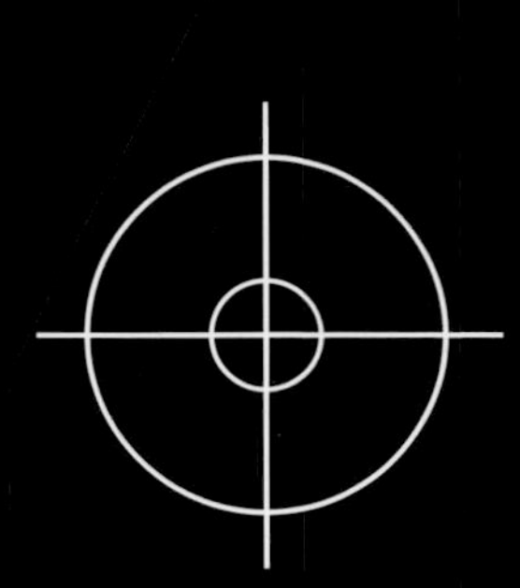

FIGHTERS FOR RIGHTS

MAHATMA GANDHI · 1948

MEDGAR EVERS · 1963

MALCOLM X · 1965

MARTIN LUTHER KING JR. · 1968

ARCHBISHOP ROMERO · 1980

WE
MARCH

Fighters for rights

The leaders in this chapter are united by having lived "a committed life," striving for rights for their people. Mahatma Gandhi, the leader of the struggle to free India from British colonial rule, is the prototype for all those brave individuals in modern times who have confronted beatings and guns armed with nothing but a profound moral conviction and the readiness, if need be, to endure suffering. Gandhi's key idea was *satyagraha,* which

Sign of the times *Segregation was common in the southern United States, as highlighted by this 1943 Greyhound Bus Station sign.*

he defined as the power "born of truth and love or nonviolence." In practice, this translated into using civil disobedience to achieve political and social reforms.

Gandhi's assassination in 1948 was a direct result of his creed of universal love and his rejection of violence. Although a Hindu, Gandhi reached out to people of all faiths and supported the rights of India's poverty-stricken masses. It was his refusal to countenance violence or hatred directed by his fellow Hindus against Muslims during the bitter aftermath of the partition of India that provoked Hindu extremists to kill him.

A man with a vision

American civil rights leader Martin Luther King Jr. was profoundly influenced by Gandhi's example. It led him to the adoption of nonviolent civil disobedience, not only as a moral and spiritual principle but also as a practical approach to achieving change in the United States. King knew that white racists would always win a violent conflict because they had more guns. The only practical way to achieve full rights for African Americans was by moral pressure, appealing to the American Constitution and demanding that the United States live up to its own promise of freedom and democracy for all its citizens.

At the time of his assassination in April 1968, King was a controversial figure. Although admired by millions across the world, he was also hated by racists, disliked by many patriotic Americans for his opposition to the Vietnam War, and rejected by black radicals who considered his policy of nonviolence demeaning and wanted to assert their power against a white-dominated society, not integrate into it. Since his death, King has been enshrined in the pantheon of American heroes—a status embodied in the public holiday that celebrates his life.

Retrospectively, historians are now more inclined to give greater prominence to grassroots movements within civil rights struggles and to local figures, such as Medgar Evers, whose leadership of the voter registration campaign for African Americans in Mississippi led to his murder in 1963.

Reaching beyond racism

Malcolm X, assassinated in 1965, was different from the other victims in this section because he did not renounce violence—on the contrary, he advocated it under certain circumstances. He wrote, "I believe it's a crime for anyone who is being brutalized to continue to accept that brutality without doing something to defend himself." He made it clear that the concept of "self-defense" could be given a broad interpretation. When Malcolm X was killed, many people were relieved.

Yet, in historical retrospect, Malcolm X's stature has grown rather than diminished. There is widespread respect for the heroic personal journey that he accomplished—how, beginning as a criminal, he first rose to a proud affirmation of black identity, then reached beyond racial separatism to a more inclusive vision in the final period of his life. In one of his last speeches, Malcolm X declared, "We don't judge a man because of the color of his skin.... We judge you because of what you do and what you practice." It was because of his move away from the Nation of Islam, with its demonization of whites, that Malcolm was killed.

A speaker for the poor

Archbishop Romero, assassinated in El Salvador in 1980, is an example of the courage needed to assert the rights of the poorest people in the world's developing countries. Romero was originally a conservative prelate, suspicious of Catholic priests who identified with the revolutionary struggle of the poor in Latin America. It was the sheer outrage at the brutality the wealthy Salvadorean elite used in defending their privilege that drove the archbishop to use his position to protest human rights abuses and call on Catholic soldiers to refuse to obey the orders of their officers. For this, he was killed.

A movement for civil rights

Two of the assassination victims in this chapter, Martin Luther King Jr. and Medgar Evers, were prominent campaigners in the civil rights movement in the United States during the 1950s and 1960s. The movement encountered a violent reaction from white supremacists. For example:

1957 Federal troops are sent into Little Rock, Arkansas, to enforce the right of black children to attend a previously all-white school

1961 Freedom Riders, traveling across the southern states by bus to protest against segregation between blacks and whites, are attacked and beaten

1962 James Meredith becomes the first black student at the University of Mississippi, but only with the provision of federal protection against white violence

1963 Medgar Evers is shot dead by a white racist; four black children are killed in the bombing of a church in Birmingham, Alabama

1964 Three young people taking part in the Freedom Summer drive for voter registration in Mississippi are killed and their bodies dumped in a swamp

1965 A voter registration campaign in Selma, Alabama, is met with extreme violence, including a series of killings

1966 James Meredith is shot in the back as he embarks on a civil rights march in Mississippi

1968 Martin Luther King Jr. is assassinated in Tennessee

In cold blood

Every evening just before 5:00 P.M., Mohandas Gandhi, known as Mahatma (meaning "great soul"), left his room in the imposing Birla House on New Delhi's Albuquerque Road, where he stayed when he was in the Indian capital. From here, he made his way down the garden to a special pavilion to hold prayer meetings for pilgrims who came from far and wide to see the famous holy man and father of the nation.

On January 30, 1948, this daily ritual was delayed by an important discussion with India's deputy prime minister, Vallabhaibhai Patel. Gandhi held no official position in India's newly established independent government, but he still had an influence over policy and was regularly consulted by Patel and Prime Minister Jawaharlal Nehru, as well as by India's Governor General Lord Louis Mountbatten. On the evening of the 30th, Gandhi tried to iron out differences between Patel and Nehru, who were vying for power.

"...a small **bomb exploded** during his evening **prayer meeting**..."

A country divided

Now at the age of 78, Gandhi was showing signs of weariness after a life of political and spiritual struggle. Gandhi had campaigned for India's independence for more than 30 years, and it had finally been won the year before, at midnight on August 15, 1947.

The country, however, was divided into two: predominantly Hindu India and Muslim Pakistan. This partition became a catastrophe. An estimated eight million Muslim refugees fled from India to Pakistan, and a similar number of Hindu refugees fled from Pakistan to India. Communal violence exploded. Muslims

Unofficial advice
Nehru (far left) consults with Gandhi (left), who held no official post.

massacred Hindus and Hindus massacred Muslims, and, at the same time, Indian and Pakistani forces clashed in disputed Kashmir.

Appalled at this bloodbath, Gandhi used his influence to end the suffering and discord. He staged a "fast to the death" in Calcutta in September 1947 to protest Hindu attacks on Muslims in the city, and almost miraculously the attacks halted. In January 1948, he repeated this technique in Delhi, fasting for six days until Hindu and Muslim community leaders agreed to make peace.

Hindu hatred

These efforts, while a triumph of nonviolent action, were not universally popular. Hindu extremists denounced Gandhi for his willingness to compromise with Pakistan and for his unwillingness to seek retaliation against Muslim attacks. Gandhi was well aware of the hatred he inspired in some quarters. On January 20, a small bomb exploded during his evening prayer meeting—a clear warning that his life was in danger.

However, Gandhi refused to take extra precautions. He told Lady Mountbatten, "If somebody fired at me point-blank and I faced his bullet with a smile, repeating the name of Rama in my heart, I should be deserving of congratulations."

Communal violence
Muslim and Hindu rioters fight on the streets of Calcutta. Thousands were killed in and around the city.

KEY DATES

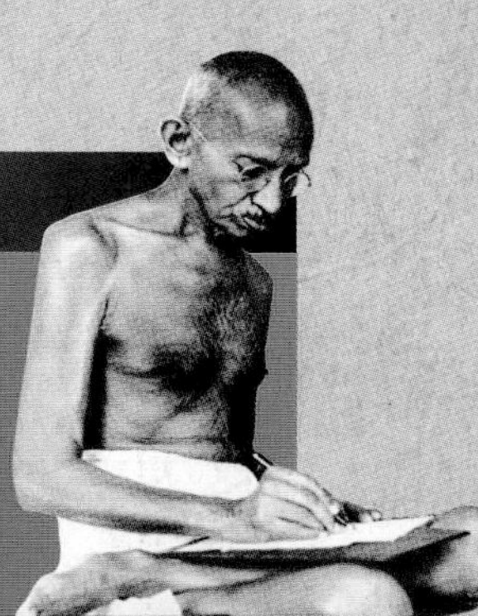

1869 Born October 2 Mohandas Karamchand Gandhi at Porbandar, India, son of the *dewan* (chief minister) to a local prince

1893 Goes to South Africa to work in Natal

1894 Founds the Natal Indian Congress to campaign for the rights of Indian workers

1914 Returns to India; campaigns for independence from Britain

1920 Launches his first civil disobedience campaign in India

1930 Leads "Salt March" against British salt monopoly; is jailed

1931 Represents the Indian National Congress at a conference in London

1939 Demands independence as the price for supporting Britain in World War II

1947 Welcomes independence; fasts to protest Hindu attacks on Muslims

1948 Fasts to end communal violence in Delhi; assassinated January 30

Mahatma's greeting
Gandhi welcomes someone by holding his hands together in the tradtional Hindu namaskar *greeting.*

On the evening of January 30, after leaving Patel, Gandhi expressed irritation at the delay in attending prayers. He walked out into the dusk, leaning on two of his devoted attendants, his great-niece Manu and Abha, another young female relative.

The prayer meeting was well attended, with about 500 people in the crowd. The majority were Hindus, but all faiths were welcomed. In protest against religious prejudice, Gandhi read from the Koran and the Bible as well as from Hindu texts.

The assassin strikes

As Mahatma walked across the lawn and up five steps to where the crowd waited for him, he put his hands together in a traditional Hindu greeting. Suddenly, a man in a green sweater and khaki jacket pushed past Manu. "Brother," she protested to the man, "Bapuji is already late for prayers. Why are you bothering him?" She thought he was about to prostrate himself at Gandhi's feet, as the devout often did. Instead, he fired three shots in rapid succession from an automatic pistol. The first hit Gandhi near the navel, the second and third in the chest. Blood seeped out across his white clothes. With his palms still together, the frail old man sank to the ground, murmuring *"Hai Rama! Hai Rama!"* ("Oh God! Oh God!"). He lay with his head in Manu's lap, already dead.

Justice for Gandhi's killers

The assassin was Nathuram Godse, the 37-year-old editor of a Hindu extremist newspaper. He made no attempt to escape or defend himself but stood immobile until he was disarmed. Assaulted by the grief-stricken crowd, he was saved from a lynching by the arrival of the police, who took him into custody. Two coconspirators, Narayan Apte and Vishnu Karkare, had been standing alongside Godse in Gandhi's garden, but they fled after the killing. The police caught them 12 days later. They were charged with Gandhi's murder along with Godse and five others, including

Godse's brother Gopal Godse and a Hindu political leader, Vinayak Damodar Savarkar.

The investigation revealed that Gandhi's assassination had been the conspirators' second attempt. They set off the bomb that exploded during a prayer meeting on January 20—it was supposed to be a signal to begin an assault with guns and grenades, but other conspirators failed to follow up. Godse showed more resolve on January 30. He was proud of what he had done, declaring, "I thought it was my duty to put an end to the life of the so-called father of the nation."

All the defendants were found guilty except Savarkar, who had no involvement with the crime. Godse and Apte were condemned to death and the other five given life sentences. The condemned men went to the gallows, each carrying a map of undivided India and the flag of the Hindu movement.

A victory for nonviolence

It would be easy to present the assassination as a victory for violence over the principle of nonviolence to which Gandhi had devoted his life, yet the aftermath demonstrated the reverse. When Gandhi was cremated, as many as a million people lined the route to the traditional funeral pyre. The emotional reaction to the killing was so powerful that the wave of massacres across India suddenly subsided. It was as if people realized the depths to which discord and hatred had dragged them, then turned back from the abyss.

Funeral pyre *Gandhi is cremated according to Hindu custom the day after his death.*

On trial *A note is passed to an assassin. Godse is to the left; Apte, center.*

GANDHI'S ASSASSINS

Nathuram Godse, the man who shot Gandhi, was born in a village between Bombay and Poona in 1910. Although his family were Brahmans—the highest caste in Hindu society—they were poor, living on his father's income as a postmaster.

In the 1930s, Godse met Vinayak Damodar Savarkar, a veteran Hindu activist who had been imprisoned for advocating violence in the independence struggle. Godse became an active member of Hindu Mahasabha, a political movement that opposed British rule and rejected the caste system. Hindu Mahasabha rejected both Gandhi's principle of nonviolence and his concern about the rights of Muslims.

Godse met his main coconspirator Narayan Apte in 1941. Apte came from a wealthy Brahman background. Unlike Godse, Apte smoked and drank and liked stylish clothes. These two different men, however, became close colleagues in Hindu Mahasabha, and, after World War II, they worked together to publish *Agrani,* a daily newspaper advocating independence and vehemently opposing the creation of the Muslim state of Pakistan. The men never expressed regret for the assassination.

MEDGAR EVERS·1963

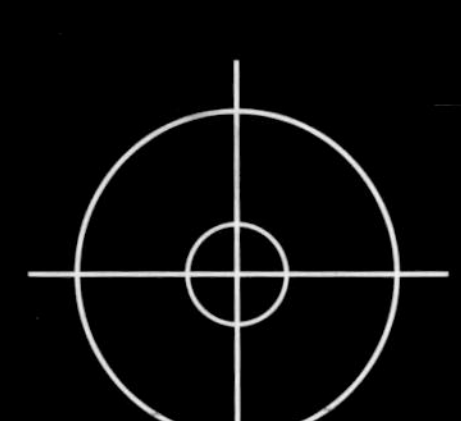

Silenced forever

In June 1963, in the southern United States, African Americans demanding equal rights confronted white supremacists prepared to use any methods to maintain segregation and racial domination. Almost daily, nonviolent black protesters were attacked with bullwhips and dogs, threatened with guns, and beaten with clubs, because they demanded the right to vote or to go to the same schools as whites.

Medgar Evers, the 37-year-old field secretary of the National Association for the Advancement of Colored People (NAACP) in the state of Mississippi, stood in the forefront of the civil rights campaign. He had been an NAACP activist since the mid-1950s. His involvement with civil rights actions, such as helping an African American enrol at the all-white University of Mississippi in 1962, had made him a prominent public figure.

Any person who stood up for black rights in the South in the 1950s and 1960s needed great courage. Death threats were a constant factor in Evers's life, as were police harassment and physical intimidation. In the spring of 1963, someone tried to firebomb Evers's house in Jackson, where he lived with his wife, Myrlie, and their three children.

An unshakable, upright man, Evers went on pursuing the cause of racial integration and refused any suggestion that he flee the state. "It may sound funny, but I love the South..," he wrote. "There is room here for my children to play and grow and become good citizens—if the white man will let them."

KEY DATES

1925 Born July 2 near Decatur, Mississippi

1943 Inducted into the U.S. Army

1951 Marries Myrlie Beasley

1953 Graduates from Alcorn College

1954 Denied admission to the University of Mississippi Law School; appointed first field secretary for the NAACP in Mississippi

1962 Helps James Meredith gain admittance to the University of Mississippi

1963 Assassinated in Jackson, Mississippi, on June 11; Byron de la Beckwith's first trial ends in mistrial

1964 Beckwith's second trial ends in mistrial

1992 Statue of Medgar Evers erected in Jackson, Mississippi

1994 Beckwith convicted

Sniper attack

On June 11, 1963, Evers was working his usual long hours to promote Jackson's civil rights protests, which were faltering in the face of routine police violence. He phoned his wife several times that evening to tell her that he loved her and would get home when he could. The children were allowed to stay up late to greet him when he got home.

It was a hot night and Myrlie fell asleep watching TV. At just after midnight, the sound of tires in the driveway woke her. She heard the car door slam shut, then there was a loud bang. The children took cover, diving to the floor as their father had taught them to do in case of a drive-by shooting.

Myrlie found her husband lying outside the front door. He had been shot in the back. The Evers children screamed for their father to "please get up," but he was mortally wounded. His last words were, "Turn me loose." He was pronounced dead at Jackson's University Hospital later that night.

Evers's death provoked demonstrations across the United States. It was the first killing of an African American in the South to make the headlines nationwide. Medgar Evers was given a hero's burial in Arlington National Cemetery, and his funeral, a moving and solemn occasion, was attended by black and white leaders from around the nation.

The criminal investigation

Surprisingly, the Jackson Police Department, known for its tolerance of white crime against African Americans, did a good job during the investigation. They found the fatal bullet, which had passed through Evers's chest, a window, and a wall to end up in the kitchen. They also identified where the sniper had hidden—in honeysuckle bushes across the street. The following morning, they discovered a 1918 Enfield rifle with a Japanese telescopic sight. On the rifle was one clear fingerprint.

JUSTICE AT LAST

The third trial *In 1994, after three trials and more than 30 years after the murder, Byron de la Beckwith is finally convicted of killing Evers.*

In 1994, 73-year-old Byron de la Beckwith was put on trial for the murder of Medgar Evers, exactly 30 years after the second mistrial. Because of Beckwith' s age and the time that had elapsed since the assassination, there were those who wanted to stop the trial; however, prosecutor Bobby DeLaughter asserted, "No man, regardless of age, is above the law."

In the 1970s, Beckwith had spent time in Louisiana State Penitentiary after being found with explosives in his car as part of a Ku Klux Klan bomb plot. A prison guard testified to hearing Beckwith say to a black nurse in the prison, "If I could get rid of an uppity nigger like Medgar Evers, I can get rid of a no-account nigger like you." This and other fresh testimony helped convince a multiracial jury of Beckwith's guilt. He was sentenced to life imprisonment. In 2001, he died in prison at the age of 80.

Path of blood *A trail of blood leads from Evers's car to the door, showing the path he took as he crawled to the house after being shot in the back.*

The FBI soon became involved with the case. The evidence led them to an outspoken white supremacist, Byron de la Beckwith, a 42-year-old fertilizer salesman from Greenwood, a town about 60 miles (96 km) from Jackson. By inspecting Beckwith's World War II military records, they found that his fingerprint matched the one on the rifle. Beckwith's car had also been seen

"Death threats were a constant factor in Evers life..."

parked near the Evers's home on the evening of the crime.

Although two Greenwood police officers swore they could place him elsewhere at the time of the killing, the case against Beckwith was strong. However, no one expected an all-white Mississippi jury to convict a white man of murdering an African American. Beckwith was tried twice, in 1963 and 1964, and both times the jury was split. Beckwith walked free—until justice won some 30 years later.

MALCOLM X · 1965

Death in Harlem

An audience of African Americans filled Harlem's Audubon Ballroom to hear a speech from the charismatic 39-year-old Malcolm X, founder of the Organization of Afro-American Unity and Muslim Mosque Incorporated, on the afternoon of February 21, 1965. There was an air of tension in the hall, because of previous threats made against the speaker's life. A week earlier, his home in Elmhurst, New York, had been firebombed in the middle of the night.

Dark-suited bodyguards surveyed the crowd from alongside the stage. At 3:08 P.M., as Malcolm X walked onto the stage, he was greeted by a prolonged ovation. His pregnant wife, Betty, and four daughters were seated in a box near the front of the stage.

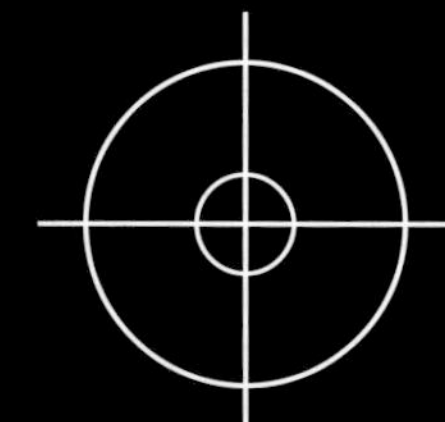

The attack begins

As Malcolm began to speak, a scuffle started. Two men jumped up, scattering chairs around. One shouted, "Get your hand out of my pocket!" Malcolm X called out, "Let's cool it, brothers!" Then there was a loud explosion as a smoke bomb went off at the back of the room.

In the moments of chaos and panic that followed, as smoke filled the ballroom, a man leaped up in the front row of the audience, pulled a sawn-off shotgun from under his coat, and fired twice. Malcolm staggered backward, clutching his chest. Two other men rushed the stage, shooting repeatedly into Malcolm's body. Even as they attempted to flee, they continued shooting. One of the assailants, Talmadge Hayer, was shot in the leg by a bodyguard. Unable to escape, he was kicked and beaten by members of the crowd before two police officers arrived. According to some reports, a second assailant was caught by the crowd and handed over to police, but there is no record of any other arrest.

Meanwhile, Malcolm X's wife and some of his aides ran to where his bullet-riddled body had fallen and made desperate efforts to revive him. A stretcher was brought from a hospital across the street, and Malcolm X

Police escort *Malcolm X's body is removed from the Audubon Ballroom and taken to a hospital across the street.*

was carried to the emergency room. Fifteen minutes later a doctor announced, "The gentleman you know as Malcolm X is dead."

The Nation of Islam

The investigation of the assassination focused on the black Muslim separatist movement, the Nation of Islam, led by Elijah Muhammad. In the 1950s and early 1960s, Malcolm X had been their star speaker and organizer. His assertion of a separate black identity and the need for black people to stand up for themselves, using violence if needed, outraged whites but appealed to African Americans who did not identify with Martin Luther King Jr.'s nonviolent integrationist policies.

Malcolm X grew disillusioned with Elijah Muhammad's corruption and ideology. In 1964, he left to develop his own organization and ideas. Rejecting the Nation of Islam view that all white men are evil, Malcolm X asserted, "We're not against people because they're white. We're against those who practice racism." Prominent figures in the Nation of Islam responded to Malcolm X's "betrayal" by calling for his death.

CONSPIRACY THEORY

Inevitably, there are many African Americans who are not satisfied with the conclusion that the Nation of Islam ordered their hero's assassination. The FBI and the CIA are known to have regarded Malcolm X as a dangerous subversive. The FBI had the Nation of Islam and Malcolm X under surveillance—and one of Malcolm X's bodyguards on the day of the killing was an undercover NYPD police officer reporting to the FBI. No wonder there is suspicion that these agencies had a hand in the assassination.

Life for a life

Three men were given life sentences for the assassination: Hayer, the man arrested at the scene, and Norman Butler and Thomas Johnson, Nation of Islam members. During the trial, Hayer denied he was a Muslim. In 1977, however, he made a sworn statement describing how he had planned the killing with four members of a Nation of Islam mosque, although not Butler or Johnson.

Malcolm X's death has been entangled in tales of witnesses who never gave evidence, key figures who disappeared, and leads never followed up by police. Yet, no evidence has yet been found to link anyone but members of the Nation of Islam to the killing.

KEY DATES

1925 Born on May 19 as Malcolm Little in Omaha, Nebraska

1931 His father, Baptist minister Earl Little, is murdered in Lansing, Michigan

1946 Sentenced to 10 years for burglary; in prison, joins the Nation of Islam

1953 Paroled; becomes a minister and spokesman for the Nation of Islam

1958 Marries Betty X (Betty Shabazz)

1964 Quits the Nation of Islam; starts his own organizations, Muslim Mosque Incorporated and the Organization of Afro-American Unity

1965 Assassinated in New York on February 21

Martyred hero

Eloquent orator *Martin Luther King Jr., who became a Baptist pastor in 1955, gives a sermon.*

On the evening of April 3, 1968, Martin Luther King Jr. made one of his most memorable speeches at the Mason Street Temple in Memphis, Tennessee. Addressing a small but enthusiastic audience who had braved torrential rain to hear him speak, King reviewed his life's work, but with death very much on his mind. During his speech he talked about how he "would like to live a long life." However, longevity wasn't important to him as long as he followed God's will. He also told his audience that "we as a people will get to the Promised Land. So I'm happy tonight...."

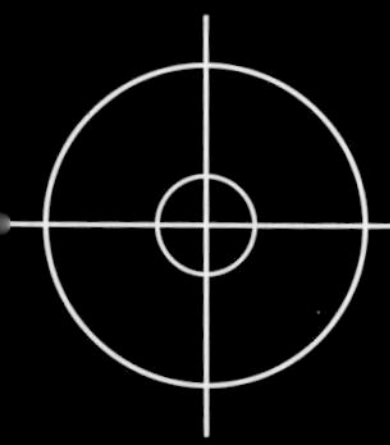

A lifetime of threats

Although he was only 39 years old, it was not surprising that King often reflected on his own death. He had endured constant harassment and threats since emerging as a prominent campaigner for civil rights in the mid-1950s. Over the years, King had been stabbed in the chest and punched in the face. His house had been bombed, and he had routinely received death threats. In fact, white supremacists had posted large cash rewards for anyone who would kill him. King had been arrested on numerous occasions, and he had been harassed and vilified by the FBI.

A visit to Memphis

King had flown to Memphis that day from Atlanta, Georgia. He intended to lead a march in support of striking Memphis sanitation workers who were engaged in a conflict with city authorities. Their dispute was a diversion from his urgent concern of the moment, the organization of a Poor People's March on Washington—scheduled for the following month—which was to involve all ethnic groups in a mass protest against economic deprivation.

An old Memphis acquaintance, Reverend Samuel "Billy" Kyles, however, had asked King to become involved in the strike dispute earlier in the year. Once he was involved in an issue, King was generally relentless and unwilling to put it aside until he achieved a successful resolution.

King checked into room 306 at the Lorraine Motel, which he was sharing with one of his oldest friends and closest colleagues in the civil rights struggle, Reverend Ralph Abernathy. King had stayed up most of the night, not getting to bed until about 6:30 A.M. As a consequence, he did not emerge from his room the following day until the early afternoon.

At around the same time, a man using the name John Willard checked into room 5B at a rundown boardinghouse on South Main Street, Bessie Brewer's, across from the Lorraine Motel. Willard's seedy room—it was lit by a single bare lightbulb—had a partial view of the balcony of room 306 of the motel; and there was an unimpeded view from the bathroom along the hall. That afternoon, there was some discontent among other guests in the boardinghouse, because the inhabitant of room 5B stayed in the bathroom for an unusually long time.

KEY DATES

1929 Born Michael Luther King Jr. on January 15 in Atlanta, Georgia, son of a Baptist pastor (his father changed his name to Martin Luther King Jr. in 1934)

1953 Marries Coretta Scott

1955 Becomes a Baptist pastor in Alabama

1956 Comes to national prominence as leader of the Montgomery Bus Boycott

1957 Forms the Southern Christian Leadership Conference (SCLC) to win civil rights

1958 Stabbed during a Harlem book signing

1960 Arrested at an Atlanta sit-in demonstration

1963 Leads the March on Washington, delivering his famous "I have a dream" speech

1964 Is awarded the Nobel Peace Prize

1967 Attacks America's war in Vietnam; launches the multiracial Poor People's Campaign

1968 Assassinated in Memphis, Tennessee, April 4

Marching for rights
Supporters of civil rights march in Montgomery, Alabama on March 25, 1965. King can be seen in the center with his wife, heading the march.

Countdown to murder

At about 5:00 P.M., King ended a meeting with his aide Andrew Young, who had spent the day in court contesting a ban on the planned march in support of the striking sanitation workers. Then King and Abernathy went back to their room to dress for dinner at Reverend Kyles's house. Sometime after 5:30 P.M., Kyles arrived in a chauffeur-driven car, ready to take his guests to his home. He found King struggling to do up the top button of his shirt. They joked about weight problems while King found a larger shirt to wear.

At about 6.00 P.M., King and Kyles stepped out onto the balcony. The car, a white Cadillac, was parked in the courtyard below. There were a small group of people alongside it, including King's aides Andrew Young and Jesse Jackson, and the driver, Solomon Jones. Some banter passed back and forth between the men on the balcony and those in the parking lot. There was a chill in the air, so Jones suggested that King should bring his overcoat. King smiled. "Solomon, you really know how to take good care of me," he said.

A fatal move

King turned slightly to call through the door for Abernathy to bring his coat. Kyles had moved away, about to head downstairs. There was a sharp sound like a car backfiring or a firecracker exploding—except that within a second all present knew that was not what they had heard. King crumpled to the balcony floor. A bullet had struck him in the jaw, slashed through his jugular artery and spinal cord, and lodged in his shoulder. Blood gushed from a gaping wound in his face and neck. Abernathy and others rushed to help King, striving in vain to stop the bleeding, calling for help, and pointing out to arriving police where the shot had come from.

"Blood gushed from a gaping wound in his face and neck."

King could neither move nor speak. Andrew Young tried to find his pulse. "Oh my God, my God, it's all over," he was moaning. "No, it's not over," Abernathy protested. "Don't you ever say that." However, it was. Abernathy traveled with King in the ambulance that took him to St. Joseph's Hospital. A team of doctors and nurses tried to save him, but King had suffered brain damage. At 7:05 P.M., the doctor leading the medical team told Abernathy, "I'm sorry, but we've lost him."

Tragic news

In Atlanta, King's wife was informed of the shooting by phone and immediately went to the airport, intending to fly to Memphis. She was told at the Atlanta airport that her husband was dead. In shock, she returned home to be with their children. King's parents, also at home in Atlanta, heard the news of his death over the radio. They wept in silence, finding no words adequate for their feelings.

While most were shocked by King's death, it was not a universal reaction. White racists celebrated—J. B. Stoner, head of the National States Rights Party, claimed to have told an audience that day, "Martin Lucifer Coon is a good nigger now." Radical "Black Power" activists who had rejected King's belief in nonviolence and integration found in his

ATTEMPTED MURDER

On September 20, 1958, Martin Luther King Jr. was in Blumstein's department store in Harlem, signing copies of his book *Stride Toward Freedom.* Izola Ware Curry, an African American woman, pulled out a letter opener and thrust it into King's chest. Surgeons removed two of his ribs to extract the blade, which had grazed his aorta. Curry, who had been suffering from mental problems, was convinced that King was persecuting her. She was later confined to a mental hospital.

King referred to this event in his "Promised Land" speech on April 3, 1968, the eve of his assassination. He noted that a newspaper report suggested that "if I had sneezed I would have died." King told his audience, "I'm so happy that I didn't sneeze."

Civil rights leaders *From left to right, Hosea Williams, Jesse Jackson, Martin Luther King Jr., and Reverend Ralph Abernathy stand on the balcony of the Lorraine Motel in Memphis, Tennessee.*

death ironic confirmation of their view that, in the words of H. Rap Brown, "violence is as American as cherry pie."

The response to the assassination in the black ghettos of major American cities was an outbreak of anarchy worse than any seen in the country's 200-year history. For the next five days, there were riots in more than 100 cities, with widespread arson and looting. In Washington D.C., buildings burned within a few blocks of the White House. At least 39 people died around the country. This was not, as the black radicals had hoped, the start of a revolution, rather an expression of frustration. It would have distressed King, who had been appalled by similar, if more scattered, outbreaks of urban rioting over the previous three years.

The search for a killer

The investigation into the assassination led toward the identification of a suspect. Immediately after the shooting, police found a green blanket on the sidewalk outside Canipe's Amusement Company, next door

Eyewitnesses *King's aides, on the balcony of the Lorraine Motel, point out the area from which the shots were fired.*

to Bessie Brewer's boardinghouse. A hunting rifle—a Remington Gamester Model 760—was wrapped inside, among other items. Eyewitnesses said the bundle had been dropped by a man who had run out of the boardinghouse and left in a white Mustang.

The rifle was traced to a sports store in Birmingham, Alabama. The man who had bought it was identified as Eric Starvo Galt, who had stayed at another hotel in Memphis before moving to South Main Street on April 4. The investigation came to a standstill until the FBI checked a fingerprint on the rifle against its records of fugitives. "Galt" was an alias for James Earl Ray, who had escaped from Missouri State Prison the previous year.

Ray's Mustang was found in Atlanta, Georgia, but where he had gone from there remained a mystery until the beginning of June, when he was identified as the man who had been issued a Canadian passport in the name of Raymon George Sneyd. During May, Sneyd had flown from Toronto to Britain, gone to Portugal for 10 days, then returned to London. He was arrested on June 8 at Heathrow airport, trying to board a plane from London to Brussels, Belgium.

BOBBY KENNEDY'S RESPONSE

When news of King's assassination was announced, Robert Kennedy was in Indianapolis, campaigning for nomination as Democratic candidate for the presidency. He drove immediately to the city's predominantly black area and gave an impromptu speech on a street corner.

His brother John F. Kennedy had been assassinated five years earlier in 1968 (see pp. 28–35), so he understood the earthshaking emotions stirred up by such a tragedy. In his speech, he suggested, "What we need is not violence but love and wisdom, and compassion toward one another, and a feeling of justice toward those who still suffer within our country, whether they be white or black." Bobby Kennedy was himself murdered two months later (see pp. 106–9).

"Over the years, other versions of the assassination have surfaced."

Evidence for a conviction

The evidence against Ray was circumstantial; however, it was convincing. He had bought the gun found on the sidewalk, had taken the room in the boarding house with a view of the motel, and had driven away in the white Mustang after the assassination. A map found in the room he had rented while staying in Atlanta prior to the killing had the position of King's house and church ringed in pencil.

It could not be proven that Ray's gun had fired the bullet that killed King—although the ammunition was of the right kind—or that he was the man who had been in the boardinghouse bathroom when the shooting took place. Based on the evidence available, however, a conviction seemed certain. On advice from his counsel, Ray pleaded guilty to avoid the death penalty. As a result, there was no trial, and Ray was locked up for life.

The killer's gun
James Earl Ray probably used this rifle to shoot Martin Luther King Jr.

A change in the story

Once in prison, Ray renounced his guilty plea, producing an elaborate and detailed story in which he was set up by others. In this version, after escaping from prison in April 1967, Ray made his way to Canada, where he was recruited by a man he knew only as "Raoul" to take part in smuggling operations. The purchase of the Mustang and the gun, the journey to Memphis, and the hiring of the room on South Main Street had all been done on Raoul's orders.

Many people, including members of King's family, believe this version of events because they think the assassination was the work of the FBI or CIA. Raoul's alleged behavior fits the profile of an FBI or CIA controller running an underground operation. By the time James Earl Ray died in 1998 of liver failure, he had convinced a large number of people that he was innocent of the crime for which he had been convicted. Far more believed that even if Ray did pull the trigger, he did so as part of a conspiracy.

LONE ASSASSIN OR PART OF A CONSPIRACY

James Earl Ray had been in and out of jail for most of his life before an armed robbery of a grocery store in 1959 led to a 20-year sentence. He escaped from prison in a bread truck in April 1967. Would such a man have been the lone killer of Martin Luther King Jr.? More than 30 years afterward, Reverend Jesse Jackson expressed the view of many people when he said, "Ray didn't have the motive, the mobility, or the money to have done it alone."

WANTED BY THE FBI

CIVIL RIGHTS - CONSPIRACY
INTERSTATE FLIGHT - ROBBERY
JAMES EARL RAY

FBI No. 405,942 G

Photographs taken 1960 — Photograph taken 1968 (eyes drawn by artist)

Aliases: Eric Starvo Galt, W. C. Herron, Harvey Lowmyer, James McBride, James O'Conner, James Walton, James Walyon, John Willard, "Jim,"

DESCRIPTION

Age: 40, born March 10, 1928, at Quincy or Alton, Illinois (not supported by birth records)
Height: 5' 10" **Eyes:** Blue
Weight: 163 to 174 pounds **Complexion:** Medium
Build: Medium **Race:** White
Hair: Brown, possibly cut short **Nationality:** American

One theory is that Ray acted for white supremacists. Ray's brother was linked to National States Rights Party leader J. B. Stoner, a man who rejoiced at King's death. Some wealthy white southerners would have paid to be rid of King. Alternatively, the FBI or CIA may have organized a conspiracy. FBI chief J. Edgar Hoover hated King, whom he denounced as a Communist. The FBI kept King under surveillance and tried to blackmail and discredit him. The CIA was also worried about King's activities.

Yet Ray's ability to commit the crime alone should not be discounted. He was a racist, and a psychiatrist noted him as dangerously obsessive and paranoid.

Attention seekers

Over the years, other versions of the assassination have surfaced. For example, in 1993, Lloyd Jowers, the former owner of Jim's Grill, a restaurant near the Lorraine Motel, claimed on television that he had been paid by mobsters to take part in a conspiracy to kill King. In 2002, a Florida minister, Reverend Ronald Denton Wilson, claimed that his father, Henry, now deceased, had carried out the assassination, motivated by anti-Communist beliefs. No evidence has ever substantiated these or other similar claims.

Headline news *People in Resurrection City, Washington D.C., home of the Poor People's Campaign, read about the capture of King's killer in London.*

No sanctuary

On the morning of March 24, 1980, Archbishop Oscar Arnulfo Romero y Galdamez was leading mass in the chapel of the Divine Providence cancer hospital in San Salvador, the capital of the Central American state of El Salvador. It was a bright, sunny day, and the doors of the chapel were open.

A red Volkswagen pulled up outside. The occupants of the car were its driver, Amado Antonio Garay, and a bearded passenger in the back seat. The bearded man told Garay to crouch down and pretend to be repairing something under the dashboard. He climbed out of the car and rested a rifle on the car door. Aiming carefully down the aisle, he fired a single .22 bullet into Romero's heart. The archbishop fell in a welter of blood, the white discs of the host scattered around him. The gunman calmly resumed his seat in the back of the car. "Drive slowly," he told the driver, and they drove off.

KEY DATES

1917 Born August 15 in Ciudad Barrios, El Salvador

1942 Ordained as a Catholic priest

1974 Becomes a bishop

1977 Appointed archbishop of San Salvador

1979 After protesting against the activities of Salvadoran death squads, nominated for the Nobel Peace Prize by a group of American congressmen and British MPs

1980 Assassinated on March 24

1983 Pope John Paul II prays at Archbishop Romero's tomb

1992 Peace agreement ends El Salvador's civil war

Motive for murder
At that time, El Salvador was slipping into civil war as left-wing guerrilla groups fought army officers, landowners, and rich businessmen. To stop El Salvador from "going Communist," the United States backed the Salvadoran army.

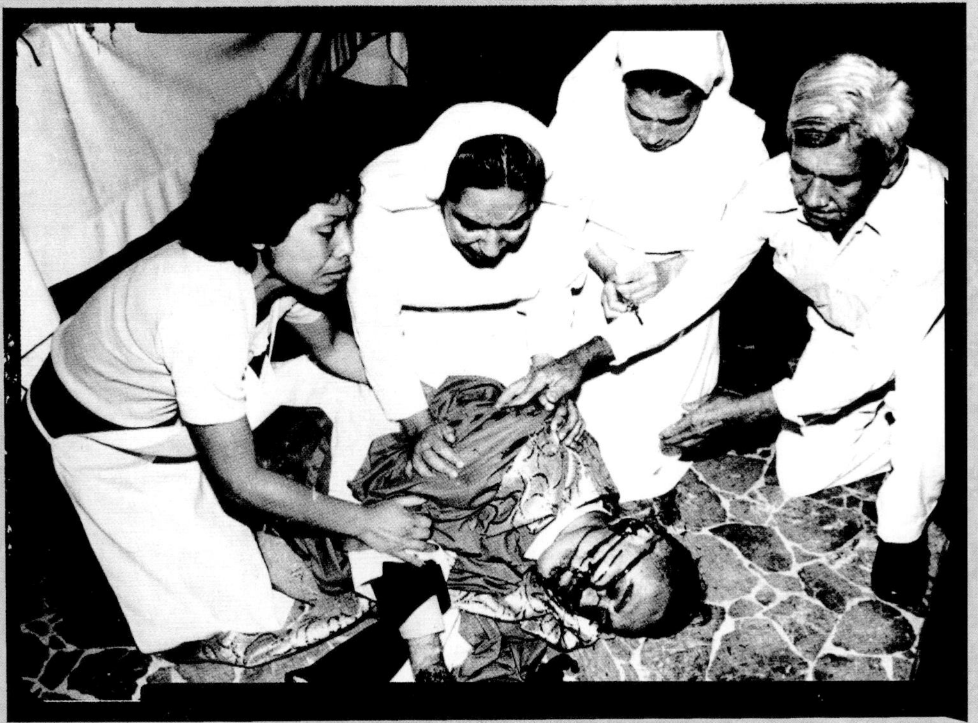

Fallen archbishop *Nuns rush to Archbishop Romero's side after he was shot and killed as he said mass.*

El Salvador's elite did not respect human rights. They ran a reign of terror using torture and murder to intimidate or eliminate anyone who wanted reform.

Archbishop Romero used the pulpit to denounce the armed forces for their "unscrupulous use of power" and "repression of the people," and he asked the United States to cut off military aid. His sermons, broadcast on radio, detailed abuses and killings.

In February 1980, the archbishop received the first of many death threats. He refused police protection, saying, "The Shepherd seeks protection not for himself, but for his flock." On March 10, explosives were found in an attaché case near the pulpit where he was to speak, but the archbishop would not be silenced.

Outspoken archbishop

On Sunday, March 23, in San Salvador's Metropolitan Cathedral, Romero delivered an eloquent denunciation of the murder of poor farmers who had tried to claim land owed them under a land reform scheme. After hearing this speech, his enemies probably decided to assassinate him the next day.

Romero's death sent shock waves across the world. Six days later, more than 30,000 people, including foreign dignitaries, gathered at the Metropolitan Cathedral for his funeral. As if to demonstrate that nothing—not even a sacred event—would halt the country's descent into violence, a bomb was set off outside the cathedral during the funeral, and snipers fired from rooftops into the crowd, killing 40 people. The assassination of Romero, followed by the massacre at the funeral, convinced many Salvadorans that armed struggle was the only way forward.

Escaping nuns *Several hours after a stampede caused by snipers and bombs at Archbishop Romero's funeral, nuns leave with hands over their heads.*

WHO WAS RESPONSIBLE?

The investigation into Archbishop Romero's assassination was held in a climate of complete intimidation. Although no one was ever arrested, most Salvadorans believe the man who ordered the killing was Major Roberto D'Aubuisson, a former leader in the Salvadoran military intelligence and a prominent commander of right-wing death squads, bands of killers who colluded with Salvadoran government security forces.

It appears that Captain Alvaro Rafael Saravia, one of D'Aubuisson's aides, was the man who told Garay to drive to the chapel on the day of the assassination, and it was to Saravia that the bearded assassin reported back after the killing. One CIA file suggests that the assassin may have been a Salvadoran National Police detective named Oscar Perez Linares.

"...a **bomb** was set off outside the **cathedral** during the **funeral**..."

IN THE NAME OF GOD OR NATION

PRINCE ITO · 1909
COUNT FOLKE BERNADOTTE · 1948
ROBERT F. KENNEDY · 1968
LORD MOUNTBATTEN · 1979
ANWAR AL-SADAT · 1981
INDIRA GANDHI · 1984
YITZHAK RABIN · 1995

In the name of God or nation

In the modern world, the political assertion of national and religious interests and identity has generated intractable conflicts in many parts of the globe. The savagery of such conflicts is reflected in the readiness of militants to kill and be killed, often with no clear aim except revenge or to win publicity for their cause.

Striving for a free country

Assassins who kill in the name of national independence are denounced as murderous criminals by their enemies as a matter of course; however, they are often regarded as heroes by the people whose cause they represent. This is the case with An Joong-Gun, who is celebrated in Korean history for assassinating Prince Ito, the Japanese statesman blamed for turning Korea into a Japanese colony.

The Jewish struggle for a homeland in the Middle East, which resulted in the creation of the state of Israel in 1948, also generated assassinations, most famously of the United Nations peacemaker Count Bernadotte and British Minister Lord Moyne. Israelis have wavered in their attitude toward those responsible for such killings—they have rarely been celebrated, but they have never been disowned.

Middle East terrorism

In the half-century since the creation of Israel, the Middle East has established itself as the world capital for all forms of terrorist violence, sometimes promoted by governments, sometimes by underground organizations, and sometimes by individuals inspired to acts of fanaticism—such as Sirhan Sirhan, the unlikely Palestinian assassin of Robert Kennedy.

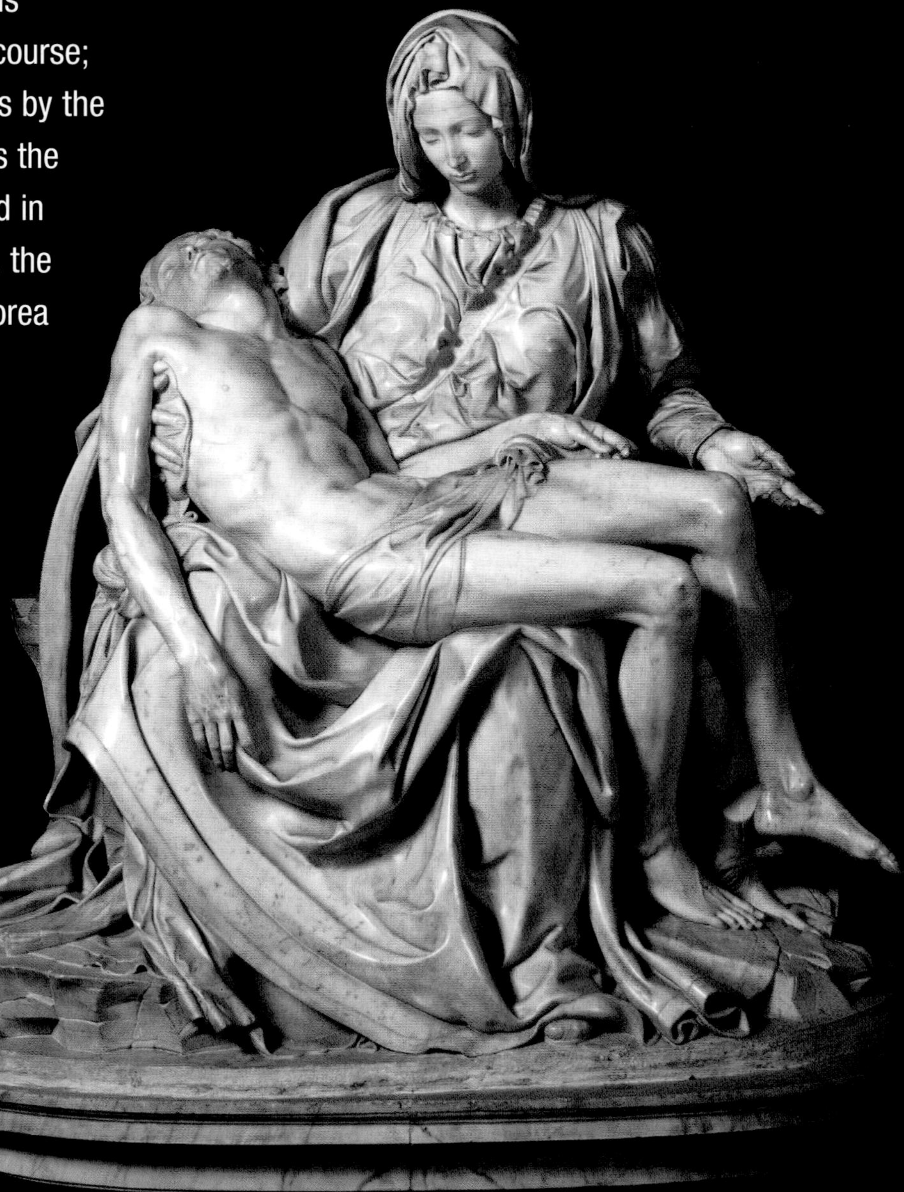

Crucified for His beliefs *The mother's sorrow shown in Michelangelo's Pietà (c. 1500) brings to life the tragedy of assassination.*

The actions of secular Palestinian liberation movements that shocked the world in the 1960s and 1970s have been completely surpassed, however, by the subsequent rise of Islamic fundamentalist extremism. Egyptian President Anwar al-Sadat made friends with the United States and sought peace with Israel; he was assassinated by Islamic extremists for these "crimes" in 1984. This attack can now be seen as the start of a process that would culminate in the destruction of the World Trade Center in 2001.

Jewish fundamentalists proved they could be as ruthless as their Muslim opponents with the killing of Israeli Prime Minister Yitzhak Rabin in 1995. His murder was almost a mirror image of the Sadat assassination, in that Rabin was killed for trying to make peace with the Palestinians.

Ethnic and religious conflicts

Although attracting less worldwide attention, conflict between India's mixture of ethnic and religious groups has generated lasting hatreds of bitter intensity. Indira Gandhi, the powerful and sometimes authoritarian leader who dominated Indian political life for almost 20 years, spent much of her life countering the ethnic separatism that has threatened to tear India apart—until Sikh separatists finally gunned her down. Her son Rajiv was also a victim of a militant ethnic group—the Tamils, who have been fighting a liberation struggle in neighboring Sri Lanka.

Ethnic conflict defined on religious grounds has largely disappeared from Europe in recent times, other than in the Balkans and in Ireland. Divided since the 1920s between an independent predominantly Catholic south and a British-ruled, Protestant-dominated north, relations between Catholics and Protestants in Northern Ireland erupted into violence in 1969.

All sides in the conflict in Northern Ireland carried out assassinations. The most prominent killings, however, were executed by the IRA, a paramilitary organization that drew support from Northern Irish Catholics. In its campaign to drive the British out of Ireland, the IRA targeted top figures in the British establishment. The decimation of three generations of Lord Mountbatten's family in 1979 even shocked some Irish Republicans. To some, however, if a cause is considered sufficiently sacred, any action that promotes it can be justified

CATHOLICS VS. PROTESTANTS

In recent times, groups based in the Middle East have been primarily responsible for assassinations with religious links. However, 400 years ago, such assassinations flourished in Europe, as the split between Catholic and Protestant versions of Christianity produced by the Reformation intensified the usual power struggles within or between nations.

The rise and fall of King Henri IV, the founder of the French Bourbon dynasty, is a remarkable illustration of the prevalence of assassination for the sake of religion at the time. In 1572, days after he married the king's sister, the St. Bartholomew's Day Massacre—in which Catholics assassinated leading French Protestants (Huguenots)—took place. Henri saved his own life by swearing to renounce Protestantism.

In 1588, his predecessor on the French throne, King Henri III, had France's two leading Catholics, the Duc de Guise and his brother, assassinated. In retaliation, a Dominican monk, Jacques Clément, stabbed the king to death the following year.

Once established on the throne, Henri IV strove to create peace between religious factions. On the afternoon of May 14, 1610, however, the king unwisely traveled in a carriage from the Louvre Palace through the Parisian streets with no armed guard, accompanied only by a few gentlemen of the court. In Rue de la Ferronnerie, the king's carriage paused as other carriages and carts blocked the road. At that moment, François Ravaillac, a Catholic fanatic, leaped onto a wheel of the carriage and stabbed the king in the chest with a dagger. Henri IV died later that day in the Louvre.

Korean revenge

Japanese statesman Prince Hirobumi Ito lived most of his life with the threat of death. As a young man in the 1860s, when Japan was ruled by Shoguns (dictators) and just starting to open its doors to Westerners, Ito's pro-Western attitude made him a target for samurai (warriors) committed to keeping foreigners out. One night they nearly ambushed Ito but failed to strike quickly enough. Ito took refuge in a teahouse, where a young woman, whom he later married, hid him in a hole where garbage was dumped.

"... Joong-Gun was waiting for him on the platform with a loaded gun."

A military leader

During the next four decades, Ito became one of Japan's most distinguished leaders, playing a vital role in the modernization process that turned Japan into a major military power, capable of defeating China in 1895 and Russia 10 years later. The Russo-Japanese War of 1904–05 represented a seismic shift in world affairs—the first victory for Asians over Europeans in modern times.

One of its immediate consequences was the Japanese occupation of Korea, a country that had been independent for 1,000 years. Ito was sent to Korea as Japan's resident general. His secret mission was to engineer a gradual, total subjection of the country to Japanese imperial rule.

Violent resistance

Korean nationalists responded to the Japanese occupation with guerrilla warfare and an assassination campaign aimed at Japanese officials and at Koreans who collaborated with the occupiers. This campaign spread to the United States.

Durham White Stevens, a former American missionary who advised the Japanese in Korea, was sent to the United States by Ito to persuade Americans that Japanese occupation was welcomed by most Koreans. This lie outraged members of the Korean immigrant community in the United States. On March 23, 1908, two Korean students, Chang In-hwan and Chon Myong-un, killed Stevens in San Francisco.

Surprisingly, Prince Ito survived four years as the top Japanese official in Korea without

KEY DATES

1841 Born October 14 in Suo Province, Japan

1863 Studies technology, government, and military organization in London

1868 Becomes a leader in the Meiji Restoration, with aims to make a Westernized Japan powerful

1886 Appointed Japanese prime minister for the first time

1890 Drafts Japan's first constitution

1895 Made marquis for role in Japan's military defeat of China

1905 Made Japanese resident general for the occupation of Korea

1907 Advances to the rank of prince

1909 Assassinated in Harbin, Manchuria, October 26

an attempt being made on his life. In July 1909, Ito returned to Tokyo, but Korean nationalists continued to hate him.

Ito's nemesis was to be An Joong-Gun, a 40-year-old former Confucian teacher. To resist the Japanese occupation, Joong-Gun had become the leader of a small guerrilla band operating out of Chinese Manchuria, carrying out raids across the border into Korea. Fate gave him the chance to make an attempt on the life of the Japanese Prince.

Slain at a train station

In October 1909, Prince Ito was sent to Manchuria. He was to meet a Russian representative in the city of Harbin to reassure the Russian government that Japan had no designs upon Manchuria (which they annexed 21 years later). When Ito's train pulled into Harbin station at 9:00 A.M. on October 26, Joong-Gun was waiting for him on the platform with a loaded gun. Ito was shot as soon as he stepped off the train.

Joong-Gun was seized by Japanese troops and taken to a prison in Port Arthur (Lushun). He endured ill treatment for five months before his execution on March 26, 1910.

VICTIM

TSUYOSHI INUKAI

Between 1912 and 1945, six Japanese prime ministers were assassinated by military officers who resented civilian rule. The most notorious of these killings occurred in May 1932. Prime Minister Tsuyoshi Inukai was an alert 75-year-old man. The assassins were nine army and naval officers, belonging to the Blood Brotherhood, a secret organization. On May 15, they went to Inukai's Tokyo home and gunned him down in front of his daughter-in-law and grandchild.

At their trial, the assassins stated that they had hoped to find the prime minister having tea with movie star Charlie Chaplin, who was visiting Japan. They believed that if they killed Chaplin, too, it would provoke a war between Japan and the United States. They pleaded patriotic motives for the killing and more than 100,000 letters in support—many written in blood—were presented in court. The men received lenient sentences.

Family man *Ito (left) is surrounded by his family, including his wife, the young woman he met in the teahouse.*

Mediator slain

The state of Israel was born in the midst of warfare. After years of a three-way conflict between Jews, Arabs, and the British—who controlled Palestine—the United Nations suggested a partition plan in November 1947: Palestine was to become independent in May 1948 as two separate states, one Jewish and the other Arab. The state of Israel was proclaimed on May 14; however, tension continued between Israel and its Arab neighbors.

KEY DATES

1895 Born January 2 in Stockholm into the Swedish royal family

1928 Marries an American, Estelle Romaine Manville

1943 Arranges the exchange of wounded German and Allied prisoners of war for the Swedish Red Cross; works with the Jewish World Congress to send food to Jews in Nazi camps

1945 Organizes the evacuation of 20,000 prisoners from Nazi camps to Scandinavia, including many thousands of Jews

1946 Plays a leading role in efforts by the International Red Cross to cope with the aftermath of war in Europe

1948 Selected by the United Nations as mediator in the Arab-Jewish dispute in May; assassinated in Israel on September 17

Working for peace

On May 20, the United Nations appointed Swedish diplomat Count Folke Bernadotte as a mediator to try to bring peace between Jews and Arabs in Palestine. Bernadotte had earned worldwide fame for his humanitarian efforts on behalf of prisoners in Nazi Germany during World War II. He was upright, incorruptible, and fair.

Bernadotte's mission began successfully when he arranged a 30-day ceasefire on June 11. However, he then produced a plan for a lasting settlement of the dispute at the end of the month, but neither side was pleased. Many Jews were incensed by his proposals that Arab refugees be allowed to return to their land in what had become Israel, and that the city of Jerusalem should become part of Arab Transjordan.

Terrorism in Israel

Members of the notorious Jewish terrorist group Lehi (an acronym for *Lohamei Herut Yisrael,* or Fighters for the Freedom of Israel), were hostile toward Bernadotte's peace plan. Known to the British as the Stern Gang, after its first leader, Avraham Stern, Lehi was established in 1940. Stern was captured by the British and shot, allegedly while trying

International challenge
His reputation as an honest man, along with his humanitarian record, made Bernadotte an ideal choice as a mediator for the United Nations.

Battle of Jerusalem *In June 1948, as Bernadotte tries to set a date for a truce, Israelis and Arabs fight in Jerusalem.*

to escape in 1942, but his organization continued to operate under other leaders, including future Israeli Prime Minister Yitzhak Shamir. In the summer of 1948, Lehi decided that Bernadotte was pro-Arab and must be eradicated. They dismissed his record for helping Jews in World War II, choosing to see it as evidence that he had close links with Nazis.

The task was entrusted to the Jerusalem branch of Lehi, headed by Yehoshua Zeitler. They planned to kill Bernadotte as he traveled to a meeting with the military governor of Jerusalem's New City, Dov Joseph, on September 17. On that day, four assassins dressed in Israeli army uniforms drove an army jeep to Palmeh Street in West Jerusalem. They parked the jeep across the road, as if it were an improvised army checkpoint.

At about 5:00 P.M., Bernadotte's convoy of three cars approached. Bernadotte was in the middle car with a French United Nations observer, André Seraut. With the jeep blocking their way, the cars stopped. Three of the assassins leaped out of the jeep. Two of them shot the car tires, while the third, Yehoshua Cohen, sprayed the interior of Bernadotte's car with bullets from a pistol. Bernadotte was hit six times, and Seraut was caught in the gunfire. Both men died instantly.

Aftermath of an outrageous act

The killing caused international outrage and was condemned in the strongest terms by the Israeli government of Prime Minister David Ben-Gurion. Lehi was forced to disband and some of its members were arrested. However, no one was prosecuted for the killing and all those arrested were soon released in a general amnesty. It is suspected that Ben-Gurion knew the identity of the assassins, because Jerusalem Lehi chief Zeitler was a close personal friend.

A Swedish official inquiry reported in 1950 that Israel's investigation had been so negligent that "doubt must exist as to whether the Israeli authorities really tried to bring the inquiry to a positive result." U.S. Ambassador Stanton Griffis wrote in his memoirs, "The murder of Bernadotte will remain forever a black and disgraceful mark on the early history of Israel."

VICTIM

Lord Moyne

Born Walter Edward Guinness, a member of the Irish brewing family, Lord Moyne was another victim of Jewish terrorism in the 1940s. In 1944, Moyne was Britain's Minister of State for the Near East. He was based in Cairo, Egypt, but his responsibility included Palestine. Moyne was a well-known anti-Zionist.

On November 6, 1944, two Lehi fighters, Eliyahu Beit-Tzuri and Eliyahu Hakim, took positions near the gates of Lord Moyne's Cairo villa. The building was not guarded because the British regarded Cairo as a safe city. At about 12:30 P.M., the British minister's car arrived, bringing him back from a morning at his office, accompanied by Major Hughes Onslow and a secretary. The car drove through the gates and pulled up in front of the villa. As the driver got out, Beit-Tzuri and Hakim ran up the driveway. Pulling open the rear door of the car, Hakim shot the British minister three times at point-blank range, while Beit-Tzuri shot the driver. The driver died immediately; Lord Moyne survived for only a few hours.

Destined to die?

In June 1968, 42-year-old New York Senator Robert F. Kennedy was in California campaigning to become the Democratic nominee in that year's U.S. presidential election. It was, in Kennedy's words, "a time of unprecedented turbulence, of danger, and questioning." Half-a-million U.S. soldiers were fighting a war in Vietnam that few thought they could win; riots flared up in the black ghettos of American cities; the youth of the American middle classes had developed countercultural lifestyles and were toying with revolutionary politics on university campuses. To many American liberals and radicals, Bobby Kennedy was the only electable politician who could end the war, right injustice in American society, and restore faith in American government.

A bright future

Voting in the California Democratic primaries took place on June 4. Kennedy had put a big effort into the California campaign during the previous week, so voting day was a chance to relax. He went to the beach, then had dinner at the Los Angeles home of movie director John Frankenheimer, where he was staying. After dinner, Kennedy and his wife, Ethel, headed to his campaign headquarters, the Ambassador Hotel, where campaign workers and the media were following the results as they came in.

It was announced at 11:40 P.M. that Kennedy had won. He emerged on a podium in the hotel's Embassy Ballroom to acknowledge the cheers of his supporters and deliver a victory speech. Many of those present believed they were listening to the next president of the United States.

Living with danger

Kennedy was aware that his campaign could make him the target of an assassination attempt. He had not only his brother's assassination in mind (see pp. 28–35), but also the killing of Martin Luther King Jr. two months earlier (see pp. 90–95). Yet security in the Ambassador Hotel was lax. There were no police or Secret Service agents protecting Kennedy. Only a few bodyguards had been hired from a local firm, Ace Security.

By the time Kennedy finished his speech, it was 12:15 A.M., June 5. With the campaign workers chanting "We want Bobby!" he stepped down from the podium and headed for the Colonial Room to meet the press. There was a choice of routes; he took the one that led through the kitchen. He and his party made slow progress through the crowded room, advancing along an aisle flanked by conveyor belts and steam tables. Karl Uecker, an assistant maitre d'hotel, led the way;

KEY DATES

1925 Born November 20 in Brookline, Massachusetts, the third son of Joseph and Rose Kennedy

1951 Admitted to the bar in Massachusetts

1957 Becomes a member of the McClellan Commission examining labor union leaders linked to organized crime

1960 Manages the presidential election campaign of his older brother, John F. Kennedy

1961 Appointed attorney general in the John F. Kennedy administration; leads a crackdown on the Mafia

1963 President Kennedy is assassinated

1964 Steps down as attorney general; elected senator from New York

1968 Begins campaign for presidency; assassinated in Los Angeles on June 5

Running for president
Early in his campaign, Bobby Kennedy waves from an open car.

AR-2839
19 COLORADO 68

Victory speech *A jubilant Kennedy and his wife, Ethel, celebrate his win in the Californian primary. He was shot a few moments later.*

behind Kennedy was an Ace Security guard, Thane Cesar.

A young man suddenly stepped toward Kennedy, pointed a .22 caliber pistol, and fired. There was chaos as bullets whizzed around the crowded space. As people tried to disarm the assailant, he continued to fire. Shot three times, in the head, chest, and neck, Kennedy lay on the ground in mortal pain. Five other people were wounded. As he was overpowered, the assailant shouted, "I did it for my country...I love my country."

The wounded were rushed by ambulance to the Central Receiving Hospital, the nearest medical facility, but Kennedy was quickly moved to the Good Samaritan Hospital for brain surgery. After a three-hour operation, Kennedy was still given a chance of survival, but he died at 1:44 A.M. the following day.

"There was **chaos** as **bullets** whizzed around the crowded space."

No room for error

Those investigating the assassination, chiefly the Los Angeles Police Department (LAPD), were conscious of accusations of a cover-up that followed President John F. Kennedy's death. Investigators wanted everything done by the book.

The facts of the case left little room for doubt. Sirhan Sirhan, a 24-year-old Palestinian immigrant, had been seen shooting Kennedy and had been arrested at the scene. His room contained notebooks expressing his intention to kill Kennedy. Kennedy had made repeated calls for the United States to supply Israel with Phantom jets—a fact mentioned in a newspaper article found in Sirhan's pocket. His motivation was anger at Kennedy's pro-Israeli—and therefore anti-Palestinian—stance on the Middle East. In January 1969, Sirhan was found guilty by a jury and sentenced to the gas chamber; his sentence was later changed to life in prison.

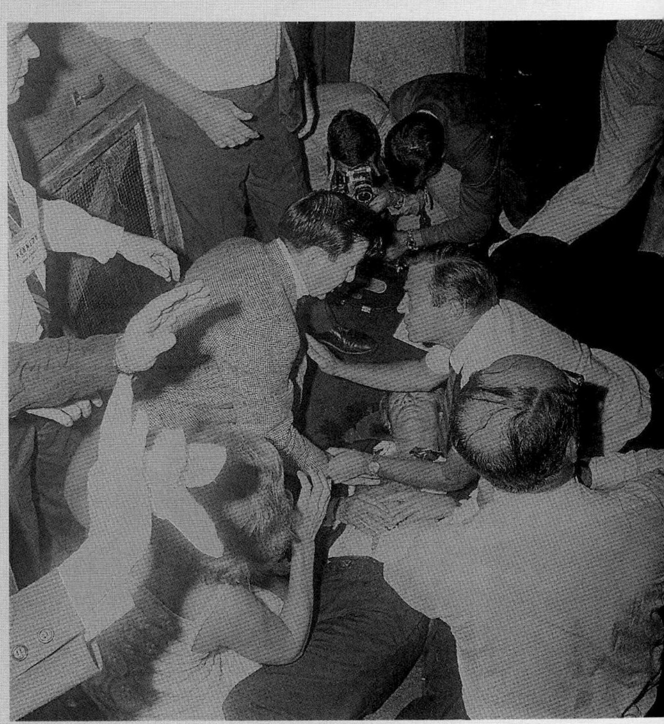

Collapsed *After being mortally shot in the chest, head, and neck, Kennedy falls to the ground.*

THE KENNEDY CURSE

The children and grandchildren of parents Joseph and Rose Kennedy have been notoriously "cursed" by sudden or violent death.

1944 Joseph Kennedy Jr., their eldest son, is killed on a World War II bombing mission

1948 Daughter Kathleen Cavendish is killed in a plane crash in France

1963 Their second son, President John F. Kennedy, is assassinated in Dallas, Texas

1968 Their third son, Robert F. Kennedy, is assassinated in Los Angeles, California

1984 Robert Kennedy's son, David Kennedy, dies of a drug overdose in Florida

1997 Robert Kennedy's son, Michael Kennedy, is killed in a skiing accident at Aspen, Colorado

1999 President Kennedy's son, John F. Kennedy Jr., is killed when his plane crashes in Massachusetts

The rumors begin

Many people remained unconvinced. Sirhan himself protested his innocence, claiming to remember nothing of the night of the killing. This was unusual for an assassin acting out of political motives, who would typically have been proud of his actions.

There was also the question of "the girl in the white polka-dot dress." Eyewitnesses described having seen this woman talking to Sirhan before the killing, and running from the scene afterward shouting, "We shot him! We shot him!" The LAPD were skeptical about this woman's existence, and later on several witnesses retracted their statements, thus contributing to rumors of a conspiracy.

The gun doesn't lie

Most disturbing of all was the ballistics evidence. There is no evidence to support the view of some conspiracy theorists that at least 10 shots had been fired—Sirhan's gun could fire only eight rounds. However, harder to explain is the coroner's conclusion that Kennedy was killed by a shot fired into the back of his head from close range. Eyewitnesses were adamant that Sirhan fired from in front of Kennedy and that his gun was never as close to the senator as the evidence implied.

The only person in the right position to fire the fatal shot was the security guard. Although Cesar's record and personality did not suggest he would have murdered Kennedy, he might have accidentally shot him while trying to shoot Sirhan. Unfortunately for this theory, Cesar's gun was a .38, whereas the bullet that killed Kennedy was a .22.

The problem raised by the ballistics evidence has never been resolved. With no other alternative, it must be assumed that in the confusion of the moment, contrary to what those present believed, Sirhan's gun came close to the back of Kennedy's head.

Conspiracy theories

Various conspiracy theories—including Sirhan having been recruited as a hitman for the Mafia, or Sirhan having been brainwashed or hypnotized to make him an unconscious killer—cannot be disproved. However, the overwhelming likelihood is that Sirhan assassinated Kennedy because of his attitude toward Palestine.

Killer in custody *Police apprehend Sirhan Sirhan immediately after the shooting.*

SIRHAN SIRHAN

Sirhan Bishara Sirhan was born in 1944, the fifth son of a Christian Arab family living in Jerusalem, then in British-ruled Palestine. His family became refugees after the foundation of the state of Israel in 1948. When he was 12 years old, they moved to the United States, settling in California. His father did not adapt to American life and soon returned to the Middle East, leaving his wife to bring up the family on her own.

Sirhan Sirhan performed well at school, but he dropped out of college in 1965. He showed an interest in horses and took jobs exercising racehorses. He worked at a ranch in Corona, outside of Pasadena, where at least one of his bosses had links to organized crime.

Sirhan followed political developments in the Middle East, identifying with the Palestinian cause. He was disgusted when American media and political leaders celebrated the Israeli victory in the 1967 Six-Day War. Sirhan seems to have initially regarded Bobby Kennedy as a figure of hope for the Palestinians because he was a politician noted for supporting the underdog. When he realized that Kennedy saw Israel as the underdog in the Middle East, as Sirhan put it during his trial, "it burned me up." There seems no solid reason not to believe Sirhan's political motivation. It was probably no coincidence that the killing occurred on the anniversary of the Six-Day War.

Bomb aboard

On August 27, 1979, a family vacationing at Classiebawn Castle, County Sligo, on the northwestern coast of Ireland, enjoyed a breakfast of mackerel fresh from Donegal Bay. The castle belonged to Earl Mountbatten of Burma, commonly known as Lord Louis Mountbatten, the favorite granduncle of England's Prince Charles. Every summer, Mountbatten spent a month at the castle with his family, relaxing in the countryside.

RETALIATION BY THE IRA

The explosion on board Mountbatten's yacht was not the only massacre on August 27, 1979. Later on the same day, the IRA ambushed British troops near the village of Warrenpoint in Northern Ireland. Two radio-controlled bombs killed 18 soldiers, the British Army's heaviest loss in a single incident during the Northern Ireland conflict.

Most of the soldiers killed at Warrenpoint were members of the Parachute Regiment, the formation that had been responsible for killing 13 Catholics on Bloody Sunday in 1972. After this day of bloodshed, a slogan appeared on walls in Catholic areas of Northern Ireland: "13 gone and not forgotten; we got 18 and Mountbatten."

Too close for comfort

In the past, concern had been expressed about Mountbatten's vacations at the castle because the border between the Irish Republic and strife-torn Northern Ireland was only 10 miles away. The Provisional IRA, which was conducting a terrorist campaign aimed at driving the British out of the part of Ireland they still ruled, was known to use County Sligo as a base for their operations. Yet, the 79-year-old Mountbatten dismissed security concerns, reportedly saying, "What could they want with an old man like me?"

After their late breakfast, at about 11:30 A.M., Mountbatten and members of his family went to the nearby fishing village of Mullaghmore, where his yacht *Shadow V* was moored. They intended to fish in the bay and check some lobster pots. Mountbatten's twin teenage grandsons Nicholas and Timothy Knatchbull; his son-

in-law and his daughter, Lord and Lady Brabourne; Lord Brabourne's mother, 82-year-old Dowager Lady Brabourne; and a local boy employed to help on the boat, Paul Maxwell, joined Mountbatten.

Remote control bomb

As the yacht headed into the bay, it was watched by an IRA bomb expert, Tommy McMahon, who was stationed on a clifftop. The IRA had been using bombs with timing devices for years, but they were now experimenting with devices detonated by radio remote control. Earlier in the morning, McMahon had hidden a bomb on the yacht. About five minutes after the boat left the harbor, while it was still close to shore, he pressed a button. The boat disintegrated in a massive explosion.

Fishermen who hurried to the site of the explosion were met with a scene of carnage. Mountbatten's legs had been blown off. He was alive when pulled from the water, but he died shortly afterward. Nicholas Knatchbull and Paul Maxwell were dead, floating face down. The other four people on the boat were rushed to County Sligo General Hospital. The Dowager Lady Brabourne died of her injuries the following day.

Capturing the assassin

McMahon was picked up by Irish police two hours after the atrocity. The car in which he was traveling, driven by Francis McGirl, was stopped for a routine check, and the two men were detained on suspicion of having stolen the vehicle. McMahon was later found to have traces of nitroglycerin on his clothing and green paint from *Shadow V* on his shoes. He was convicted of the four murders and sentenced to life imprisonment; McGirl was acquitted. McMahon was released in 1998, along with other terrorist prisoners, under the Good Friday Agreement, which was designed to end the Northern Ireland conflict.

There was revulsion at the assassination. Although many Irish Republicans accepted that an aging relative of the Queen constituted a "legitimate target," they were upset that a local boy had been killed. The IRA issued a statement justifying their actions as a way to "bring to the attention of the English people the continuing occupation of our country."

Beyond rescue *Workers remove a victim, one of Mountbatten's party, who was fatally injured during the boat explosion.*

KEY DATES

1900 Born June 25 on the grounds of Windsor Castle, as Prince Louis Francis of Battenberg, great grandson of Queen Victoria

1913 Joins the Royal Navy, serving in World War I

1917 Changes name from Battenberg to Mountbatten in response to wartime anti-German sentiment

1922 Marries Edwina Ashley

1939 Commands a destroyer flotilla at the start of World War II

1942 Appointed chief of combined operations

1943 Appointed supreme allied commander in Southeast Asia

1947 Sent to India as viceroy to oversee independence; becomes governor general after independence

1949 Returns to the navy, holding a series of senior posts

1959 Appointed British chief of defense staff

1979 Assassinated in County Sligo, Ireland, on August 27

Jihad attack

In March 1979, Egyptian President Anwar al-Sadat signed a peace treaty with Israel, an event hailed in the West as a major breakthrough in the search for a permanent solution to the problems of the Middle East.

"...assassins **stormed** the stand, **spraying bullets**..."

To many in the Arab world, including Sadat's own country, however, the peace treaty was an act of betrayal, a surrender to the forces of Zionism and American imperialism. By signing the treaty, Sadat had signed his own death warrant.

Celebrating victory

On October 6, 1981, a military parade was staged in Cairo to celebrate the anniversary of the start of the 1973 Yom Kippur War, when Egyptian forces had successfully attacked Israeli positions on the east bank of the Suez Canal. Wearing a blue field marshal's uniform glittering with gold braid and medals, President Sadat took his place in the center of the front row of the stand, with Vice President Hosni Mubarak alongside him. About a thousand guests, including American military advisers, diplomats, and journalists, were seated around them. The stand was separated from the parade ground in front of it by a concrete wall.

Surprise attack

An hour into the parade, jet fighters flew past, trailing colored smoke that drew all eyes to the sky. Unnoticed, a truck towing a field gun stopped on the parade ground opposite where Sadat was sitting. An officer, Lieutenant Khaled Ahmed Islambouli, jumped out of the driver's cabin, walked toward Sadat, and began lobbing grenades into the stand. At the same time, a group of soldiers stood up in the back of the truck and opened fire. Security guards were unable to react quickly enough as the assassins stormed the stand, spraying bullets over the front rows as the audience sought cover behind overturned chairs.

As the assailants tried to escape, Sadat's bodyguard opened fire, killing one of them. Three others, including Islambouli, were captured. Sadat's bullet-ridden body was taken by helicopter to a military hospital, but he was already dead. Ten other people were killed in the carnage and 28 were wounded.

Fundamentalism at work

The assassination plot had emerged from a network of Islamic extremist movements, including Islamic Jihad. These groups were formed by Islamic fundamentalists, Muslims who reject secularism and modern Western civilization, advocating a return to their

KEY DATES

1918 Born December 25, one of 13 children of a clerical worker

1952 Takes part in the coup that overthrows Egypt's King Farouk

1967 Israel defeats Egypt in the Six-Day War

1969 Appointed vice president under Nasser

1970 Becomes Egyptian president on Nasser's death

1973 Leads Egypt in the Yom Kippur War with Israel

1978 Signs the Camp David accords with Israeli Prime Minister Menachem Begin; both are awarded the Nobel Peace Prize

1979 Signs a peace treaty with Israel

1981 Assassinated by Islamic fundamentalists on October 6

version of Islamic government, law, and customs. Egypt was the cradle of Islamic fundamentalism, and Sadat's predecessor, Gamal Abdul Nasser, had repressed these militants. Sadat treated them more leniently, but there was an upsurge in fundamentalist agitation. Sadat knew that extremists were plotting against him and had 1,500 militants arrested in 1981, enraging his enemies.

A 28-year-old electrical engineer, Abdel Salem Faraj, who was associated with the Islamic Jihad, had been one of the prime movers. The blind Sheikh Omar Abdel Rahman, who was later linked to the bomb explosion at the World Trade Center in 1993, was also implicated. They had hoped to provoke an uprising to allow fundamentalists to seize power and found an Islamic state. Twenty-four people were tried for the attack. Five were condemned to death and hanged, including Faraj and Lieutenant Islambouli.

MUBARAK SURVIVES

After Sadat's death, his successor, Hosni Mubarak, instituted a crackdown on the Islamic extremists. Thousands were arrested, while many were expelled from Egypt or fled into exile. Inevitably, Mubarak became a target for terrorists.

On July 3, 1995, President Mubarak flew to Addis Ababa, Ethiopia, to attend a summit meeting of the Organization of African Unity. An assassination squad waited along the route from the airport into the city. As his convoy approached an intersection, a vehicle drew out and blocked its path. Gunmen ran into the road, firing AK-47s. Fortunately, Mubarak's limousine was armored and the bullets ricocheted off. Security guards returned the terrorists' fire, killing two of them. Mubarak's driver drove back to the airport, and Mubark returned to Cairo.

The group responsible for the attack were members of Islamic Jihad—the organization that had killed Sadat. Islamic Jihad was based in Sudan, a country with a fundamentalist government. Three years later, in 1998, they joined forces with Osama bin Laden to become a major component of the Al Qaeda network.

Camouflaged gunman *Dressed in an Egyptian Army uniform, an assassin with a submachine gun fires into the stand.*

Scene of carnage *During the chaos after the attack, men seek cover behind overturned chairs, amid the dead and wounded.*

Revenge attack

In June 1984, the Punjabi city of Amritsar was the scene of horrific bloodshed, resulting from a conflict between militant Sikh separatists, led by Jarnail Singh Bindranwale, campaigning for an independent Sikh homeland, and the Indian government, headed by 66-year-old Prime Minister Indira Gandhi.

Bindranwale's militants had established a headquarters in Amritsar's Golden Temple, the holiest shrine of the Sikh faith, where they were besieged by the Indian Army. Prime Minister Gandhi ordered the army to occupy the temple. By the time all resistance was crushed on June 6, more than 1,000 people were dead, including Bindranwale—several thousand more were wounded. The desecration of the Golden Temple was a shocking act.

"He pulled out his revolver and shot Gandhi three times."

Can the Sikhs be trusted?

The Sikhs made up a substantial part of India's armed forces, including those defending the compound where the prime minister lived and worked in New Delhi. After the storming of the Golden Temple, many said that the Sikh guards could no longer be trusted, but Gandhi refused to dismiss them. She was the daughter

Guard of Honor *As India's prime minister, Indira Gandhi inspects the troops on India Republic Day in 1967.*

of India's first prime minister, Jawaharlal Nehru, and had inherited his commitment to a united India without religious prejudice.

Her life in his hands

One of Gandhi's Sikh guards was Beant Singh, a man with an unblemished record. He arranged to be on duty inside the prime minister's compound on October 31, 1984. Satwant Singh, a constable of the Delhi Armed Police, was alongside him. Beant Singh was armed with a .38 revolver; Satwant Singh carried a Sten gun, a World War II-vintage light machine gun.

Surrounded by aides, Gandhi left her residence at 9:10 A.M. and was on her way to a television interview with British actor Peter Ustinov. As she approached Beant Singh, she gave some slight gesture of acknowledgment. He pulled out his revolver and shot Gandhi three times. As she collapsed, Satwant Singh opened up with the Sten gun. A dozen bullets hit the prime minister.

Gandhi's blood-soaked body was driven to the hospital. Surgeons failed to save her. At 1:45 P.M., Gandhi's death was announced. Mobs attacked Sikh temples and businesses. More than 1,000 Sikhs are thought to have been killed.

The two assassins did not try to escape, but both were shot by Indian special forces after being arrested. Beant Singh was killed but Satwant Singh survived. The investigation revealed no conspiracy beyond Beant Singh's circle. Despite rumors of a wider plot behind the assassination, no evidence has emerged to support any alternate version of events.

KEY DATES

1917 Born November 19 in Allahabad, India, the child of future Prime Minister Jawaharlal Nehru

1942 Marries Feroze Gandhi (unrelated to Mahatma Gandhi)

1959 Elected president of Congress Party

1964 Elected to parliament; appointed minister of information

1966 Becomes prime minister

1971 Leads India to victory in a war against Pakistan that results in Bangladesh independence

1975 Declares a state of emergency in India and suspends many civil liberties after being found guilty of electoral malpractice

1977 Congress Party defeated in elections; resigns as prime minister

1980 Reelected as prime minister

1984 Orders assault on the Sikh Golden Temple in Amritsar; assassinated on October 31

VICTIM

Rajiv Gandhi

Indira Gandhi was succeeded as Indian prime minister by her son Rajiv Gandhi. He lost the premiership in 1989 but sought reelection in 1991. His campaign arrived in Sriperumbudur, in the Tamil Nadu state, on May 21. Many Tamils—an ethnic group living in southern India and in neighboring Sri Lanka—despised Rajiv. As prime minister, he ended Indian support for the Tamil Tigers, a guerrilla movement fighting against the Sri Lankan government. The Tamil Tigers were waiting for Rajiv in Sriperumbudur. A young woman with a belt of grenades and explosives tied around her waist stepped forward and hung a garland around Rajiv's neck; then she activated a detonator, killing herself, Rajiv, and 16 bystanders.

Family photo *Indira poses with her two sons. Rajiv's arm is draped around her shoulders.*

Act of respect *Indira's son Rajiv lights her funeral pyre as part of a traditional cremation.*

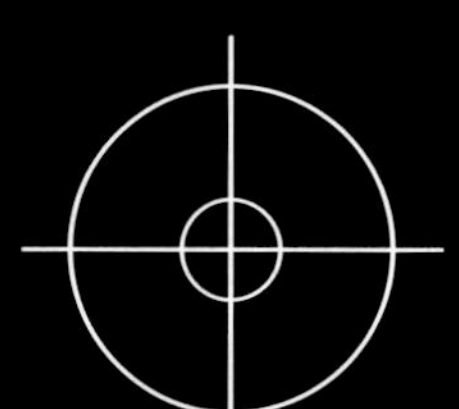

Soldier of peace

Yitzhak Rabin spent most of his life as a soldier, and he was in charge of the Israeli forces that fought their Arab neighbors in the Six-Day War. However, in his later years, Rabin became a man of peace, accepting the need to compromise with the Palestinians living in the territories occupied by Israel since 1967. After becoming prime minister of Israel in 1992, Rabin began pushing through an accord to give Palestinians self-rule in the West Bank and Gaza.

The handshake *President Clinton (center) encourages Rabin (left) to shake hands with Arafat (right).*

Violent protests against the prime minister

Many Israelis opposed the agreement reached between Rabin and Yasser Arafat, leader of the Palestinians. Among them was Yigal Amir, a 25-year-old student at Bar-Ilan university outside Tel Aviv. He was involved in a protest campaign against the Rabin government and the peace accords. Amir took part in political rallies, which often turned into riots, and in mass demonstrations of support for Jews who had established illegal settlements on the West Bank. The protests had become extreme, with demonstrators holding up placards showing Rabin in Nazi uniform or with the crosshairs of a sniper's rifle sight printed over his face.

KEY DATES

1922 Born in March in Jerusalem

1940 Joins Zionist Palmach commandos

1948 Commands the Harel Brigade in Israel's War of Independence

1967 Commander of Israeli forces in the Six-Day War

1974 Elected prime minister of Israel

1992 Becomes prime minister for second time

1993 Negotiates peace accord with Yasser Arafat

1995 Shakes hands with Yasser Arafat during a visit to the White House; assassinated at a peace rally on November 4

1996 Yigal Amir tried for his assassination

Give peace a chance

In response to these protests, a rally was held to demonstrate support for the peace process and to condemn political violence—the slogan was "Peace Yes, Violence No." The rally was set for the evening of November 4, 1995, in Tel Aviv's Kings of Israel Square.

By the time Rabin and his wife, Leah, arrived, more than 100,000 people packed the square. Rabin made a powerful speech, declaring that "the way of peace is preferable to the way of war." He ended, "This rally must send a message to the Israeli public, to the Jews of the world, to the multitudes in the Arab lands, and to the world at large: that the people of Israel want peace, support peace."

Shots in the night

One person who didn't join in this emotional celebration of peace was Yigal Amir. The young extremist was waiting in the area to the left of the stage where Rabin's car was parked. A pistol loaded with a mixture of normal and dumdum ammunition was in his pocket. Although a security pass was needed to enter the parking area, Amir attracted no attention, and his right to be there was never questioned.

As the triumphant evening drew to a close, Rabin left the stage. He had five bodyguards, one walking in front and four closed in around him. Rabin reached the car and was about to climb in, when Amir stepped forward and fired three shots into his back. As the shots were fired, someone—possibly the assassin—shouted, "They're not real bullets. They're blanks. It's not real."

One of the bodyguards, himself injured in the shooting, pushed Rabin into the car. The driver asked the prime minister how he was, and he replied, "It's not so bad." These were his last words.

Although the hospital was only half a mile away, dense crowds slowed the car's progress. When the car finally did arrive, medical staff had not been alerted and the driver had to search for a doctor. Treatment proved futile. Rabin's death was announced about an hour later.

CONSPIRACY THEORY

The Israeli Secret Service, Shin Bet, was criticized for failing to protect Prime Minister Rabin. Some alleged that Shin Bet was culpable of more than incompetence. Amir reportedly received weapons training from Shin Bet in 1992, and one of his closest associates, Avishai Raviv, overtly a right-wing activist, was covertly a Shin Bet agent.

The shout of "they're blanks" during the shooting has led to the suggestion that Amir was told by Shin Bet to fire blanks, but that he had substituted live bullets. Another theory is that Rabin was not shot by Amir—who was using blanks—but was killed in the car on its surprisingly slow journey to the hospital. However, if the latter theory is true and Amir was set up, it is strange that the Israeli secret agents didn't instantly shoot him rather than arrest him.

On trial *Arrogant and unrepentant, Yigal Amir did not attempt to escape arrest. He stated, "I acted alone on God's orders and I have no regrets."*

A fallen soldier *Just after the shooting, Israeli security personnel pushed Rabin into a car. Only his legs can be seen in the photograph.*

SECRET SERVICE

REINHARD HEYDRICH · 1942
PATRICE LUMUMBA · 1961
NGO DINH DIEM · 1963
ZORAN DJINDJIC · 2003

00:02:21

Secret service

It is in the nature of organizations such as secret police and espionage agencies that the truth about their operations rarely emerges with any certainty. Some people might believe that few assassinations are carried out by secret services; others suspect that almost all political assassinations are the result of their influence.

Soviet spies

In this shadowy area, unanswered questions abound. For example, was the Soviet Secret Service responsible for the killing of Leningrad Communist Party boss Sergei Kirov in 1934 (see box, right)? Did it assassinate Czech Foreign Minister Jan Masaryk, who apparently killed himself by jumping out of an upstairs window after the Communist takeover of Czechoslovakia in 1948? Did it order the Secret Service of their satellite state Bulgaria to arrange the assassination of Pope John Paul II in 1981 (see pp. 180–81)? Did the Soviets, indeed, persuade Lee Harvey Oswald to assassinate President John F. Kennedy in 1963 (see pp. 28–35)?

The answer to all these questions might well be in the negative, yet there is no doubt that Communist bloc assassins did operate in the West. For example, in 1978, exiled Bulgarian writer Giorgi Markov—an outspoken critic of the Bulgarian Communist regime—was murdered in London. He was poisoned when his assassin stabbed him in the leg with the tip of an umbrella—which contained a capsule of ricin poison.

VICTIM

Sergei Kirov

The most famous—and mysterious—assassination case in the Soviet Union was the killing of Leningrad Communist party chief Sergei Kirov in 1934. Kirov was an intimate friend of Josef Stalin and his family, but he was also possibly the only man popular enough in the party to have stood as a rival to the Soviet dictator.

On December 1, 1934, Kirov went to his office in Leningrad's Smolny Institute late in the afternoon. He arrived surrounded by guards of the Soviet Secret Police, the NKVD, but they left him when he reached the third floor of the building. His personal bodyguard, a man named Borisov, remained. Allegedly, as Kirov advanced along the corridor, a man stepped out of the door of a men's room, walked up behind him, and shot him in the back of the neck with a revolver.

The killer was identified as Leonid Nikolaev, a party functionary who had lost his job. How he had penetrated the tight security around the Leningrad party headquarters, and how he had known Kirov would turn up for work at that late hour, was never explained.

The day after the shooting Stalin arrived in Leningrad to head the investigation. According to some accounts, Nikolaev was brought to Stalin and asked by NKVD men why he had killed Kirov. He pointed to the Secret Police and screamed, "They made me do it." Borisov, the only eyewitness to the assassination, was killed by the NKVD shortly afterward—probably thrown out of a fast-moving truck. The purported assassin Nikolaev disappeared, presumably executed by the Secret Police.

The official version of the assassination given to the Soviet media presented Kirov as a Communist hero struck down by enemies of the revolution. Stalin assumed emergency powers to crush these supposed enemies and the NKVD embarked on mass arrests and executions in Leningrad. It was the first wave of the Great Terror, which claimed the lives of millions of Soviet citizens.

Serbian Slobodan Milosevic's "special forces" have continued the ruthless Communist tradition of secret operations into the 21st century. They are almost certainly responsible for the killing of Prime Minister Zoran Djindjic in 2003.

The original spies for the West

In the West, modern secret agencies can trace their origins to World War II, when the British Special Operations Executive (SOE) and the American Office of Strategic Services (OSS) were established to promote subversion and sabotage in Nazi-occupied Europe. Assassination was considered an acceptable part of such operations, as in the SOE-backed killing of SS Chief Reinhard Heydrich.

The OSS was the direct ancestor of the postwar CIA, which maintained the tradition of encouraging subversion, at times playing a supporting role in the overthrow of governments in countries as diverse as Iran, Guatemala, Chile, and South Vietnam.

The American CIA

It has been publicly known since the 1970s that the CIA dabbled in assassination plots against foreign heads of state. There were identifiable projects to kill Patrice Lumumba in the Congo and Fidel Castro in Cuba, although these were not carried out with any real energy or purpose. Either the will to kill was not really there, or the CIA was too incompetent for the job.

Many people believe that the CIA or other shadowy U.S. secret services were behind assassinations inside the United States, including the deaths of President Kennedy, Martin Luther King Jr. (see pp. 90–95), and even Robert F. Kennedy (see pp. 106–9). It is impossible to either prove or disprove these theories. However, looking at the ineptitude of the plans to kill Castro, one might conclude that the CIA was not responsible for the assassination of President Kennedy in 1963.

American intelligence agencies were unquestionably complicit in the overthrow of the regimes of Ngo Dinh Diem in South Vietnam in 1963 and of Salvador Allende in Chile a decade later, as well as in the downfall of Lumumba. They must bear their share of the responsibility for the deaths of these leaders that followed. However, evidence of successful direct assassination of leading political figures by the CIA or any other U.S. covert agency remains elusive.

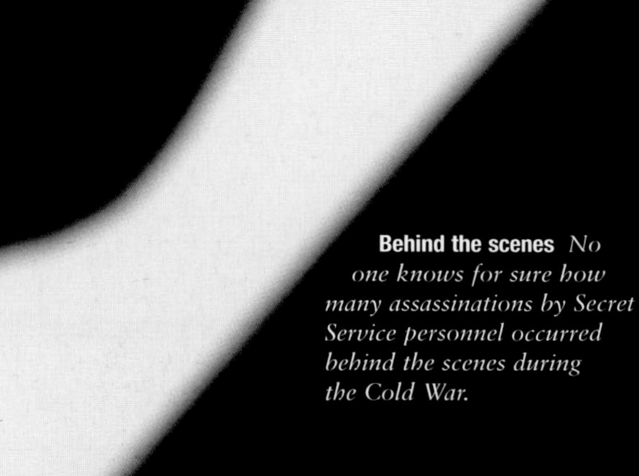

Behind the scenes *No one knows for sure how many assassinations by Secret Service personnel occurred behind the scenes during the Cold War.*

Grenade attack

On May 27, 1942, SS Obergruppenführer Reinhard Heydrich left his luxurious residence in the village of Penenske Brezany to drive to his headquarters in Hradcany Castle in Prague. Heydrich was the most powerful and feared man in the Nazi-occupied Protectorate of Bohemia and Moravia (now the Czech Republic).

For many weeks, Heydrich's movements had been observed. He had been chosen for assassination by the Czech government in exile in London, and by Britain's Special Operations Executive (SOE), established to promote resistance in Nazi-occupied Europe. Heydrich's brutality and success in pacifying the Czechs had made him a prime target. His assassination would be a direct blow to the Nazi hierarchy and stimulate the Czechs to a more hostile attitude toward their occupiers.

"...he **leaped** out of the car...gun in hand, before **collapsing**..."

Heydrich was also a skilled manipulator, offering inducements, such as improved food supplies, so that the Czechs would collaborate with their Nazi rulers. His nine months in charge of the Czech lands had been a striking success for the Nazis. The population was largely quiescent, and the Czech resistance movement was almost nonexistent.

Pride before the fall

Heydrich's weak point was overconfidence. A tall, blond, blue-eyed embodiment of the Nazi "Aryan" ideal, he liked to flaunt his contempt for the allegedly racially inferior Czech Slavs, spurning the most elementary security precautions. He always drove into Prague by the same route at the same time, in an open-topped, unarmored Mercedes, accompanied only by his driver, who also functioned as a bodyguard.

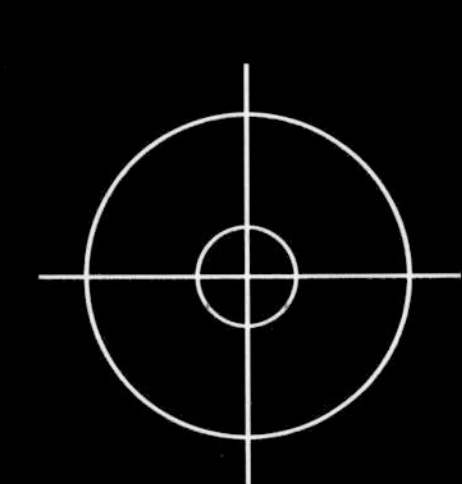

The butcher of Prague
Heydrich ordered the mass execution of hundreds of Czechs accused of opposing Nazi rule in Prague.

RETALIATION IN BLOOD

The Nazis were brutal in their revenge on the Czech people for the killing of Heydrich. It is estimated that around 2,000 people died in more or less direct reprisals for the assassination. The most notorious incident was the destruction of the village of Lidice on June 9, 1942, five days after Heydrich's death.

The SS had information that connected at least one Czech resistance fighter with the village. SS troops entered Lidice and ordered its entire population out of their houses. Of the 199 men in the village, 173 were shot; the other 26 were burned to death in a barn. The women and children who had witnessed this mass murder were sent to concentration camps. The village was razed to the ground and grain was planted over it to make sure no trace remained.

Destruction *Nazi soldiers burn the buildings of Lidice before using explosives to level the village.*

The mission was entrusted to two Czech soldiers serving with the Free Czech forces in Britain, Sergeant Jan Kubis and Sergeant Josef Gabcik. They parachuted into Czech territory from an RAF aircraft in December 1941 and linked up with local resistance fighters. After observing Heydrich's routines, they decided to ambush him at a point along his daily route in the Prague suburbs where his car had to slow to a crawl to negotiate a tight hairpin bend.

Waiting to strike

On the morning of May 27, Kubis and Gabcik positioned themselves at the hairpin bend. Another resistance fighter, Jan Valcik, stood farther along the road to signal Heydrich's approach. At 10:25 A.M., a flash from the lookout's mirror indicated that the Mercedes had come into view.

Heydrich was seated in the back, reading some documents. As the car slowed down, Gabcik pulled a Sten gun from under his coat, pointed it at Heydrich's head, and pulled the trigger. Nothing happened—the gun had jammed. Instead of speeding away, Heydrich's driver stopped the car and reached for his own weapon. Heydrich also pulled out his gun.

They had not noticed Kubis, who stepped forward and threw a grenade at the back of the car. The explosion blew fragments of grenade and car into Heydrich's body, but he leaped out of the car and pursued Kubis, gun in hand, before collapsing on the sidewalk. Meanwhile, Gabcik had a shoot-out with the driver, wounding him in the legs, and boarded a nearby tram to escape. Kubis fled the scene by bicycle.

Heydrich was driven to a hospital in Prague in the back of a truck. At first, his chances of survival seemed good, despite internal injuries. However, infection set in and he died on June 4.

An accusation and the assassins

The Germans alleged that Heydrich had been poisoned by botulism toxin applied to the weapon used to attack him. The British denied using biological warfare, and no evidence to support the allegation has ever been found.

The assassins were betrayed by a member of the Czech resistance in return for money. On June 18, Kubis, Gabcik, Valcik, and four others were cornered in the crypt of a Prague church. They put up a fierce struggle. Three of the men were killed in the fighting, which also cost 14 German soldiers their lives. The other four, including Gabcik, took cyanide.

KEY DATES

1904 Born on March 7 in Halle, near Leipzig, Germany, into a family of classical musicians

1919 Joins the local Freikorps, right-wing irregulars fighting left-wing revolutionaries

1922 Joins the German navy

1931 Forced out of the navy; joins the Nazi Party, becoming a member of the SS (Schutzstaffel)

1932 Accepts sole command of the SD (Sicherheitsdienst), the SS's Security Service

1934 As second in command to Heinrich Himmler, controls the Gestapo Secret Police

1939 Fakes an attack by Poles on a German radio station to justify Germany's invasion of Poland

1941 Sets up special SS squads to massacre Jews in conquered territory

1942 Assassinated on May 27; dies on June 4

PATRICE LUMUMBA · 1961

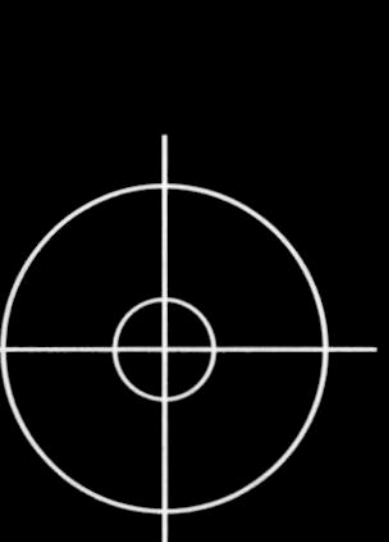

Executed

In the 1950s, European powers that had ruled in Africa began to decolonize more than 20 African countries. In most, colonialists arranged an orderly transfer of power, but not in the Belgian Congo.

The Belgian Congo occupied a vast area of central Africa. It had poor communications and a population of more than 200 tribes, so it was bound to be difficult to rule. Despite this, the Belgians failed to prepare the African population for independence—for example, the senior ranks of the army and the civil service were almost exclusively white.

KEY DATES

1925 Born on July 2 in the village of Onalua in Kasai Province, Belgian Congo

1951 Marries Pauline Opango

1955 Becomes regional president of a trade union of government employees

1958 Founds the National Congolese Movement (Mouvement National Congolaise—MNC)

1959 Imprisoned for inciting riots against Belgian plans to delay granting independence

1960 Congo becomes independent, with Lumumba as prime minister in June; Colonel Mobutu takes power in Congo in September; Lumumba is arrested by Mobutu's soldiers on December 2

1961 Executed in Katanga on January 17

An enthusiastic nationalist

The decision to grant independence was made in January 1960, and five months later, on June 30, the country was handed over to an inexperienced government headed by a newly elected prime minister, Patrice Lumumba. He was an idealistic young man who used anti-imperialist rhetoric. His chief ambition was to make the Congo a truly independent, united country.

The U.S. government was convinced that Lumumba was pro-Communist and would provide an opening for Soviet influence in Africa. CIA Director Allen Dulles wrote that "his [Lumumba's] removal must be an urgent and prime objective."

The Soviets to the rescue

Only days after independence, the Congo was plunged into chaos by a mutiny in the army. Belgium sent troops in, allegedly to save white lives but

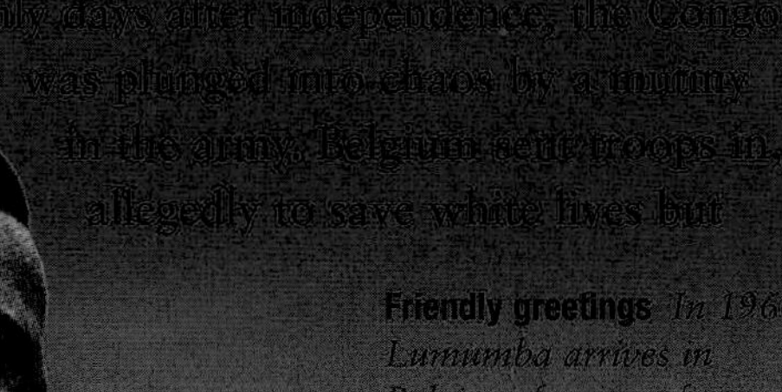

Friendly greetings *In 1960, Lumumba arrives in Belgium for a conference.*

mostly to dismember the country. Most of the Congo's mineral wealth was in the province of Katanga. Belgium backed a local politician, Moïse Tshombe, who declared Katanga's secession from the Congo.

Lumumba appealed to the United Nations to send in troops to oust the Belgians. By July, 10,000 United Nations troops were in the country, but they refused to attack Katanga—so Lumumba asked for aid from the Soviet Union. The Soviets flew in supplies and technicians. The Americans saw their worst fears confirmed.

Captured: *Congolese soldiers roughly handle Lumumba while his arms are tied behind his back.*

The CIA plots a murder

By September, Congolese Army Chief Colonel Mobutu had seized power and Lumumba was held prisoner in a house in Leopoldville (now Kinshasa), under United Nations guard for his own safety. Meanwhile, the CIA was plotting to kill him.

CIA technical officer Sidney Gottlieb was sent to Leopoldville with a tube of poisoned toothpaste—designed so that its symptoms would resemble a tropical disease. According to Lawrence Devlin, CIA Head of Station in Leopoldville, the poison plot was abandoned. However, the CIA then began to plan an assassination using a sniper.

Before this could come to fruition, on November 27, Lumumba escaped and headed for Stanleyville (now Kisangani), where his supporters were in control. Both the CIA and the Belgians helped Mobutu find Lumumba. He was captured by Mobutu's soldiers on the banks of the Sankuru River on December 2 and taken back to Leopoldville.

"... they were shot one at a time by firing squads commanded by Belgian officers."

Taken to a firing squad

Lumumba was then taken to Thysville military barracks, about 100 miles from Leopoldville. On January 17, apparently on the insistence of the Belgian government, he was flown to Katanga and handed over to Tshombe and his Belgian advisers. That night, after more brutal mistreatment, he was driven into the bush with two of his colleagues. With Tshombe present, they were shot one at a time by firing squads commanded by Belgian officers.

The bodies were buried in shallow graves. Then, under the supervision of Belgian police, the bodies were dug up, dismembered, and dissolved with acid until no traces remained.

Salvador Allende

U.S. intelligence services also plotted against Salvador Allende, the democratically elected president of Chile. Because they feared that his mildly left-wing government might steer Chile toward Communism, the CIA and U.S. military intelligence backed a coup planned by the Chilean Armed Forces and led by General Augusto Pinochet Ugarte. It was apparently hoped that Allende would take his own life; if not, he was to be killed and his death announced as suicide.

The coup was carried out on September 11, 1973. When rebel troops stormed the presidential palace in the Chilean capital, Santiago, Allende was killed by gunfire during the fighting. Once the palace was in rebel hands, his body was seated upright on a sofa. A gun was placed under his chin and his head was blown apart by a single shot. It was then announced that he had committed suicide. General Pinochet ruled Chile under a military dictatorship until 1990.

NGO DINH DIEM · 1963

Coup d'état

Thich Quan Duc, a Buddhist monk, doused himself in gasoline and set himself on fire in Saigon, South Vietnam, on June 11, 1963. His self-immolation was a protest against South Vietnam's President Ngo Dinh Diem, who was responsible for the killing of nine Buddhists by South Vietnamese soldiers the previous month—their crime having been to display religious flags. The president's brother, Ngo Dinh Nhu, who headed the feared South Vietnamese Secret Police, was not impressed by the suicide. "If the Buddhists want to have another barbecue," he is quoted as saying, "I will be happy to supply the gasoline."

Making the headlines

Reports about burning monks and cynical police chiefs were not what President John F. Kennedy and his administration wanted to see on the front pages of newspapers. The United States had supported Diem in 1954 as a leader capable of defending South Vietnam from the spread of Communism in Southeast Asia.

By the end of 1963, despite huge American financial and military aid, including the presence of about 16,000 U.S. military advisers, South Vietnam faced an increasingly menacing Communist insurgency. Diem was barely fulfilling his purpose, and his American backers were concerned about his regime.

Diem pursued his own agenda, which had little to do with the Communism that obsessed the United States. Diem's priorities had been first to ensure his own power, then the power and financial advancement of his family, and finally to enhance the position of Vietnam's Catholic minority, to which his family belonged. In pursuit of these goals, he repressed his opponents, failed to implement a land reform program supported in the countryside, and alienated adherents of his country's majority religious group, the Buddhists.

The CIA to the rescue

The Americans wanted Diem to win popular support, not alienate it, so he could defeat the Communist insurgents. By the time a new U.S. ambassador, Henry Cabot Lodge, arrived in Saigon in late August 1963, the future of Diem was the main issue on his agenda. Could the South Vietnamese leader reform his regime, or would he have to be replaced—and if so, by whom?

The answers were provided by the CIA, which had a substantial presence in Saigon. CIA agent Colonel Lucien E. Conein had built up a strong relationship with South Vietnamese Army officers, many of whom were unhappy with Diem's rule. It emerged that General Duong Van Minh—known as Big Minh for his impressive build—was willing to lead a coup if the Americans would give their support.

Throughout September and October the situation hung in the balance. The Kennedy administration wavered, still willing to give

KEY DATES

1901 Born January 3 into an aristocratic Catholic family in the Quang Binh province of Vietnam

1926 Serves as a governor under French rule

1933 Becomes a minister in the government of Emperor Bao Dai, who ruled under the French

1945 Refuses an invitation to join independent Vietnamese government headed by Ho Chi Minh

1950 Leaves Vietnam for the United States, where he contacts politicians, including John F. Kennedy

1954 Becomes prime minister of South Vietnam

1955 With U.S. support, elected as first president of the Republic of Vietnam, displacing Bao Dai

1960 National Liberation Front established to fight against Diem's regime in South Vietnam

1963 Assassinated on November 2 in a coup

Diem another chance to reform his regime while at the same time indicating that it would not oppose a coup if one happened.

The Vietnamese generals sweated, aware that Diem's brother Nhu was plotting to use his secret police to strike against opponents of the regime. Eventually, the generals decided—on the basis of what they were told by Ambassador Lodge and Conein—that they had backing from the Americans to act.

Inside the palace *A member of South Vietnam's rebel military forces searches the reception room in Diem's presidential palace during the November 1 coup.*

KENNEDY AND DIEM

The question of President John F. Kennedy's responsibility for Diem's assassination has been much debated. President Richard M. Nixon once said bluntly, "Kennedy killed Diem." However, there seems to be no evidence to substantiate this view.

As a senator in the early 1950s, Kennedy had met and admired Diem. In 1963, it seems that he preferred to see reform in Diem's regime, something he had not given up on—even in discussions on the eve of the coup. Moreover, Kennedy had clearly said that if there were a coup, Diem should be exiled and not physically harmed. There seems no reason to disbelieve his shock when told the news of the killings. Perhaps the most that can be said is that Kennedy should have realized Diem was unlikely to have survived a coup d'état.

The fall of Diem's regime

On November 1, at 1:30 P.M., South Vietnamese troops loyal to General Minh seized key installations in Saigon. Diem's presidential palace was surrounded. As mortars were fired into the palace, Diem phoned Lodge to ask if he had American support. All the ambassador would say was that he could arrange safe passage out of the country for Diem.

Diem refused to surrender. With his brother Nhu, he fled the palace through a secret tunnel, hiding in a house in the Cholon district, the Chinese quarter of Saigon. Early on the morning of November 2, he and Nhu took refuge in a nearby Catholic church, disguising themselves as priests. There they were arrested by rebel troops.

The two men were led out to an armored personnel carrier, their hands tied behind their backs, to be driven to military headquarters. What happened once they were inside the vehicle is contested. According to some accounts, the officer in charge of arresting the men (whose name is unknown) had an intense hatred of Diem and Nhu, so he bayoneted Nhu, then shot both men in the back of the head. Many others believe that Diem and Nhu were killed on direct orders from General Minh. Regardless of the circumstances of their deaths, the bodies were carried away and buried in unmarked graves, while the people of Saigon celebrated the fall of the regime.

"...he bayoneted Nhu, then shot both men in the back of the head."

Shot by a sniper

As workers streamed out of their offices at lunchtime on March 12, 2003, three men in blue overalls walked into 14 Admiral Geprat Street, an office building in the center of the Serbian capital of Belgrade. Signs of Serbia's recent troubled past were visible all around—the two buildings on either side of No. 14 were still ruined shells after having been bombed by NATO aircraft during the Kosovo War of 1999.

KEY DATES

1952 Born January 1 in Bosanski Samac, Bosnia

1974 Jailed for forming a non-Communist student movement at Belgrade University

1990 Elected to the Serbian Parliament in first free elections

1992 Becomes leader of Serbia's Democratic Party

1996 Elected mayor of Belgrade

2000 Plays a leading role in the downfall of the Milosevic regime

2001 Appointed prime minister under President Vojislav Kostunica

2003 Assassinated in Belgrade on March 12

Waiting for their victim

The three men, one carrying a toolbox, walked up the stairs to the second floor and entered an empty office. Once inside, one of the men took out a Heckler & Koch high-velocity rifle. The window of the office looked down on a small parking lot about 220 yards (200 m) away, at the rear of the building where Serbia's prime minister, 51-year-old Zoran Djindjic, worked.

Djindjic was regarded by the West as Serbia's best hope for the future. He had helped to overthrow the feared Serbian President Slobodan Milosevic in 2000 and had authorized his extradition to face charges in front of the War Crimes Tribunal in the Hague. As prime minister, Djindjic was an advocate of free-market reforms in the former Communist state. He also led a crackdown on Serbian organized crime.

Democratic leader

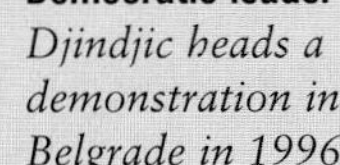
Djindjic heads a demonstration in Belgrade in 1996.

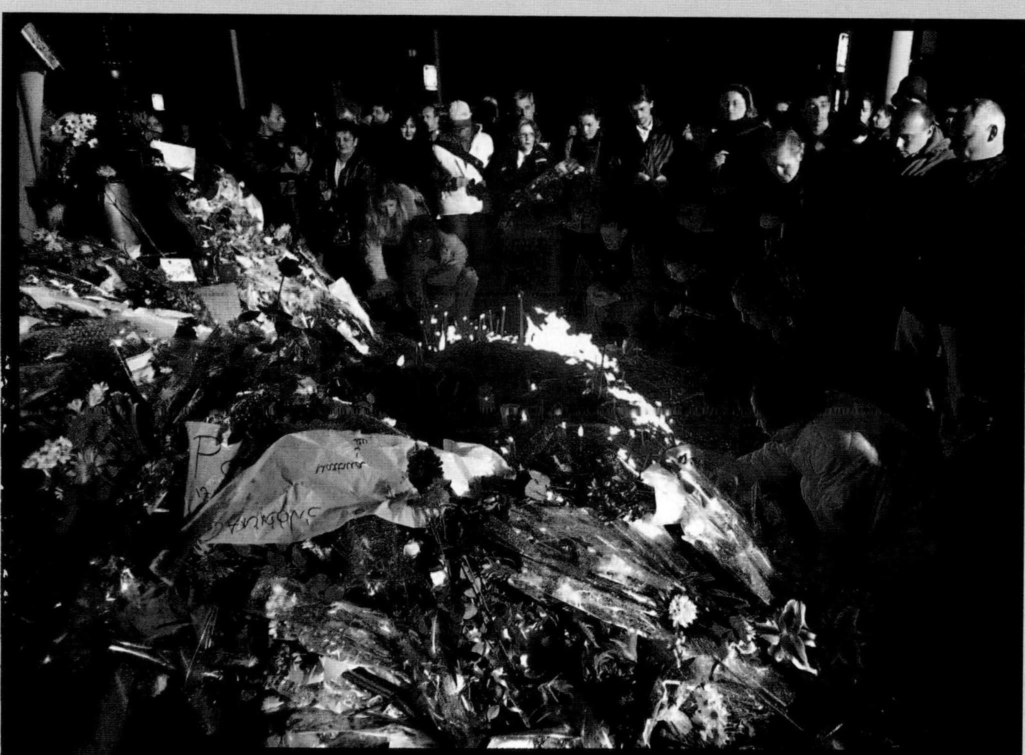

In tribute *Mourners light candles and leave flowers as a memorial for assassinated Prime Minister Djindjic.*

About 20 minutes after the three men entered the office, the prime minister's armored BMW entered the parking lot. Djindjic got out of the car, using crutches because of an ankle injury. As he balanced himself on the crutches, a shot rang out. A bullet struck him in the back, passed through his heart and intestines, and exited to wound a bodyguard. Djindjic was rushed to a hospital, but he was already dead. Meanwhile, the assassins ran out of the building and disappeared into the crowds.

Hunting down the killers

The Serbian government made mass arrests, targeting organized crime and ex-Milosevic death squads. Milorad Lukovic (also known as Legija), a leader of both the criminal Zemun gang and Milosevic's feared special operations unit, the Red Berets, topped their list of suspects. Like Milosevic, Lukovic was wanted by the Hague Tribunal, accused of responsibility for massacres during the Balkan conflicts of the 1990s. Hundreds of other suspects were arrested, but Lukovic could not be found.

A dangerous friendship

As an investigation of the assassination continued, it became clear that the picture of Djindjic as a human-rights supporter shot down by thugs was too simplistic. Djindjic himself once said, "A man must have friends in both heaven and hell."

Although he led the Red Berets, Lukovic had been Djindjic's temporary ally. Just before the demonstrations that brought Milosevic's fall from power, Djindjic had met secretly with Lukovic in an armored car, where they agreed that the Red Berets would not defend Milosevic. When Djindjic wanted Milosevic arrested in 2001, the Red Berets did the job. What Djindjic offered in return is not known but, by 2003, Lukovic was saying that the prime minister had not delivered.

In May 2004, Lukovic surrendered to the Serbian police after a year on the run, raising hopes that the truth might emerge at last.

VICTIM

Jill Dando

On April 26, 1999, 37-year-old British TV presenter Jill Dando was murdered outside her London home. Her killer walked up to her in broad daylight, pointed a gun at her head, and fired a shot. Although a celebrity-obsessed local man, Barry George, was convicted of Dando's murder, many people still believe he is innocent and that she was killed by a Serbian hit man.

It has been suggested that Dando's killing, which took place during the Kosovo War, was ordered in retaliation for the NATO bombing of a TV station in Belgrade. She may have been selected as a victim because she had recently made a high-profile appeal on behalf of Kosovan refugees. The killing was allegedly ordered by Arkan (real name Zeljko Raznatovic), a Serbian paramilitary leader with a vicious record during the "ethnic cleansing" in Croatia and Bosnia in the 1990s.

Arkan was also the victim of an assassination. On January 15, 2000, four men in running outfits approached him and his bodyguards outside Belgrade's Intercontinental Hotel and opened fire at close range with submachine guns. Arkan was hit three times in the face and died on the way to the hospital. He may have been killed because he knew too much about Milosevic's involvement in war crimes.

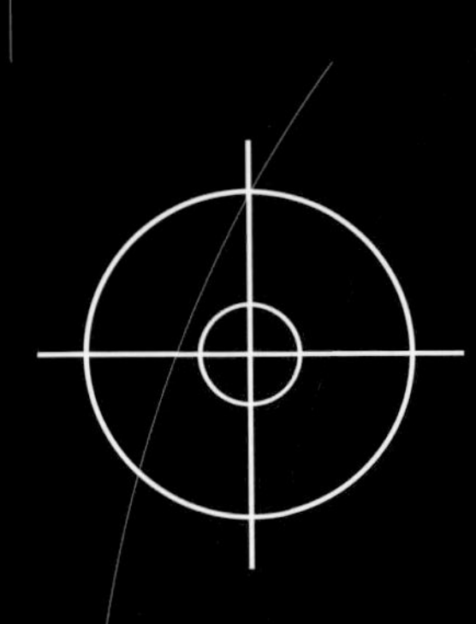

STALKERS AND LUNATICS

JAMES GARFIELD · 1881
HUEY LONG · 1935
OLOF PALME · 1986
ANNA LINDH · 2003

Stalkers and lunatics

Anyone who becomes famous—whether as a politician, movie star, rock musician, or other type of celebrity—will inevitably enter the fantasy lives of thousands of people whom he or she has never met or has only briefly encountered and swiftly forgotten. This usually harmless phenomenon becomes dangerous when fantasy turns into obsession. Often, the admirer's love transforms swiftly to hate—the celebrity is seen as rejecting or failing the admirer.

Alternatively, an individual confronted with his or her own failures may need to acquire some type of meaning or value. That person focuses his or her resentment or bitterness on a single powerful public figure.

Legal sanity

As courts of law around the world have discovered, it is often difficult to establish whether a killing should be considered a sane act. For example, Sirhan Sirhan had a rational political motive for assassinating Senator Robert F. Kennedy (see pp. 106–9), yet he seems in other ways to fit the profile of a classic stalker. He was a loner who at first admired Kennedy, seeing him as a source of hope, then he felt that his idol had let him down.

Few people would doubt that President James Garfield's assassin, Charles Guiteau, was insane, despite a court ruling to the contrary. This is not just because of his claim to have acted on God's orders, but also because the relationship he developed with the president was a complete fantasy. In his own eyes, the assassin had served Garfield well, then gone unrewarded. In reality, the president only became aware of Guiteau's existence because of several irrational letters requesting a diplomatic post the delusional man had sent to him.

A murderer's weapon *This knife was used to kill the Swedish Foreign Minister Anna Lindh. The killer's DNA was found on it.*

VICTIM

Assassination of Spencer Perceval

Only one British prime minister has ever been assassinated—Spencer Perceval. A 50-year-old father of five, Perceval had been the head of government for three years when, in 1812, he was shot by John Bellingham, a 35-year-old failed businessman.

Bellingham had once run a profitable Liverpool based company trading in timber. In 1803, on a visit to Russia, he became involved in a complex dispute over the insurance of a cargo. He was arrested and spent time in a Russian jail. When he was freed, he was bankrupt and embittered. Bellingham returned home convinced that the British government owed him compensation for his financial disaster. However, the government did not agree. Bellingham wrote to the prime minister, but the answer was brief and negative.

In February 1812, Bellingham moved to London and began visiting the Houses of Parliament, talking to anyone who would listen about his case. It must have become evident to him that no progress was being made. Late in April, he bought two pistols and ammunition from a shop in a nearby street, and he had a tailor make a deep pocket inside his coat.

At 5:00 P.M. on May 11, Bellingham entered the lobby at the entrance to the House of Commons and sat down by a fireplace. Fifteen minutes later, Prime Minister Perceval walked into the lobby with some colleagues. Bellingham rose to his feet, approached the prime minister, pulled a gun out of his hidden pocket, and fired. Perceval cried out "I am murdered! I am murdered!" He fell to the floor with a hole in his chest, blood spreading across his clothes. Perceval had been shot in the heart.

Bellingham made no attempt to escape. He was handcuffed, led out of the building, and taken to Newgate Prison. A large crowd had gathered, but it was not hostile toward the assassin—Perceval had been an unpopular prime minister among the poor of London. The crowd might even have helped Bellingham to escape, but soldiers arrived to escort him to jail.

Justice was swift. Bellingham was tried on May 15. A plea of insanity was refused, after which Bellingham pleaded his own case with considerable eloquence. He told the court that "my family was ruined and myself destroyed, merely because it was Mr. Perceval's pleasure that justice should not be granted," and he asserted that, "when a minister sets himself above the laws…he does it at his own personal risk." Such revolutionary theories did not appeal to the jury, which took only 10 minutes to return a guilty verdict. Bellingham was hanged at Newgate Prison on May 18.

However, what of Dr. Carl Weiss, the presumed assassin of Senator Huey Long? He may have killed Long because the senator threatened his family's status and reputation—a threat that was real enough—and yet still not be considered to have acted sanely. Long seems to have taken on a significance in Weiss's psyche that went far beyond the rational offense to his interests and social standing.

Acts of lunacy

In the case of Swedish Prime Minister Olof Palme, the question turns on the identity of his assassin. If he had been killed by Gustav Christer Pettersson, as was once believed—a man with no political opinions, no acquaintance with Palme, and a history of random violence—then it remains a truly lunatic assassination. Yet most people suspect that some still unknown politically motivated assassin was really responsible.

The killing of Swedish Foreign Minister Anna Lindh provides almost a mirror image of the Palme case. The police wanted to believe in a political motive, but they found evidence that Mijailo Mijailovic, a man with a history of psychiatric problems, was responsible for the crime.

The assassination of Dutch politician Pim Fortuyn presents a borderline case. His killer was ruled sane by a Dutch court, yet doubts remain about the balance of mind of a person who felt that Fortuyn's anti-immigration polices were such a threat to Europe's future that he had to be killed. As with Sirhan Sirhan—or for that matter Lee Harvey Oswald (see pp. 28–35)—perhaps a killer's political views are best regarded as part of a fantasy life that has gotten fatally out of hand.

Fatally wounded

In the spring of 1881, newly inaugurated U.S. President James Abram Garfield received a series of letters from a man he had never met, Charles J. Guiteau, who apparently wanted to enter the diplomatic service. First Guiteau wanted to be sent to Austria. "Next spring I expect to marry the daughter of a deceased New York Republican millionaire," he informed the president, "and I think we can represent the United States government at the court of Vienna with dignity and grace." However, France soon caught Guiteau's fancy. "I think I prefer Paris to Vienna," he wrote in another letter.

No doubt President Garfield and his secretary of state, James G. Blaine—who had also received Guiteau's job applications—paid no attention to these solicitations. They were absorbed by disputes inside the Republican Party in the administration's early months.

"The first shot grazed the president's arm, but the second shot hit him in the back."

Feeling betrayed, seeking revenge

During the 1880 campaign, Guiteau had written, printed, distributed, and delivered a speech in favor of Garfield. Although this incoherent address had no impact on the election results, Guiteau believed he had played a crucial role in Garfield's election victory. He therefore saw the president's failure to give him a position as a sign of ingratitude.

In May 1881, Guiteau decided to kill Garfield. Guiteau was already a familiar figure near the White House—where he had been harassing staff about his employment prospects—when he began following the president's movements. By mid-June, he was writing letters, which he never sent, beginning: "I have just shot the president...."

On July 2, Garfield went to the Baltimore and Potomac Railroad Station, intending to take a train north to his college reunion. As he walked through the waiting room with Secretary of State Blaine, Guiteau came up behind him and fired two rounds from a .44 caliber Bulldog pistol. The first shot grazed the president's arm, but the second hit him in the back. He fell, crying out, "My God, what is this?" Guiteau was seized by security guards while Garfield was taken to the White House for medical treatment.

An agonizingly slow death

There was a bullet lodged somewhere inside the president's body, but doctors could not find it, although no fewer than 16 of them probed his wound with fingers and metal instruments. Inventor Alexander Graham Bell

KEY DATES

1831 Born on November 19 near Orange (in Cuyahoga county), Ohio

1856 Graduates from Williams College, Williamstown, Massachusetts

1858 Marries Lucretia Rudolph

1859 Elected to the Ohio Senate as a Republican

1861 Commands a Union Army regiment in the Civil War

1863 Takes his seat in the House of Representatives as congressman from Ohio

1880 Narrowly wins presidential election

1881 Shot on July 2; dies of infection on September 19

turned up with his patented "induction balance," an early form of metal detector, but he could not locate the bullet either.

In the days before doctors understood what caused infections, hands were not always washed and surgical equipment was often not sterilized. Consequently, all the probing infected the wound, which was then repeatedly reinfected by operations to remove infected material, similarly conducted with unsterilized surgical equipment. Garfield was subjected to this painful treatment without anesthesia, then not in general use.

Two months after the shooting, Garfield was still alive but fading. On September 6, he was moved by train to a house by the sea in Elberon, New Jersey, where he died on September 19. The autopsy revealed the elusive bullet had lodged near his spine.

An act of insanity?

When Guiteau went on trial two months after Garfield's death, one main thread of his defense was that the president had died of medical malpractice, rather than of the gunshot the defendant had fired. This assertion was turned down by the court—as was Guiteau's plea of insanity, which he expressed in religious terms: "It was God's act and not mine."

Neurologists and phrenologists—experts who "scientifically" deduce character from the shape of a person's skull—were called to testify by both defense and prosecution. Guiteau's behavior in court was itself evidence of his mental instability. At times he was foul-mouthed and abusive; at other times, he vainly played to the crowd. However, at the end of a lengthy trial, the jury took only an hour to find Guiteau guilty.

On June 30, 1882, Guiteau was hanged in the District of Columbia Prison in front of a huge crowd, many of whom had paid large sums to witness the event. Before the hangman put the hood over his head, Guiteau recited a poem of his own composition, with the refrain "I am going to the Lordy, I am so glad...."

CHARLES JULIUS GUITEAU

President Garfield's killer, Charles Julius Guiteau, was born in 1841 in Freeport, Illinois. From an early age, he had an unstable life. He seems to have combined an aversion for working with a habit of spending money, which led to a lifetime of scrounging, petty fraud, and failure to pay his bills.

In his 20s, Guiteau became associated with the Oneida Community in New York, a religious group professing free love and communal property. Later, he left the group and moved into journalism, then law. He qualified as a lawyer in Chicago in 1869 and married a looal librarian.

After his wife divorced him in 1874 for abusive behavior, Guiteau became an itinerant religious revivalist—something between a preacher and charlatan. In 1880, he appointed himself as a campaigner for the Republican Party. By 1881, he was penniless and losing grip on reality.

Crime scene *Guiteau chose the Baltimore and Potomac Railroad Station on Missouri Avenue in Washington as the place to shoot President Garfield.*

A hail of bullets

In 1935, Senator Huey P. Long from Louisiana was one of the most controversial figures in American political life. Known as "Kingfish," Long had established a virtual dictatorship in his home state, using ruthless methods—bribery, vote fixing, intimidation, and gerrymandering—to suppress political opposition.

However, Long was also immensely popular, presenting himself as the champion of the little man against big business. Among his major achievements, he helped to improve education and set up an impressive road-building program, financed by taxes on large corporations.

KEY DATES

1893 Born August 30, near Winnfield, Louisiana

1915 Passes bar examination to become a lawyer

1921 Becomes chairman of the Louisiana Public Service Commission

1928 Elected governor of Louisiana

1930 Elected to the U.S. Senate but continues as governor until he arranges a successor of his own choice

1932 Campaigns on behalf of Franklin D. Roosevelt in presidential election

1933 Criticizes Roosevelt's New Deal policies

1934 Launches the Share Our Wealth Society

1935 Announces his intention to run for president in August; assassinated on September 8; dies on September 10

Take from the rich, give to the poor

During the Great Depression of the 1930s, Long's voice began to be heard on a national scale. In a speech to the U.S. Senate, he made his message clear. "Unless we provide for redistribution of wealth in this country, the country is doomed."

In 1934, Long established the Share Our Wealth Society, a nationwide movement dedicated to the straightforward transfer of money from the rich to the poor . No individual would be allowed personal wealth of over 5 million dollars, and the money taken from millionaires would be used to give every American a minimum annual income of $2,500. This was the beginning of Long's bid for the presidency in 1936.

Fighting off the enemy

Naturally, Long's unscrupulous political tactics won him plenty of enemies in Louisiana. One was Judge Benjamin Pavy of St. Landry Parish. Although only a minor figure, Pavy was a persistent opponent of Long's policies. In 1935, Long decided to unseat him from his post. A bill was brought before the Louisiana legislature to redraw county borders and give Long's supporters a majority in St. Landry Parish.

At the same time, Long applied pressure on the judge by attacking his family. Two of the judge's daughters were fired from their teaching posts, and a rumor was spread that Pavy's wife had "coffee blood"—that she was the daughter of her father's black mistress. This was a very damaging accusation among whites in Louisiana in the 1930s.

Protecting his family

Long's actions seem to have infuriated Judge Pavy's son-in-law, 29-year-old Carl Weiss, a respected physician living in the Louisiana capital, Baton Rouge. On the evening of Sunday, September 8, 1935, he put on a white linen suit and left the house, telling his wife he was going to make calls on patients. He was carrying a Belgian .32 automatic pistol.

Weiss drove to the State Capitol Building, an expensive, monumental brass and marble structure that Long had recently had constructed. When Weiss arrived, Long was in the governor's office, so Weiss waited in the marble-pillared corridor outside. At about 9:20 P.M., Long came out into the corridor surrounded by armed bodyguards. Weiss stepped forward to confront him. According to the most widely accepted version of events, Weiss then pulled out his gun and shot Long in the abdomen. The bodyguards opened fire on Weiss, shooting about 60 rounds. His bullet-riddled body fell to the floor.

Turbulent political life
The National Guard protects Long in 1934, during a probe into political violence in New Orleans. Long made many enemies during his political career.

Death arrives

Long stumbled unattended down the stairs of the Capitol building, dripping blood. Meeting a political associate, James O'Connor, he cried, "Hell, man, take me to the hospital!"

A bullet had entered Long's body below the ribs and exited his back. Unbeknownst to the doctors who treated him, it had perforated his kidney. An operation was performed, but internal bleeding continued. Long grew weaker through the following day and died the morning of September 10.

There was no official investigation of Long's death, no autopsy was performed on his body, and the inquest was perfunctory—leaving several questions unanswered (see box, left). Long was buried in the grounds of the Louisiana statehouse.

DID WEISS REALLY KILL LONG?

There are some who doubt the accepted version of Huey Long's death. Dr. Weiss's behavior before the killing gave no clue that he was contemplating such a desperate action. One theory is that he planned only to confront Long and punch him—after the shooting, Long had an unexplained cut on his lip. Some believe Weiss punched Long, and his bodyguards overreacted and opened fire, killing both men. Others claim that Long was shot by both Weiss and a bodyguard.

There is also the possibility of a conspiracy. One of the bodyguards could have been paid to kill Long, seizing this chance to fulfill the contract. Or if Weiss was the killer, he may have been convinced to do it by Long's enemies. In August 1935, Long told the U.S. Senate of a private meeting allegedly held in New Orleans, during which some of his opponents discussed plans to have him killed. Some claim that wealthy men who feared his redistribution policies had him killed.

Shot in the back

On the evening of February 28, 1986, Swedish Prime Minister Olof Palme and his wife, Lisbet, went to the movies. They traveled to the center of the Swedish capital, Stockholm, by subway train, where they met their son Marten and his girlfriend and waited in line at the box office. There were no police or bodyguards with them. Palme was accustomed to walking around the streets of his peaceful country without fear.

Unafraid to speak out

Palme had gained international fame for his campaigns on issues such as disarmament and the rights of developing countries. He had ruffled the feathers of the United States many times—for example, by denouncing the U.S. role in the Vietnam War. He was an active supporter of liberation movements in the Third World. Some right-wing governments and extremists saw his actions as those of an enemy.

KEY DATES

1927 Born January 30 in Stockholm

1949 Joins the Swedish Social Democrat party

1953 Acts as personal secretary to Social Democrat Prime Minister Tage Erlander

1955 Becomes leader of the Social Democrat Youth Movement

1963 Enters the government, holding various posts

1969 Becomes prime minister and leader of the Social Democrat party

1976 Social Democrats lose power; Palme joins the Brandt Commission on Third World problems

1982 Becomes prime minister once again

1986 Assassinated on February 28

The end of innocence

The movie ended after 11:00 P.M. Palme and his wife left their son and walked toward the subway station. There were plenty of people about. At 11:21 P.M., a man came up behind the prime minister and shot him twice in the back. Lisbet, who was walking slightly ahead of her husband, turned as she heard the shots and saw the assailant, a man in a dark coat with a cap pulled down over his eyes. He fired

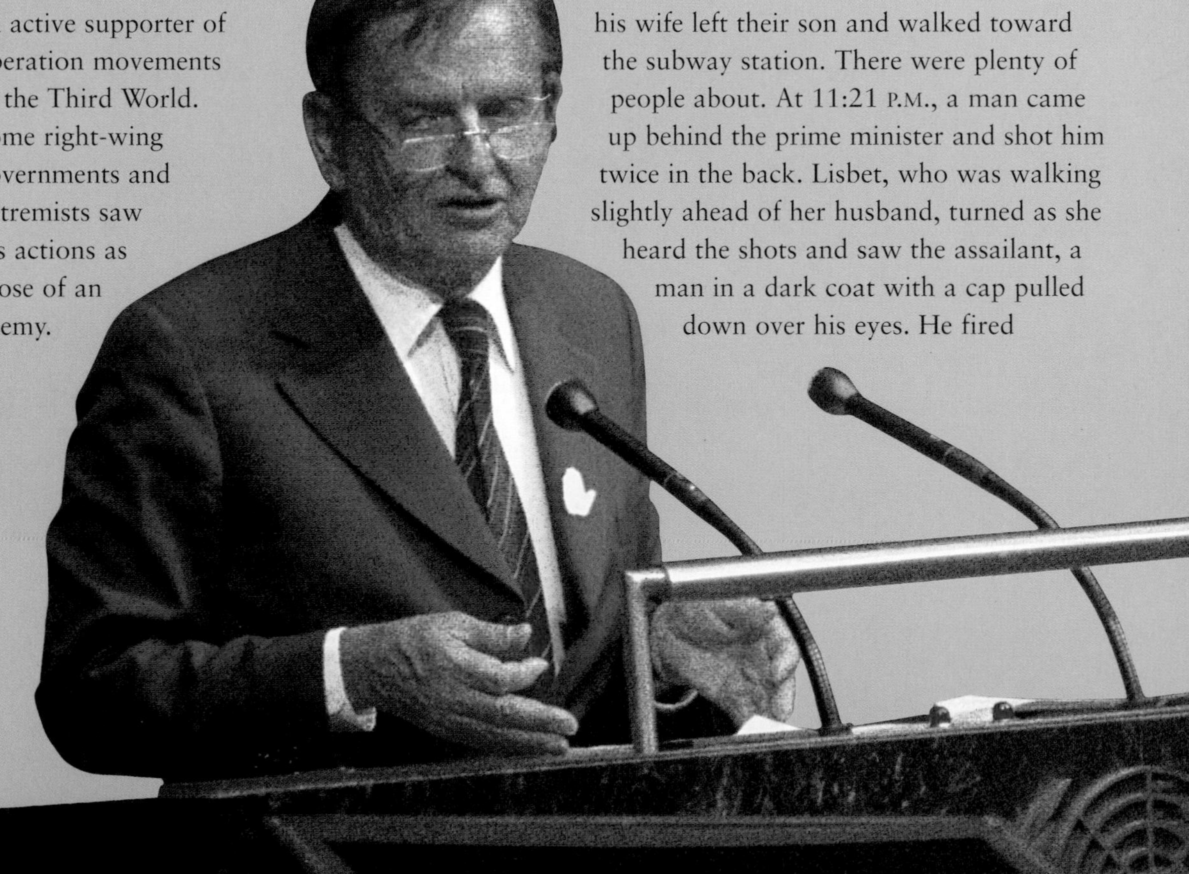

another shot, narrowly missing her, and ran off. Palme was dead within minutes.

The assassination came as a shock to the Swedish people, who regarded their country as a civilized haven in an otherwise dangerous world. It seems to have been a shock to the Swedish police, too. Immediately after the killing, they reacted too slowly to catch the assassin fleeing the scene. They also failed to secure the crime scene—the bullets that killed Palme were later found by members of the public. (The gun has never been recovered.)

In remembrance *Roses and other flowers are left by a plaque near the place where Palme was shot and killed by an unknown assassin.*

A chaotic investigation

Ake Viktor Gunnarsson, a member of a right-wing movement founded by American extremist Lyndon LaRouche, was picked up as a suspect two weeks after the shooting. Witnesses had placed him at the scene of the crime and powder marks were found on his clothing. However, the police lineup had been botched and the powder did not match that found on Palme's coat, so police let him go.

As the months passed, police began to focus on foreigners living in Sweden. In particular, they targeted the Kurdish Workers' Party, a left-wing group dedicated to creating an independent Kurdish state in parts of Turkey and Iraq. Because this was exactly the kind of cause that Palme was famous for supporting, it is hard to see why this group's members came under suspicion. Thirteen Kurds were arrested and three were charged, but they were all released because of an almost total lack of evidence against them.

Gustav Christer Pettersson was arrested in December 1988, 22 months after the crime. He was an alcoholic and drug abuser who had spent most of his life in prisons or psychiatric hospitals. He had previously been convicted of killing one person and attempting to kill two others with a bayonet.

> **"A man came up behind the prime minister and shot him twice in the back."**

There was no forensic evidence to connect Pettersson to Palme's assassination, and he had no known motive. However, after viewing a videotape of a police lineup, Lisbet declared she was certain that he was the man she had seen on the evening of the shooting. Pettersson was found guilty and sentenced to life imprisonment. However, an appeals court later reversed this decision and freed him, arguing that an identification made two years after the event was not safe grounds for a conviction. Palme's assassination still remains unsolved.

Speaking up *Prime Minister Palme addresses the United Nations General Assembly a few months before being shot.*

SOUTH AFRICAN ANGLE

In 1996, Euguene de Kock, the former head of the South African Secret Police, told a court in Pretoria that a South African agent had assassinated the Swedish prime minister. De Kock claimed that the shooting had been organized by Craig Williamson, the man behind the killing of Ruth First (see p. 151).

Palme opposed apartheid and supported the African National Congress (ANC), which might have made him a target for the South African Secret Police. Links between the Swedish police and the South African apartheid regime have been discovered, suggesting a cover-up. However, De Kock and Williamson were enemies, so it could have been a malicious allegation.

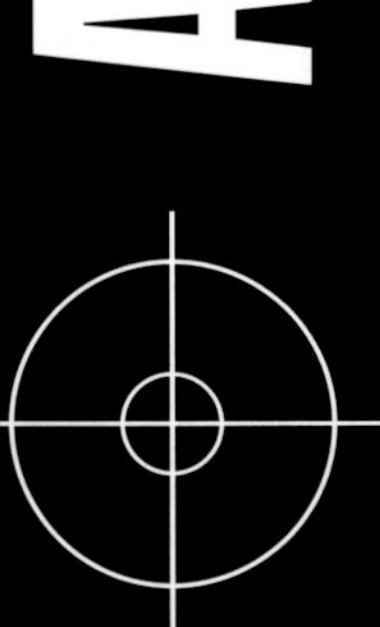

Brutally stabbed

Sweden's 46-year-old Foreign Minister Anna Lindh was out shopping at one Stockholm's most luxurious department stores with her press secretary, Eva Franchell, on the afternoon of September 10, 2003. Lindh wanted to look her best for an upcoming TV debate on adopting the euro as Sweden's currency. She had recently been devoting all her charm and energy to persuading the Swedish people to vote "yes" in a referendum on the issue. As was traditional in Sweden—despite Olof Palme's assassination in 1986 (see pp. 138–139)—Lindh had not been assigned a bodyguard.

KEY DATES

1957 Born on June 19 in Enskede, a suburb of the Swedish capital Stockholm

1982 Gets a law degree from Uppsala University; elected to parliament as a Social Democrat, supporting Prime Minister Olof Palme's government

1984 Heads the Social Democrat Youth League

1991 Elected to the Social Democrat Party's executive committee; marries politician Bo Holmberg

1994 Appointed Sweden's minister for the environment, reflecting her concern for green issues

1998 Promoted to foreign minister in the government of Prime Minister Goran Persson

2003 Heads the campaign to persuade Swedes to vote to join the Euro Zone; fatally attacked in Stockholm on September 10; dies September 11

A mindless attack

Mijailo Mijailovic, a 25-year-old Swede of Serbian parentage, was also in the store. Security camera footage showed him wearing a baseball cap, wandering from floor to floor. In his jacket pocket, he was carrying a craft knife.

Lindh had just tried on a sweater when Mijailovic pushed her against a clothing rack. She fell to the ground, raising her arms to shelter herself from the attack, which lasted 56 seconds. Franchell had not seen the knife and thought the man was punching Lindh in the stomach. Mijailovic then went down an escalator, tossing the knife onto the floor before running out of the store.

The campaigner *Just days before her death, Lindh stands in front of a poster in favor of a "yes" vote for the euro.*

Carried away *After being mortally stabbed, Lindh is taken from the department store on a stretcher.*

Lindh had been stabbed in the chest, stomach, and arms 10 times. Franchall recalled, "I looked down at her stomach. Blood was oozing out." Lindh was rushed to the hospital, where surgeons battled to stop the internal bleeding. However, the knife had sliced into her liver. She died 13 hours after the attack on the morning of September 11.

Catching the killer

Lindh was a popular personality in Sweden. Even her opponents acknowledged her as a politician with style and integrity. A combination of charm and competence had made her stand out as a possible candidate for prime minister in the future. After her death, tributes of flowers and candles were left in the streets around the department store and the hospital as a public expression of grief.

The pressure on the Swedish police to catch the killer was immense. They possessed three assets: security camera footage from inside the store, the murder weapon that had been abandoned as the killer escaped, and the assassin's baseball cap found near the scene.

Police first assumed that the killing had been planned by right-wing extremists and arrested Per-Olof Svensson, a man with neo-Nazi connections, on September 16. He was in custody eight days later when a tip led the police to Mijailovic, whose DNA matched material on the knife and the cap. He had a history of violence; he had been convicted of wounding his father with a knife in 1997. At that time, psychiatrists had declared him "in great need of psychiatric and psychotherapeutic efforts," but he had not been treated.

At his trial in 2004, Mijailovic claimed that antidepressants that caused "voices" in his head had sparked the killing. He told the court, "the voices came and said I should attack her." Prosecutors argued that he had recognized and followed Lindh before killing her. Mijailovic was found sane at the time of the attack and sentenced to life in prison.

VICTIM

Pim Fortuyn

On May 6, 2002, right-wing Dutch politician Pim Fortuyn was walking to his car when a man came up from behind and shot him five times. The assassin, Volkert van der Graaf, was arrested as he fled the scene.

Fortuyn was a controversial political figure. He was gay and flaunted a lavish lifestyle that contrasted with the low-key style of most Dutch politicians. He was outspoken and his views were controversial. He had called for a halt to immigration and criticized Islam as "culturally backward." His assassination occurred nine days before national elections in which his party, Lijst Pim Fortuyn, had been expected to make a strong showing.

A vegan morally troubled by such abuses as the use of fruit flies in research, van der Graaf was unrepentant about shooting a human. He claimed to have killed Fortuyn on behalf of the Netherlands' Muslim minority. In 2003, he was sentenced to 18 years in prison.

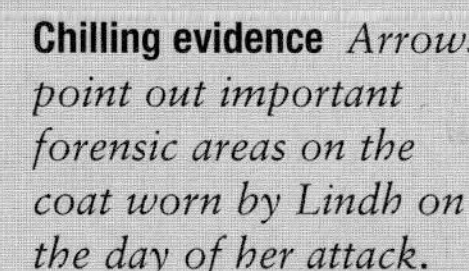

Chilling evidence *Arrows point out important forensic areas on the coat worn by Lindh on the day of her attack.*

Goodbye

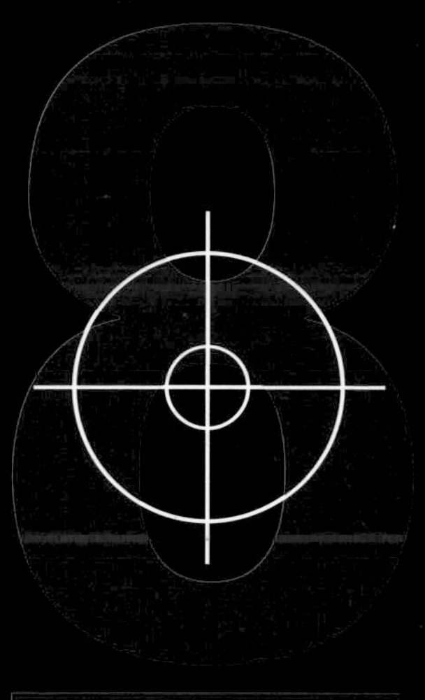

ASSASSINATION OR MURDER?

THE ROMANOVS · 1918

STEPHEN BIKO · 1977

JOHN LENNON · 1980

Assassination or murder?

Everyone can agree that the intentional killings of Archduke Franz Ferdinand (see pp. 22–27), President John F. Kennedy (see pp. 28–35), and Martin Luther King Jr. (see pp. 90–95) can be classified as assassinations. However, there are other cases involving the killing of prominent individuals in which the application of the term "assassination" is less certain.

Execution or assassination?

Should people killed in cold blood by their political enemies be described as victims of assassination, although the act takes the form of an execution? Firing squads killed the Romanov family of Czar Nicholas II of Russia in 1918; Patrice Lumumba, first prime minister of the independent Congo, in 1962 (see pp. 124–25); and the Emperor Maximilian of Mexico in 1867 (see box, opposite). Could these be considered "assassinations"? Perhaps what gives special credibility to the term when applied to the Romanovs is the clandestine disposal of the bodies by their Bolshevik killers and the denial by authorities that the killings had taken place. Lumumba's death was similarly followed by a desperate effort to hide the remains—and he had in any case been the target of more obvious assassination plots.

Inconclusive evidence

In the case of South African Black Consciousness activist Stephen Biko, who died in police custody in 1977, time has failed to clarify satisfactorily the events surrounding his death. In effect, it may have been manslaughter—the accidental result of gross mistreatment—or plain murder by police officers at the scene. However, if his killing was ordered by members of the white South African government, who were afraid of Biko's growing political influence over young black South Africans, assassination would certainly be the correct word.

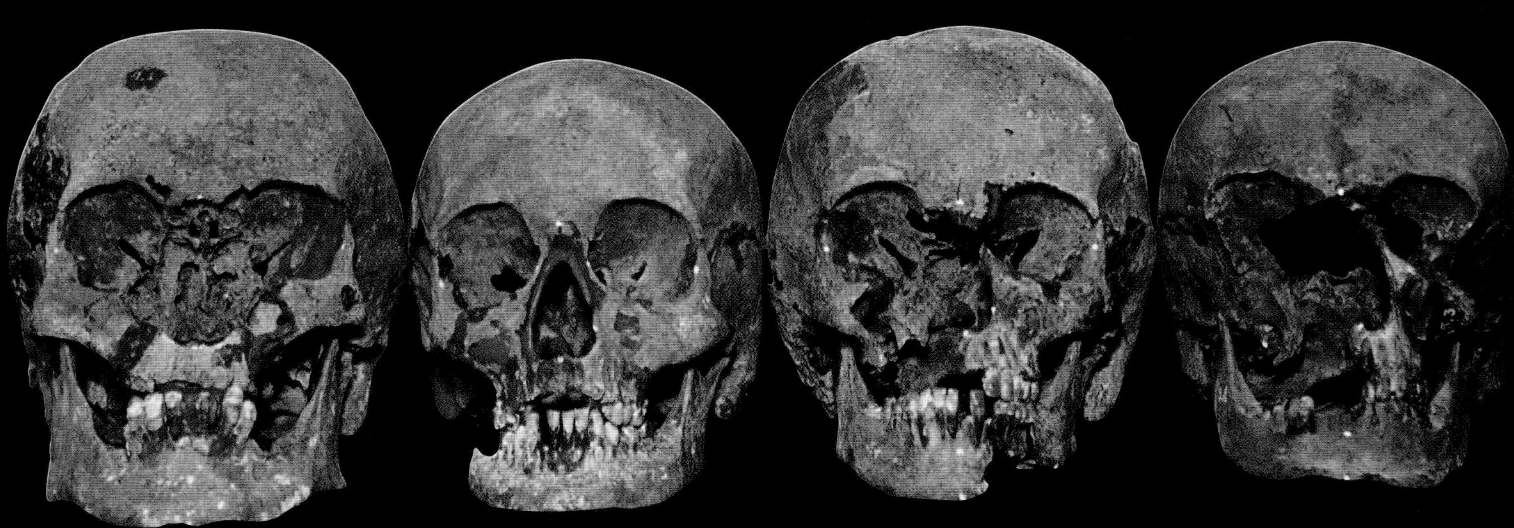

Dynastic remains *These skulls from the Romanov family were excavated from a shallow grave in Ekaterinburg, Russia.*

VICTIM

Emperor Maximilian of Mexico

Mexico's 35-year-old Emperor Maximilian, the younger brother of the Hapsburg ruler of Austria, Emperor Franz Joseph, was a tragic victim of "assassination" by firing squad. Maximilian's life came to this grim end through the machinations of France and his own naive idealism.

During the American Civil War in 1862, Napoleon III, the ruler of France, sent troops into Mexico to back a revolt by Mexican Conservatives against the Liberal President Benito Juárez. Because the Conservatives wanted someone of royal blood to rule the country, the French and the Conservatives invited Maximilian to take the throne of Mexico—a country he had never even seen.

Maximilian arrived in Mexico in 1864 with his 24-year-old Belgian wife, Carlota. He hoped to bring good government, freedom, and prosperity to the country. Instead, as Juárez fought back, Mexico was plunged into civil war. The end of the American Civil War in 1865 allowed the United States to assert its influence in support of Juárez and against the French.

Although Napoleon III withdrew his forces in 1866, Maximilian refused to abandon Mexico. His wife returned to Europe and attempted to raise support for her husband, while he stayed at his post. However, in May 1867, Maximilian was under siege by Juárez's army at Queretaro, and he was taken prisoner.

On June 19, Maximilian was led out to a square on top of a hill with two of his generals. Seven of Juárez's soldiers formed a line to carry out the execution. Completely calm in the face of his impending death, Maximilian gave each of the soldiers some gold in an attempt to bribe them. He wanted them to aim for his heart and not disfigure his face when they killed him. His last words were—in Spanish—"Long live Mexico! Long live independence!" The volley of shots rang out over the hillside, and he fell to the ground. An officer stepped forward to deliver a final shot at close range, in case Maximilian were still alive. The firing squad then reloaded to execute his two companions.

Maximilian had left instructions for his body to be mummified and shipped back to Europe, where he was buried in the Hapsburg vault in Vienna. Carlota never recovered from the shock of these events. She became severely depressed and lived as a recluse in a Belgian chateau for 60 years until her death in 1927.

The case for murder

It could be argued that all cases involving killers who are deranged or have purely private motives should be seen as simply murders. In addition, some people contend that a celebrity cannot, by definition, be assassinated, because political motivation is lacking.

The killer of Anna Lindh (see pp. 140–41), for example, probably did not have any political motives and is believed to have been unaware of his victim's political background. If he did recognize Lindh, it is likely that he killed her because she was famous—a celebrity—not because she was politically powerful. Her killing could be seen as a murder, not an assassination.

Following this view, the death of former Beatle John Lennon in 1980 was murder, not assassination. However, it could be argued that Lennon's songs frequently expressed political beliefs, and he was certainly regarded as a political subversive by the U.S. government, which spent four years trying to have him deported. Above all, however, Lennon's death deserves to be described as an assassination because of the way in which it happened—the lone crazed killer with a gun.

Ronald Reagan was a president (see pp. 178–79) and Lennon a musician, but their shootings, only a few months apart, had a great deal in common—in fact, they were directly linked. Like Lennon's assassin, the man responsible for shooting Reagan, John W. Hinckley Jr., was mentally unbalanced, obsessive, and suffered from depression. When Lennon was shot, Hinckley used the killing as a template when planning to shoot the president.

In some ways, perhaps it is legitimate to regard celebrities as the popes and kings and emperors of the modern world—prominent, almost magical individuals who populate the often violent fantasy lives of the lonely and the unstable.

A dynasty falls

In March 1917, a revolutionary uprising forced Czar Nicholas II of Russia to abdicate the throne, bringing an end to the rule of the Romanov dynasty after more than 300 years in power. Nicholas was not suited to the strains of ruling, so abdication was partly a relief to him. After the abdication a visitor remarked that "it was as if a heavy burden had fallen from his shoulders."

The czar and his family—his wife Alexandra, their four daughters, Olga, Tatiana, Maria, and Anastasia, and their only son, Czarevich Alexis—were held in a palace in Tsarskoe Selo, near Petrograd (St. Petersburg), waiting for the new provisional government to decide their fate. They played tennis and dominoes, read novels, and worked in the garden in luxurious confinement.

Unwelcome visitor

Nicholas's cousin, King George V, invited the Romanovs to take refuge in Britain, and the Russian provisional government accepted this solution. However, the czar and his regime were hated by those on the political left, who saw them as brutal oppressors. The Petrograd

KEY DATES

1868 Future Czar Nicholas II is born on May 18, eldest son of Czar Alexander III

1872 Alix, the future Czarina Alexandra, is born on June 6 in Germany, daughter of Grand Duke Louis of Hesse-Darmstadt and granddaughter of Queen Victoria

1894 Nicholas and Alexandra marry; Nicholas succeeds to the Russian throne

1898 Czar Nicholas II initiates the Hague Peace Conference to end all wars

1904 Czarevich Alexis, heir to the czarist regime, is born on August 12

1905 The czarist regime survives a revolutionary uprising in Russia

1914 Nicholas reluctantly leads Russia into war with Germany and Austria–Hungary

1917 The czar is deposed after a revolution in March; the family is moved to Tobolsk, Siberia, in August; the Bolsheviks seize power in November

1918 The family is killed in Ekaterinburg (now Sverdlovsk) in July

Soviet—a body representing revolutionary workers and soldiers—objected to the former czar being let off so lightly. And so did many trade unionists in Britain. George V withdrew the invitation after he was warned that the former czar's arrival might cause trouble.

To get the Romanovs out of the way, they were packed off to the Siberian town of Tobolsk in August 1917. They established themselves in a former governor's residence and were cared for by a large retinue of servants, including 7 cooks, 10 footmen, a butler, and a barber. The family's life was still comfortable and easy, although their son, a hemophiliac, had persistent health problems.

Power struggle for the czar

In Petrograd, Vladimir Ilyich Lenin and Leon Trotsky led the Bolshevik revolutionaries to seize power from the provisional government in November. As Bolsheviks took control of cities across Russia, forces were organized to fight against them. In 1918, civil war broke out between the Bolshevik Red Army and the White anti-revolutionaries.

At first, the Bolshevik leaders wanted to put the czar on trial to expose the alleged crimes of the czarist regime. A Bolshevik agent was sent to Tobolsk to bring Nicholas to Moscow. However, in the chaos of revolutionary Russia, this was no easy task. Local Bolsheviks controlling the city of Ekaterinburg, which lay between Tobolsk and Moscow, wanted the former czar themselves. They won an acrimonious debate with the Moscow authorities. The Romanovs were delivered to Ekaterinburg in April 1918.

The family were confined in a building the Bolsheviks called the House of Special Designation (also known as the Ipatev house, after its former owner). They were shut in their rooms except at mealtimes and were subjected to harassment by guards. They were accompanied only by their physician, Dr. Botkin, who looked after Alexis, and a handful of servants. In July, Yakov Yurovsky, the head of the local Bolshevik secret police,

The last Romanovs *Tzar Nicholas II, along with his wife and children, pose for one of the last official portraits before abdicating the throne (far left).*

Civilian action *The residents of Petrograd (now St. Petersburg) burn the Romanov coats of arms, torn down from city buildings in 1917.*

THE PROPHECY OF RASPUTIN

Before his death in 1916, Rasputin allegedly left a letter prophesying the fate of the Romanov dynasty. This document—the authenticity of which is not certain—states that if Rasputin is killed by Russian peasants, the "czar of Russia [will] have nothing to fear." However, it also claims that if he is killed by the nobility and the czar's relatives, "then no one of your [the czar's] family, that is to say none of your children or relations, will remain alive for more than two years." Rasputin declared that the Romanovs would be killed by the Russian people. Members of the Russian nobility were, indeed, among Rasputin's assassins, including the tsar's nephew Grand Duke Dmitri Pavlovich (see pp. 52–55)—and the Romanovs were killed by the Russian people.

The execution room *This is the room in which Czar Nicholas II and his family were murdered.*

the Cheka, took control of the Romanovs' imprisonment.

Decision time

By the second week in July, the Bolsheviks were struggling and Ekaterinburg was under threat from the White forces (it fell to the anti-Bolsheviks on July 25). According to one of Lenin's colleagues, Yakov Sverdlov, the Bolshevik leadership feared that if Nicholas were rescued by the Whites, he might become "a live banner" behind whom the anti-revolutionaries could rally.

On July 16, the Bolsheviks in Ekaterinburg sent a coded telegram to Lenin in Moscow saying that Nicholas was to be executed without delay. "If your opinion is contrary," it ended, "inform immediately." Lenin made no reply.

Rude awakening

What happened on the night of July 16 is partly known from an account by Pavel Medvedev, the commander of the guard in the House of Special Designation. According to Medvedev, Yurovsky called him into his office at about 8:00 P.M. and said, "We must shoot them all tonight, so notify the guards not to be alarmed if they hear shots." By "them all," Medvedev also meant the servants and the doctor—there would be no witnesses.

Sometime after midnight, Yurovsky went into the rooms occupied by the Romanovs and told Dr. Botkin to wake them. He was told that there was fighting in the town and the family needed to move into the basement for their own safety. It was after 1:00 A.M. by the time the Romanovs, their doctor, and the servants had washed and dressed.

> "The room filled with **smoke** as **bullets ricocheted** around...."

The emperor emerged first, carrying Alexis down the stairs. His wife and their daughters followed, then the doctor and servants—there were 11 in all. Anastasia was carrying Joy, their dog. They were led across a courtyard and down into the basement. "There were," Medvedev recalled, "no tears, no sobs, and no questions."

Three chairs were brought in for Nicholas, Alexandra, and Alexis. The daughters put pillows on Alexandra and Alexis's chairs. The Romanovs were simply

The remains *An expert examines the skeletons of the Romonav family, which were dug up from their grave in 1991.*

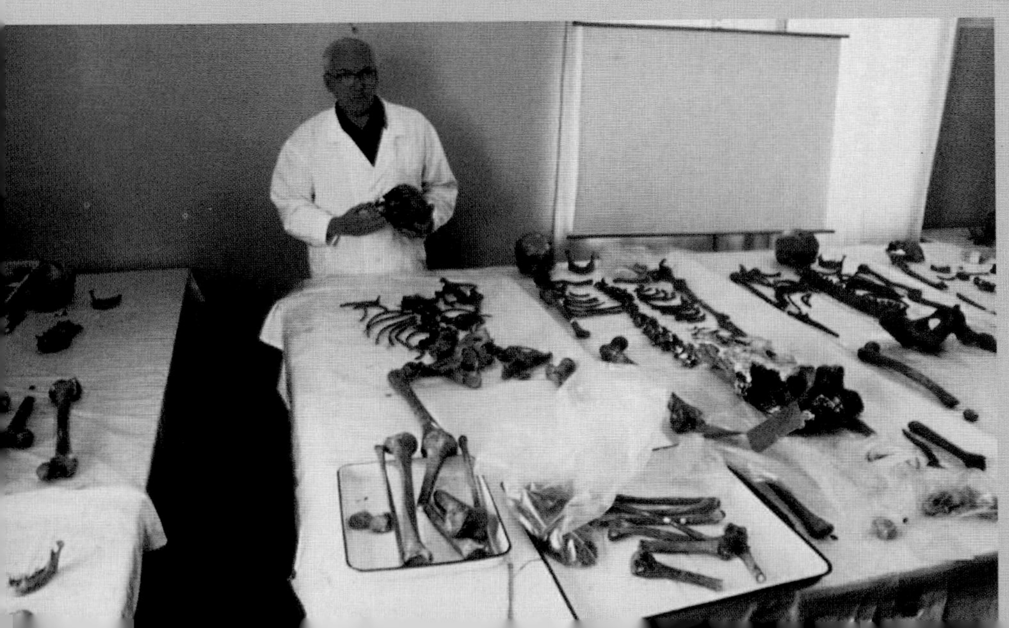

dressed, with Nicholas and Alexis wearing soldiers' shirts and caps.

An executioner for each victim

Yurovsky entered with the execution squad, consisting of five Russians and six Hungarians (sometimes cited as Latvians). Medvedev was ordered to go outside and keep watch. Each man in Yurovsky's squad had orders to kill a specific person—there were 11 executioners and 11 to be killed. However, the room was too small for the squad to line up with each opposite his intended victim.

The planned firing squad quickly degenerated into a chaotic bloodbath. As Yurovsky read out the order for the Romanovs to be killed, Nicholas protested, shouting, "What? What?" Yurovsky responded by pulling out his pistol and shooting Nicholas at point-blank range. At this, all the others opened fire. The room filled with smoke as bullets ricocheted around the constricted space.

When the shooting stopped, Medvedev returned to the basement. He saw "all the members of the czar's family lying on the floor with numerous wounds to their bodies." Alexis was still alive and moaning, so Yurovsky shot him at point-blank range. Anastasia also showed some signs of life. She was bayoneted to make sure she was dead.

SURVIVING ROMANOVS?

The secrecy surrounding the killing of the Romanovs has led to speculation that some of the family might have survived. Several people later claimed to be the czar's youngest daughter, Anastasia, who allegedly survived the shooting because of diamonds sewn under her dress.

The most impressive claim was from a woman who turned up in a mental hospital in Berlin in 1920. She used the name Anna Anderson; she later claimed to be Anastasia, and many people believed her. Anderson died in 1984. Later, DNA analysis of her remains revealed no connection between her and Europe's closely interbred royal families.

The first graves

The bodies were taken to a truck while the basement was cleaned of blood. Medvedev's involvement had ended by 3:00 A.M., but Yurovsky had to dispose of the bodies. That night they were dumped in local mine shafts, but, after reconsidering, the killers decided this was not a safe hiding place.

According to Yurovsky, the bodies were later retrieved and buried in a shallow grave, where they were doused with sulfuric acid so they would not be recognizable. A truck was driven back and forth over the top of the grave to obliterate all traces of digging.

Resting place for a czar
Eighty years after their deaths, on July 16, 1998, a funeral with full pomp and ceremony is held for the exhumed bodies of the czar and his wife.

The final burial

In 1991, after the fall of the Communist regime in Russia, the burial place of the Romanovs was excavated—its site had apparently always been known, despite the efforts of the killers to keep it a secret. Examination of DNA from the corpses established without question that they were the Romanov family. However, only nine bodies were found. The consensus of expert opinion is that Alexis's and Maria's bodies were not in the excavated grave.

In 1998, Nicholas and Alexandra were reburied in the cathedral of St. Peter and Paul in St. Petersburg, the traditional burial place of the czars. In August 2000, all seven members of the Romanov family who had died in Ekaterinburg were declared Orthodox martyrs and saints by a council of the Russian Orthodox church.

Death in custody

On August 21, 1977, for the fourth time in two years, the Eastern Cape security police detained Stephen Biko. As the most prominent leader of young blacks opposed to the segregationist apartheid regime of white-ruled South Africa, Biko had become used to police harassment. Because the South African police routinely used torture, Biko may have been worried, but he would have had no reason to think he was about to be killed.

Black power

The developing political situation in South Africa had caused the authorities to view Biko as a threat to white rule. The South African regime had suppressed the oldest established antiapartheid movement, the African National Congress (ANC)—most of whose leaders were in exile or in prison—but a new wave of unrest among black students had erupted in 1976. These young black South Africans were inspired not by the integrationist views of imprisoned ANC leader Nelson Mandela, but by Biko's Black Consciousness movement—an assertion of pride in black identity akin to the Black Power movement in the United States.

A brutal interrogation

After his arrest, Biko was held in a police cell in Port Elizabeth. He was brought to the Sanlam Building, the police headquarters, for interrogation on September 6 and taken to a soundproof chamber used for torture sessions.

A five-man police interrogation squad stripped Biko and beat him savagely. At one point, three men—Harold Snyman, Daniel Siebert, and Gideon Nieuwoudt—seized hold of Biko and rammed him headfirst into a wall. He must have sustained brain damage, because from then on he was never lucid. Although he was

KEY DATES

1946 Born on December 18 in King William's Town, Eastern Cape, South Africa

1948 White South African government introduces apartheid laws creating racial segregation

1969 Becomes founder member and first president of the all-black South African Students Organization

1972 Helps establish the Black People's Convention, uniting a large number of black South African organizations around Durban

1973 His movements and freedom are restricted

1975 First detention by South African police

1976 Riots, believed to be inspired by Biko, occur in Soweto township, outside Johannesburg

1977 Dies on September 12 in police custody

1997 Truth and Reconciliation Commission holds hearings on Biko's death

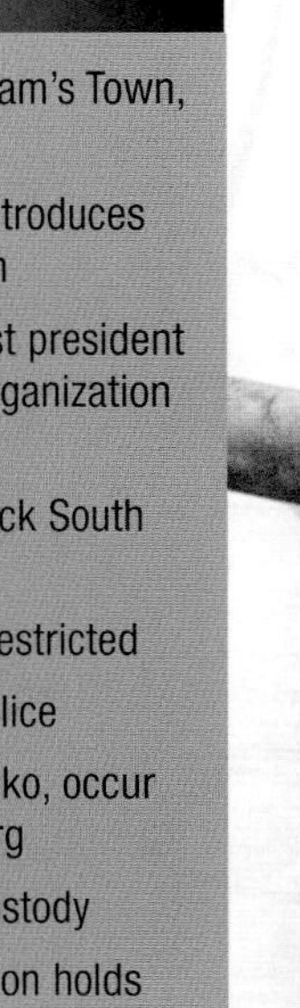

uncoordinated and unable to respond to their interrogation, the police officers manacled Biko naked to a metal grille.

Five days later, the police doctor suggested that Biko be taken to a hospital. Instead, on September 11, he was thrown into the back of a Land Rover and driven for 12 hours to a prison in the South African capital of Pretoria. He died there on September 12, still naked, lying on the floor of a prison cell.

The official story

The South African minister of justice, James Kruger, initially announced that Biko had died while on a hunger strike, although his body was covered with bruises. Later, a white magistrate conducting an inquest found that Biko had died of brain damage, allegedly after hitting his head against a wall in a scuffle while attacking his interrogators.

In 1997, in front of the Truth and Reconciliation Commission—which examined the crimes of the apartheid era—some of the police officers involved stuck to the story of a scuffle, while others asserted that Biko had been rammed into a wall. However, it has never been determined if the South African government instructed the police to kill Biko.

VICTIM

Ruth First

Antiapartheid activists were assassinated in the 1970s and 1980s in a campaign sanctioned by the South African government to eradicate opposition to white rule. Ruth First, a leading South African Communist and ANC supporter, was one prominent victim. In order to escape detention by the South African police, she lived in exile with her husband, Joe Slovo, the leader of the South African Communist Party. By the early 1980s, as a writer and academic, First was working at Eduardo Mondlane University in Mozambique. On August 17, 1982, when she opened a letter in her office, it exploded, killing her.

Testimony to the Truth and Reconciliation Commission (TRC) revealed that the letter bombing had been planned by secret agent Craig Williamson and a bomb maker, Roger Raven, on instructions from the South African Ministry of Police.

Funeral procession *Biko's body is transported in a coffin on an oxcart to its final resting place.*

A killer strikes

In December 1980, singer John Lennon's life was on an upward swing. The 40-year-old former Beatle had started making music again after a five-year break, recording with his wife Yoko Ono. The couple were living with their five-year-old son Sean in the celebrity-packed Dakota apartment building on New York's 72nd Street.

Meeting his killer

On December 8, as Lennon and Ono left the Dakota for a recording session, they were approached by a pudgy man holding a copy of Lennon's latest album, *Double Fantasy.* The young man's name was Mark David Chapman. In his coat pockets he had a copy of the novel *The Catcher in the Rye*—whose hero, Holden Caulfield, like Chapman, saw all those around him as phonies—and a five-shot .38-caliber revolver. Chapman had flown to New York from Hawaii to kill Lennon.

Lennon was at ease with the fans who hung around the door of the Dakota day and night. He signed the album cover, handed it

KEY DATES

1940 Born on October 9 in Liverpool, England

1955 Forms a rock band, The Quarrymen

1959 Forms the Beatles with Paul McCartney

1963 Beatlemania hits Britain; his son Julian is born

1964 The Beatles take the United States by storm

1966 Meets conceptual artist Yoko Ono

1968 Divorces his wife Cynthia

1969 Marries Yoko; the Beatles break up

1971 Moves to the United States

1975 His son Sean Ono Lennon is born

1980 Killed in New York on December 8

The happy couple *John and Yoko head to a recording studio in New York on August 22, 1980, a few months before his untimely death.*

back with a polite word, got into the white limousine waiting at the curb, and drove off. Chapman was stunned by this brief friendly contact with his intended victim. Not for the first time, he wavered in his mission.

Chapman had first flown to New York with the revolver on October 30, but after assessing the Dakota and obtaining bullets, he had a change of heart and flew home again. He arrived in New York for the second time on December 6, staying at the YMCA, then at the Sheraton Center—where on the night of December 7, in imitation of the hero of *The Catcher in the Rye,* he engaged the services of a prostitute to talk to him.

The stalker takes aim

By December 8, Chapman was a familiar figure to the doormen at the Dakota. They had seen him waiting there for hours on the previous two days, part of the throng of celebrity watchers on the sidewalk. The weather was exceptionally warm for December in New York. No one thought it odd that Chapman stayed outside the Dakota throughout the afternoon and evening, waiting for Lennon and Ono to return.

Just before 11:00 P.M. his patience was rewarded. The couple had spent the day recording Ono's song *Walking on Thin Ice* for their new album. Their limousine could have driven into the Dakota's private drive, safely behind security gates. Instead, it stopped in the street, and they walked across the sidewalk toward the front door of the apartment building, Ono in front, Lennon following her, carrying cassettes from the recording session.

Chapman was standing in the shadows near the stone arch of the doorway. He later told police that as Lennon walked past him, he heard a voice in his head. "It said, 'Do it, do it, do it,' over and over again."

Chapman called out "Mr. Lennon!" As Lennon turned, he fired all five rounds from his gun. Four of them hit their target. Lennon stumbled up the steps into the Dakota and fell face downward onto the ground, blood streaming from his mouth and chest.

A doorman disarmed Chapman, who made no effort to escape. He stood on the sidewalk reading *The Catcher in the Rye*, waiting for police to arrive and take him away. Lennon was taken to Roosevelt Hospital in a police car, but he was already dead.

As news spread of Lennon's death, hundreds of fans gathered outside the Dakota and chanted his anthem "Give Peace a Chance" into the early hours of the morning. It was the start of an outpouring of public grief that showed how much Lennon had been loved worldwide.

Chapman might very possibly have succeeded in a plea of insanity, but instead insisted on pleading guilty. Sentenced to life imprisonment, Chapman is still locked up—in solitary confinement for his own safety—more than 20 years after the killing.

MARK DAVID CHAPMAN

The killer of John Lennon was born near Fort Worth, Texas, in May 1955. His family later moved to Decatur, Georgia. As a youngster, Chapman rebelled against his parents, but, at the age of 16, he found God and became an exemplary member of the local YMCA.

In 1977, during a time of severe depression, he bought a one-way airline ticket to Honolulu, intending to have a good time, then kill himself. The suicide attempt failed, and two years later he married Gloria Abe. Marriage did not stabilize his mental state. He engaged in private conversations with imaginary friends and began praying to the Devil as well as to God.

His disturbed feelings focused on John Lennon after he saw a photo of the singer in the book *One Day at a Time,* by Anthony Fawcett. His wife later told an interviewer that the book made her husband feel Lennon was the ultimate phony. "He was angry that Lennon would preach love and peace but yet have millions," she said.

Final tribute *A large crowd gathers outside the Dakota, a week after John Lennon was shot.*

FAILED ASSASSINATIONS

QUEEN VICTORIA · 1882
VLADIMIR ILYICH LENIN · 1918
FRANKLIN D. ROOSEVELT · 1933
ADOLF HITLER · 1944
HARRY S TRUMAN · 1950
CHARLES DE GAULLE · 1944–66
FIDEL CASTRO · 1959–65
GEORGE WALLACE · 1972
RONALD REAGAN · 1981
POPE JOHN PAUL II · 1981
MARGARET THATCHER · 1984

Failed assassinations

Assassination attempts that have failed open up some of the great "what if's...?" of history. What if President-elect Franklin D. Roosevelt had been killed in February 1933 before he reached the White House? Would the future history of the United States have been fundamentally changed, with no New Deal, perhaps no American involvement in the war against Hitler?

If Lenin had been killed in 1918, would the attempt to establish a Communist state in Russia have failed—hence no Stalin, no Cold War? And what if Hitler had been killed, not in the famous bomb plot of 1944, but in the less well-known attack in 1939, when World War II had hardly begun?

There is no denying the fascination of the idea of the course of history being determined by the trajectory of a bullet traveling just a few millimeters to the side of a vital organ, or a bomb going off a few minutes early or late.

Dangerous weapon *This .22 caliber revolver was used by John Hinckley Jr. when he shot President Ronald Reagan in 1981. Fortunately, the president survived.*

Luck and medical intervention

Some survivors of assassination attempts were just plain lucky. This was certainly true of Hitler, who interpreted survival as a sign of his destiny, and of Pope John Paul II, who thanked the Virgin Mary for interceding in his behalf when he was shot in 1981. British Prime Minister Margaret Thatcher could thank the timing of a trip to the bathroom for surviving an IRA bomb in 1983.

People targeted by assassins in recent years have also been beneficiaries of improvements in surgery and medical care. You only have to compare the stories of Presidents James Garfield (see pp. 134–35) and William McKinley (see pp. 64–65)—virtually killed by their doctors as much as by their assassins—with the case of President Ronald Reagan in 1981 to understand why assassination attempts that have failed are concentrated in the modern period. Governor George Wallace and artist Andy Warhol are other examples of men who depended on the skill of doctors for survival.

Seekers of fame and fantasy

Not all failed assassinations are a sign of the victim's luck or the high standard of medical care. Often assassins may be more committed to self-dramatization and fantasies of heroism than to practical effectiveness. French leader General Charles de Gaulle survived several spectacular assassination attempts, yet his enemies could surely have found a simpler and more effective way to kill him than a bomb attack on a car traveling at high speed or an ambush in the street. Somehow, a shot from a sniper's rifle might just not have satisfied their desire for flamboyant show.

The would-be assassins of President Harry S Truman in 1950 chose to shoot their way into the presidential residence, an action unlikely to end with the death of the president. It was a gesture that satisfied their self-image and was bound to bring maximum publicity for their cause.

In some cases, the would-be assassins seem to lack the implacable will or sheer insanity—required to execute a cold-blooded killing. Roderick Maclean, the man who fired at Queen Victoria in 1882, shot only once, leaving five bullets unused in his revolver. Squeaky Fromme's assault on President Gerald Ford in 1975 was so bungled that many commentators believe that she did not actually intend to shoot him.

It is tempting to put in this same category the plots against Cuban leader Fidel Castro that were backed by the CIA in the 1960s. These were generally so overingenious and bizarre, it is difficult to tell whether he was the victim of any genuine assassination attempt at all.

VICTIM

Andy Warhol

On June 3, 1968, 39-year-old Pop artist, filmmaker, and cultural entrepreneur Andy Warhol drifted into the Factory, his workplace at 33 Union Square West, New York City, at about 4:15 P.M. Valerie Solanas, a 32-year-old woman who knew Warhol, was waiting for him on the sidewalk. She was carrying two handguns in a paper bag.

Solanas was an unbalanced individual who had used drugs and thought of herself as a creative genius. She had attracted some attention as the author of an antimale tract, The SCUM Manifesto. SCUM stood for Society for Cutting Up Men, a nonexistent organization of which Solanas claimed to be the leader.

Solanas had played herself in one of Warhol's films and had given him a script, which she hoped he would turn into a movie. Warhol not only did not make the movie, but he also lost the only copy of the script. When she decided to put her violent fantasies into action, he was an obvious target.

The would-be assassin went up with Warhol in the elevator to his office-cum-studio. After a few minutes, while Warhol was talking on the phone, she took out a .32 automatic and opened fire, missing her target. Closing in on the terrified artist as he cowered under a desk, she shot him in the chest at point-blank range. She also wounded art critic and curator Mario Amaya, a visitor to the Factory. The bullet that struck Warhol passed through both lungs and other internal organs. He survived after prolonged surgery.

Valerie Solanas gave herself up to police. She was adopted by some feminists as a hero. She spent the rest of her life in and out of mental institutions and died in 1988.

A poet's shot

On March 2, 1882, 62-year-old Victoria, queen of the United Kingdom and empress of India, took a train from London to Windsor, accompanied by the youngest of her nine children, 24-year-old Princess Beatrice, and her own beloved Scottish servant John Brown.

During the 45 years of her reign, Victoria had been attacked in public at least half-a-dozen times, although only one of those assaults, the first in 1840 (see box, opposite), could seriously be called an attempted assassination. Other incidents—such as being shot at with pistols loaded with powder but no ball or, in 1850, being struck in the face with the knob of a walking stick—had been frightening but hardly life-threatening.

Nonetheless, these events might have led the queen to exercise caution. Yet she rejected what she called "the security which nervous monarchs throughout Europe insisted upon," and continued to travel without guards separating her from the people.

"It is **worth** being **shot** at—to see **how much one is loved.**"

An unruffled queen

Outside Windsor's train station, Victoria climbed into a carriage that was to take her to Windsor Castle. A group of schoolboys from nearby Eton College, spotting their monarch, gave her a patriotic cheer. As the horse-drawn carriage moved away, Princess Beatrice saw a young man a few yards away raise a revolver and fire straight at them. The queen was not only unhurt but completely unaware that anyone had fired a shot. She had been looking the other way at the time and had thought that the loud bang had come from a steam engine in the train station.

The princess said nothing about the incident because she did not want to alarm her mother. It was only when Queen Victoria saw a man being jostled and shoved by angry Eton boys that she asked what had happened and was told by her servant John Brown, "That man fired at Your Majesty's carriage."

Sent to an insane asylum

The would-be assassin Roderick Maclean, a Scot, wrote verse and aspired to be a poet. He had sent Queen Victoria a poem dedicated to her, but it had been returned with a note saying the queen "never accepts manuscript poetry."

KEY DATES

1819 Born May 24 in Kensington Palace, London

1837 Accedes to the British throne on the death of her uncle, King William IV

1840 Marries Prince Albert; survives first attempted assassination; gives birth to the first of nine children

1861 Prince Albert dies; the queen goes into seclusion, supported by her servant John Brown

1877 Proclaimed empress of India

1882 Survives assassination attempt by Roderick Maclean

1887 Celebrates her Golden Jubilee; Irish Republicans are arrested for plotting to blow her up

1897 Celebrates her Diamond Jubilee

1901 Dies January 22 on Isle of Wight

THE FIRST ASSASSINATION ATTEMPT

On June 10, 1840, Queen Victoria was only 21 years old and four months pregnant when the first assassination attempt was made on her life. The queen had just left Buckingham Palace and was driving up Constitution Hill with Prince Albert seated alongside her in a small open carriage when a shot was fired at the carriage. The prince wrote that he had seen "a little mean-looking man...barely six paces from us." As the prince looked at the man, who hadn't moved from his position, he noticed that he held a pistol in each hand. The man fired again into the carriage, yet the royal couple were unhurt.

The "mean-looking man," who was apprehended by passersby, was Edward Oxford, an 18-year-old employed as a barman in a pub. There were suggestions that he might be part of a conspiracy headed by the queen's uncle, Ernest Augustus, the king of Hanover, who might have claim to the throne if the queen died. The pistols bore the monogram "E.R."—possibly for "Ernestus Rex," "King Ernest" in Latin—and letters from Hanover were allegedly found in his room. However, it was accepted that Oxford had acted alone. Oxford was found guilty of high treason—a hanging offense—but then declared insane and confined in an asylum. He was released in 1867.

Maclean had spent much of his life in a lunatic asylum. At his trial, eight medical experts testified that, as the defense lawyer put it, "insanity had marked him for its own." He was found not guilty but was sent back to a mental hospital, where he eventually died.

The royal reaction

Queen Victoria was not pleased with the "not guilty" verdict, but she was otherwise very satisfied with the aftermath of the assassination attempt. It brought a flood of protestations of loyalty and affection from her people. She wrote to one of her daughters, "It is worth being shot at—to see how much one is loved."

The Scottish poet William McGonagall was inspired to write a poem celebrating the queen's survival. He wrote "Maclean must be a madman, Which is obvious to be seen, Or else he wouldn't have tried to shoot, Our most beloved Queen."

Apprehending the criminal *Indignant Eton school boys and other bystanders try to intervene as a shot is fired at Queen Victoria.*

Attempted murder

The head of the Russian Bolshevik government, Vladimir Ilyich Lenin, was driven to the Mikhelson factory in the suburbs of Moscow on the afternoon of August 30, 1918. He was planning to deliver a speech to the workers.

Warring factions

Lenin's Bolsheviks, who had seized power in November 1917, were struggling to found the world's first Communist state. The regime had many enemies, including other revolutionary parties excluded from power.

Russian anarchists and members of the Socialist Revolutionary (SR) Party had found their dream of a workers' revolution turning into a nightmare. The Bolshevik Secret Police, the Cheka, cracked down on anyone who stepped out of line. These revolutionaries had plotted assassinations against the old czarist regime; now they were ready to fight the Bolsheviks.

The assassins strike

On August 30, the head of the Cheka in Petrograd (St. Petersburg), Moisei Uritsky, was killed by an SR assassin, Leonid Kanegiser. Lenin hesitated over his factory visit, but he finally decided to go ahead with his speech.

As Lenin came out of the building, walking through a crowd toward his car, some women called out to him, wanting

The Bolshevik leader *Lenin waves his hat to a large crowd in the streets of Moscow in 1919.*

to ask questions. Lenin turned to answer. Another woman pushed through the crowd, pulled a revolver out of her bag, and fired three times. Hit by two of the shots, the Bolshevik leader fell to the ground, bleeding.

Lenin was rushed to the Kremlin. One bullet was lodged in his neck, the other in his lung. The doctors who treated him—chosen for their Bolshevik political views, not their skill—decided that extracting the bullets was too risky.

A reign of red terror

Meanwhile, Lenin's bodyguards had seized Fanya Efimovna Kaplan at the Mikhelson factory gates. Kaplan made a full confession to her Cheka interrogators—presumably under torture—claiming that she had tried to kill Lenin because he was "a traitor to the revolution." On the night of September 3, she was shot in the back of the head by the commandant of the Kremlin guard, Pavel Malkov. He had orders to ensure that her remains were destroyed without a trace.

Kaplan was one of thousands who lost their lives after the assassination attempt. The Cheka unleashed a "Red Terror" upon the SRs and other enemies, carrying out arrests and executions without trial on a huge scale.

Lenin pulled through, but his health was never fully restored. Even so, he established a Communist system that lasted nearly 70 years.

FANYA KAPLAN

Fanya Efimovna Kaplan was born into a Jewish family in the Ukraine in 1887. Jews were oppressed under czarist rule, so many joined revolutionary organizations. In 1906, Kaplan joined a group plotting to blow up the governor general of Kiev. The bomb went off early, killing a maid. The police arrested Kaplan, and she was sentenced to hard labor in the Siberian salt mines. She was not released until the revolution in 1917.

After the attempt on Lenin's life, Kaplan claimed that she had acted alone. However, she may have been recruited by the SR Combat Organization (see p. 59), the group behind many assassinations before the revolution. Some investigators have argued that Kaplan may not have fired the shots that hit Lenin. He could have been shot by a fellow SR conspirator, a person whom her confession was protecting. It is rumored that the bullet extracted from Lenin's neck in 1922 did not match the gun found on Kaplan. However, given the lack of evidence to the contrary, most historians accept Kaplan's confession.

Lenin is shot *Kaplan runs away after shooting Lenin in this 1918 painting by M. Sokolov.*

KEY DATES

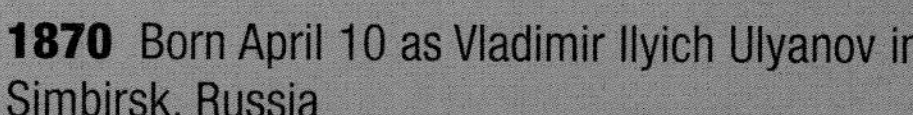

1870 Born April 10 as Vladimir Ilyich Ulyanov in Simbirsk, Russia

1887 Expelled from Kazan University

1895 Arrested for socialist agitation; exiled to Siberia

1898 Marries fellow socialist Nadezhda Krupskaya

1903 Leads the more radical Bolshevik ("majority") faction of the Russian Social Democratic Labor Party

1907 Leaves Russia for exile in Western Europe

1917 Returns to Russia after the overthrow of the czar and leads the Bolsheviks to seize power

1918 Survives assassination attempt August 30

1924 Dies on January 21; his embalmed body is displayed in a mausoleum in Red Square, Moscow

The bullets miss

KEY DATES

1882 Born January 30 in Hyde Park, New York

1910 Elected to the New York State Senate

1913 Appointed assistant secretary of the navy

1920 Is the Democratic vice presidential candidate

1921 Becomes partially paralyzed by polio

1928 Elected governor of New York

1932 Wins presidential election

1933 Escapes assassination attempt on February 15; in his first 100 days as president, introduces New Deal to counter the effects of the Depression

1936 Reelected by a landslide majority

1940 Elected for a third presidential term

1941 United States enters World War II

1944 Elected for a fourth term in a wartime election

1945 Dies three weeks before Germany is defeated

In February 1933, Franklin Delano Roosevelt was enjoying a yachting vacation in Florida. His presidential inauguration was less than three weeks away, and he was relaxing before taking on his new leadership role. However, he planned to make a speech in Miami's Bayside Park on the evening of February 15.

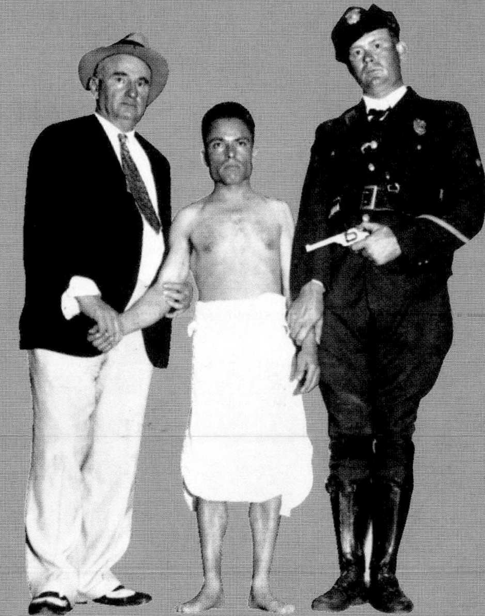

Making an arrest *Clad only in a towel, Zangara is held by police. The sheriff (right) holds the pistol used in the shooting.*

A tale of two immigrants

Among the people gathered in the park were two strangers who had never met: Anton Cermak, the Czech-born mayor of Chicago, and Giuseppe Zangara, an Italian-born bricklayer. In December 1932, Chicago Mafia chief Frank Nitti had been wounded by police. Cermak was blamed for the attack on Nitti, so he left Chicago to escape Nitti's gunmen.

Zangara had emigrated from Italy to New Jersey in 1923. He moved to Florida hoping that its climate might cure his stomach pain. This chronic pain supposedly contributed to a resentment against society that made Zangara fantasize about killing heads of state. While in Italy, he had plotted to kill King Victor Emmanuel III. In the United States, he had dreamed of killing President Herbert Hoover. When he read in a newspaper that Roosevelt was going to be in Miami, he bought a .38 pistol.

A shot from the crowd

Roosevelt, who was partially paralyzed by polio, preferred to disguise the fact that he could not stand unaided. He had developed techniques for unobtrusively supporting himself while making speeches. That February evening he was driven in an open car into the park. Near the bandstand he raised himself up in the car to sit on top of the seat back. In this position, he was visible to those in the bandstand, but Zangara, eight yards (7 m) back in the crowd, had to climb onto a chair to see Roosevelt.

After Roosevelt had finished his speech, Cermak approached him. Zangara opened fire at the president over the crowd. Standing on a wobbly chair, and with no experience using a gun, Zangara shot five people, including Cermak, but failed to hit Roosevelt.

Cermak was driven to the hospital with an abdominal wound. He believed that he had been the target and that Zangara had been sent by the Mafia. Cermak died on March 3, one day before Roosevelt's inauguration.

Meanwhile, Zangara was disarmed and arrested at the scene. Within five days of the crime, Zangara was sentenced to 80 years in prison for the five shootings. Once Cermak died, Zangara was tried for murder and executed in the electric chair on March 20.

Working the crowd *Roosevelt shakes hands with supporters in Warm Springs, Georgia, in December 1933.*

VICTIM

Theodore Roosevelt

Franklin D. Roosevelt's distant relative President Theodore Roosevelt also survived an assassination attempt. On October 14, 1912, while campaigning in Milwaukee, Wisconsin, for a third presidential term, Teddy Roosevelt was about to make a speech when he was shot in the chest by a New York bartender, John Schrank. The bullet first struck Roosevelt's metal spectacle case and the manuscript of his speech. Nonetheless, it penetrated his chest, lodging behind one of his ribs. Roosevelt still made his speech, opening with, "I have just been shot; but it takes more than that to kill a bull moose."

Schrank was found insane and confined to an institution for life—he had apparently been driven to the act by dreams of assassinated William McKinley (see pp. 64–65). Roosevelt died in his sleep from a blood clot in 1919, the bullet still in his chest.

Surviving a bomb

Colonel Claus Schenk von Stauffenberg arrived at Rastenburg, East Prussia, on July 20, 1944. Along with Lieutenant Werner von Haeften, he was driven to Adolf Hitler's "Wolf's Lair," the headquarters from which the Führer was directing Germany's resistance to the advancing Soviet Red Army. As chief of staff of the German reserve army, Stauffenberg was able to pass through the gates of the headquarters without being searched. He was carrying plastic explosives in his briefcase.

Unhappy officers

Discontent with Hitler's rule had been simmering among members of the German officer corps since 1938, when General Ludwig Beck, then chief of the German general staff, had considered overthrowing Hitler to avoid a war with Britain and France. However, it was after the German surrender at Stalingrad in early 1943 that plotting began in earnest. The conspirators included army officers, civil servants, diplomats, intelligence officers, and conservative politicians. Most were traditional German patriots. They opposed Hitler because his policy of massacre and extermination brought dishonor upon the army and the nation. They also wanted to save Germany from defeat in the war.

The conspirators' plan was to replace Nazi rule with a military government led by General Beck, which would then negotiate peace with the Western allies and save Germany from being overrun by the Soviet Union. For this they needed the support of many senior army officers, but they would only back the plot once Hitler was dead and success ensured. As a result, any coup attempt had to start with the Führer's assassination.

Against the odds

At first the Führer was lucky—a series of attempts on his life had failed. A bomb put on his aircraft failed to explode; a would-be assassin with a revolver was not allowed into a meeting with Hitler at the last moment; a suicide bomber had to rapidly dismantle the bomb strapped to his body when Hitler left a public exhibition early.

The conspirators hesitated at key moments. These were men of duty who had taken an oath of loyalty to Hitler and whose lives were devoted to upholding order and authority. To assassinate their head of state and commander in chief, especially in a time of war, required a psychological leap that many could not take when the time came.

"With a flash of flame and a deafening shock wave of sound, the bomb went off."

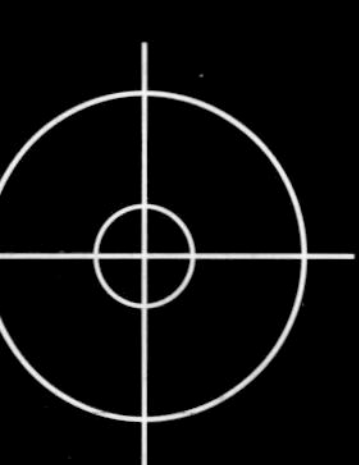

A new conspirator

Stauffenberg was a late addition to the conspiracy, but he brought a fresh resolve to the bid to assassinate Hitler. He was a living example of the struggle in which Germany was engaged. By the age of 37, he had lost an eye, his right hand, and two fingers of his left hand in the fighting in North Africa. He was appointed chief of staff to General Friedrich Fromm, head of the reserve army, in July 1944, so Stauffenberg had access to briefings between Hitler and his generals.

The briefing with Hitler on July 20 was to take place at 12:30 P.M. First Stauffenberg

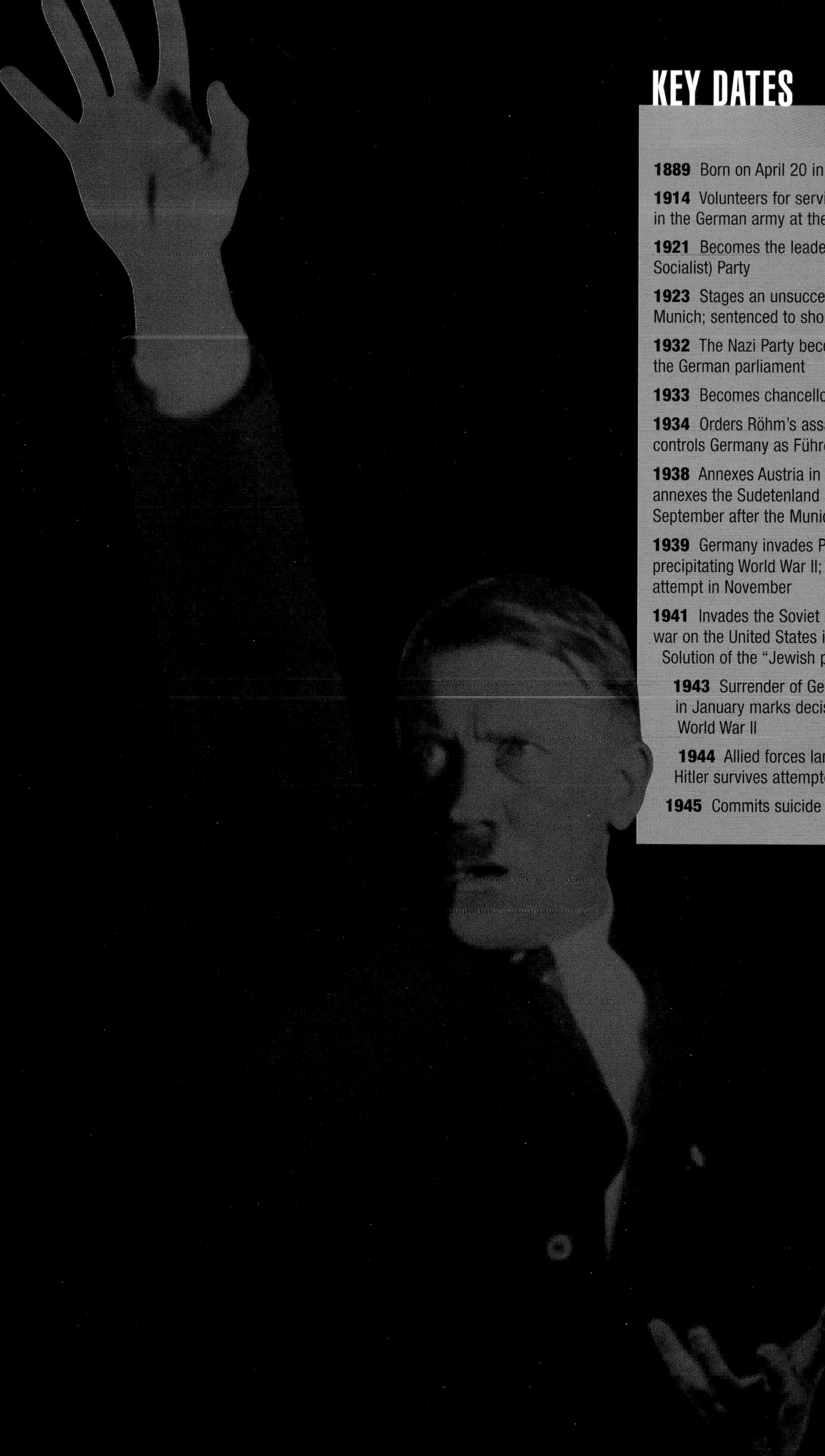

KEY DATES

1889 Born on April 20 in Braunau, Austria

1914 Volunteers for service with Bavarian forces in the German army at the start of World War I

1921 Becomes the leader of the Nazi (National Socialist) Party

1923 Stages an unsuccessful coup (or *Putsch*) in Munich; sentenced to short prison term

1932 The Nazi Party becomes the largest party in the German parliament

1933 Becomes chancellor of Germany

1934 Orders Röhm's assassination (see pp. 70–71); controls Germany as Führer of the Third Reich

1938 Annexes Austria in the *Anschluss* in March; annexes the Sudetenland area of Czechoslovakia in September after the Munich crisis

1939 Germany invades Poland on September 1, precipitating World War II; survives an assassination attempt in November

1941 Invades the Soviet Union in June; declares war on the United States in December; initiates Final Solution of the "Jewish problem"—the Holocaust

1943 Surrender of German forces at Stalingrad in January marks decisive turning point of World War II

1944 Allied forces land in Normandy in June; Hitler survives attempted assassination in July

1945 Commits suicide on April 30 in Berlin

Der Führer *After his release from prison, Hitler poses to a recording of one of his speeches in 1925.*

attended a preparatory meeting chaired by Field Marshall Wilhelm Keitel, Hitler's military right-hand man. Afterward, he said he wanted to freshen up. Accompanied by Haeften, they locked themselves in the men's room, opened the briefcase, and started setting the timers on the two devices inside. However, they were interrupted by a knock on the door—there was an urgent phone call for Stauffenberg. He left with only one of the devices primed in his briefcase. Haeften hid the other, unprimed, in his own bag.

The aftermath *Hitler and Mussolini survey the damage after the attempt on the Führer's life in July 1944.*

Planting the bomb

The Hitler briefing meeting was already under way when Stauffenberg arrived. It was being held in a wooden barrack hut. Stauffenberg took his place at the heavy oak table that filled most of the room. He sat to the right of Hitler, who was at the center of one side of the table. Stauffenberg placed his briefcase under the table, leaning it against a table leg.

Almost as soon as he entered the room, Stauffenberg excused himself and left. No one paid attention—officers were always coming and going because of the need to deal with urgent business of various kinds. The meeting continued without him. At 12:45 P.M., Hitler was leaning on the table, studying a map. With a flash of flame and a deafening shock wave of sound, the bomb went off.

Stauffenberg and Haeften were arranging for a car to take them back to the airfield when they heard the explosion. Sure that

Hitler was dead, they flew to Berlin, where fellow conspirators were waiting for the signal to put a coup into motion. It was code-named Operation Valkyrie.

Surviving the blast

The bomb blew out doors and windows and set fire to part of the hut. A stenographer had his legs blown off; one general had a large chunk of wood driven through his body; two other generals lost limbs. Those four later died; other men had burns and concussions.

Hitler, however, was not dead. His eardrums were shattered, his face was cut by glass, splinters of wood were embedded in his hands and legs, and his clothing was shredded and partly on fire, but he walked unaided from the wreckage of the hut. That afternoon he went ahead with a planned meeting with Italian Fascist leader Benito Mussolini.

The bomb had failed in its planned effect partly because only half the intended amount of explosive had been used; partly because the wooden hut allowed the blast to spread outward; and partly because the oak table took much of the force of the blast.

Aftermath of the failed bombing

Stauffenberg arrived at the War Office in Berlin at 4:30 P.M. and told the conspirators Hitler was dead. Beck declared himself head of state, and regional military commanders were informed of the Führer's death. However, the conspirators did not arrest key Nazi leaders, and communications centers were not seized. Soon, the news spread that Hitler was unhurt. At 6:30 P.M., Nazi propaganda chief Joseph Goebbels made a radio broadcast informing the Germans of Hitler's survival.

Stauffenberg's superior General Fromm had been aware of the plot but hesitated to support it. Once he knew the assassination plot had failed, he presented himself as the man who crushed the coup. Taking charge in the War Office, Fromm allowed Beck to commit suicide. He had Stauffenberg, Haeften, and two other conspirators taken into a courtyard and shot.

The People's Court

Fromm's action angered Hitler. He became one of the thousands arrested in the repression that followed. The Führer wanted slow revenge. He ordered that the leading conspirators should be tried by a People's Court, then "hung up like meat carcasses." In the execution room at Plötzensee Prison in Berlin, many were hanged, dangling from meat hooks with piano wire around their necks, their agony prolonged by skillful executioners.

Even with the consequences of the failed assassination, many of the more idealistic conspirators still felt it was worthwhile as a way of redeeming the soul of Germany. Major General Henning von Tresckow, one of the driving forces behind the plot, said that what mattered was "showing the world and history that the German resistance movement at risk of life has dared the decisive stroke." In that sense, at least, some honor had been retrieved.

The would-be assassin *Claus Schenk von Stauffenberg was doomed once the assassination attempt failed.*

THE MUNICH BOMBING

There were many plots to assassinate Hitler, but apart from the attempt in July 1944, only one was acted upon. November 8 was the anniversary of Hitler's failed Munich *Putsch,* or coup, of 1923, which he always celebrated with a speech to the "old fighters" in the Munich beer cellar where the *Putsch* had been launched. In 1939, the Führer's speech was shorter than usual, ending at 9:07 P.M. Hitler left immediately afterward to catch a train to Berlin. At 9:20 P.M., a bomb concealed in a pillar behind the speaker's dais exploded, killing 8 people and injuring another 63.

The bombing was the work of a carpenter and electrician, Georg Elser, who had apparently decided that the elimination of the Nazi leadership could bring peace and better living conditions to Germany. He spent a year building his own bomb and hollowing out the pillar in the beer cellar. He was arrested on the night of the bombing by border guards as he tried to cross into Switzerland. He was carrying a postcard of the beer cellar, which linked him to the bombing.

Hitler refused to accept that Elser had acted alone and instructed the Gestapo to use every means possible to make him reveal his accomplices. However, Esler remained adamant that he had planned and executed the bombing alone. He was sent to Sachsenhausen concentration camp. In early 1945, with the Nazis facing defeat, he was moved to the camp at Dachau. He was executed on April 9.

Under fire

On the afternoon of November 1, 1950, two well-dressed Puerto Rican men, 36-year-old Oscar Collazo and 25-year-old Griselio Torresola, took a taxi from Hotel Harris, near Union Station in Washington D.C., to Blair House on Pennsylvania Avenue. Blair House had been adopted as a temporary residence by U.S. President Harry S Truman while the White House was undergoing structural repairs. The two men were carrying concealed handguns and ammunition with the intention of shooting their way into Blair House and assassinating the president.

"...the **shooting** was over. It had lasted less than three minutes."

Seeking Puerto Rican independence

Collazo and Torresola were members of the New York branch of the Puerto Rican Nationalist Party. Led by Pedro Albizu Campos, the Nationalists were dedicated to freeing their country from American rule, using violence if necessary. They believed that killing Truman would give a major boost to the cause of Puerto Rican independence.

Collazo, a family man, was angry that Puerto Ricans were being discriminated against in New York and that the United States was ruling his native island. Torresola came from a dedicated Nationalist family. Two of his siblings had been involved in a failed insurrection in the Puerto Rican capital of San Juan only three days before the attempt on the president. Torresola was skilled in using guns; Collazo was not.

A crude plan

The two men were not prepared for their act. Arriving in Washington the previous day, they had briefly visited Blair House, which was open to attack. The front of the building was near a busy sidewalk, with three guarded entrances: two at street level leading into the basement, and a main entrance at the top of a flight of steps. The would-be assassins decided to simply approach from opposite directions and try to shoot their way past the guards.

Collazo and Torresola were not certain if Truman would be in Blair House when they attacked. In fact, as they approached the building at about 2:20 P.M., the president was inside taking a nap. Seven guards were on duty that afternoon, with five of them in front of the building at the moment of the attack.

A shoot-out

Collazo walked up to Private Donald Birdzell, the guard on the steps to the main entrance,

KEY DATES

1884 Born May 8 in Lamar, Missouri

1919 Marries Elizabeth ("Bess") Wallace

1922 Elected a judge in Jackson County

1934 Elected to the U.S. Senate as a Democrat from Missouri

1945 Sworn in as vice president in January; becomes president on the death of Roosevelt in April; authorizes dropping of atom bombs on Japan in August

1947 Commits the United States to defending countries worldwide against Communism (the Truman Doctrine)

1948 Wins second term as president

1950 Survives assassination attempt

1972 Dies of natural causes on December 26

pointed a gun at him, and pulled the trigger. Nothing happened. Either the gun had jammed or the safety catch was on. Collazo banged his fist against the gun, and suddenly it fired, hitting Birdzell in the leg.

At the same time Torresola walked up to the white sentry box in front of the basement door and shot Private Leslie Coffelt three times at point-blank range. Private Joseph Downs, standing behind Coffelt's sentry box, was also shot three times before he had time to draw his weapon. Torresola was now free to enter Blair House through the basement door, but Coffelt, although mortally wounded, managed to raise his gun and shoot Torresola in the head, killing him.

Meanwhile Collazo was pinned down on the main steps, under fire from two guards at the east end of the building and the wounded Birdzell lying in the road. A shot fired by Secret Service Agent Floyd Boring hit Collazo in the chest, and the shooting was over. It had lasted less than three minutes.

Apprehending the leader *Nationalist politician Pedro Albizu Campos is arrested in San Juan, Puerto Rico.*

After the fracas

Private Coffelt died in the hospital; a plaque outside of Blair House marks his courage. The other wounded guards survived, as did Collazo. He was sentenced to death for his part in Coffelt's murder and the attempted assassination of the president. Truman commuted his sentence to life imprisonment. Collazo was released by President Jimmy Carter in 1979 and died of natural causes in Puerto Rico in 1994.

A fallen man *One of the would-be assassins, Oscar Collazo lies at the steps of Blair House after being shot by guards.*

VICTIM

Gerald Ford

President Gerald Ford was the target of two assassination attempts in the same month. On September 5, 1975, Lynette "Squeaky" Fromme, a follower of cult leader Charles Manson, approached Ford in California. Aiming an automatic at his stomach, she pulled the trigger, but the gun did not go off. There may have been no bullet in the chamber or Secret Service Agent Larry Buendorf may have blocked the hammer with his hand as he grabbed the gun.

Sara Jane Moore was a 44-year-old mother of four and was associated with leftist radicals. Ford arrived in San Francisco on September 21. The following day Moore bought a pistol and shot at the president outside the St. Francis Hotel. Jostled by a bystander, she missed. Both women were given life imprisonment.

Survivor

Late in 1944, General Charles de Gaulle, leader of the Free French movement during World War II, was visiting the port of Dakar, capital of French West Africa. French naval vessels in the colonial port were decked out with flags in celebration of the liberation of France from German rule.

A bungled assassination attempt

De Gaulle was unpopular with the French Navy. He had supported Britain, and in 1940 the British Royal Navy had sunk French warships, with great loss of life, to prevent them from falling into German hands. The bitterness French naval officers felt toward the British was transferred to de Gaulle.

As the general stood on the bridge of the cruiser *Georges Leygues,* a junior officer on an escort vessel raised a rifle and aimed it at his neck. At that moment, another officer, Jean le Guichet, walked by and the attempt was abandoned. No arrest was made. The story only emerged later, and the would-be assassin's name has never been revealed. De Gaulle had survived the first of 31 assassination plots.

KEY DATES

1890 Born on November 22 in Lille, France, son of a teacher

1925 Promoted to the Conseil Supérieur de la Guerre (Supreme War Council)

1940 When France is occupied by Germany, establishes the Free French movement

1944 Heads a provisional government

1946 Resigns the presidency when the Fourth Republic is established

1958 Founds the Fifth Republic and is elected its first president

1961 Survives assassination attempt by the OAS (Organisation Armée Secrète)

1962 Grants Algeria independence; survives second OAS assassination attempt

1963 Would-be assassin Bastien-Thiry executed on March 11

1966 Survives a final assassination attempt by right-wing students

1970 Dies of natural causes on November 9

Right-wing politics and the colonial empire

De Gaulle was a conservative authoritarian who believed in tradition—he was no friend to the political left. However, as leader of the Free French in World War II, he had opposed the right-wing Vichy government, which had collaborated with the Nazis. After the war, he maintained an ambivalent relationship with right-wing generals and politicians who had no time for democracy and a passionate devotion to France's colonial empire.

In 1954, France was forced out of Indochina, defeated by Ho Chi Minh's guerrillas in Vietnam. Two years later, a liberation movement began in Algeria that aimed to oust France from its massive North African possession. The French right regarded a further defeat as unthinkable.

Foreign visit *De Gaulle travels through the streets of Algiers during a visit on June 4, 1958.*

Algeria had a large European population committed to maintaining domination over the Muslim majority. The settlers and the officers commanding the French Army in Algeria formed a close bond in a bid to defeat the rebel FLN (Front de Libération Nationale) and to resist any defeatism on the part of the French government in Paris.

A sniper takes aim

In May 1958, General Raoul Salan, the French commander in chief in Algeria, staged what was in effect a military coup at a distance. He demanded the installation of a French government that was committed to keeping Algeria French; otherwise, his troops would be flown in to occupy Paris.

"...a **sniper** had a telescopic sight **trained** on him."

De Gaulle, by then in his late 60s, stepped out of retirement to take over as French head of government. On June 4, 1958, he visited Algiers. As he addressed a vast public meeting, standing alongside Salan, a sniper had a telescopic sight trained on him. De Gaulle's speech seemed to make plain that he intended to keep Algeria French; the sniper never pressed the trigger.

Celebration *Muslim girls carry banners in the streets of Algiers after de Gaulle announces Algeria's independence on July 3, 1962.*

By the early 1960s, de Gaulle's views had changed. He was in charge of the French Fifth Republic, and he wanted to unburden France of its colonial commitments. The French generals and Algerian settlers felt betrayed.

Salan turns to terrorism

At the end of 1960, Salan retired from the army and became leader of the OAS (Organisation Armée Secrète), a terrorist organization dedicated to attacks on Muslims and on the Gaullist government. The OAS hit squads, commanded by a Foreign Legion deserter, Lieutenant Roger Degueldre, used machine guns and plastic explosives to spread a reign of terror in Algeria and France. In 1961, it was de Gaulle's turn to be a target.

> **"...the napalm threw a jet of fire across the road ahead."**

Throughout the late summer, an OAS squad made elaborate plans to assassinate the president on one of his journeys from Paris to his home at Colombey-les-Deux-Eglises. They concealed plastic explosives and a canister of napalm in a pile of sand on a straight stretch of road near the village of Crancey. The OAS practiced timing the explosion so that a car traveling at 70 mph (113 kph) would be hit by the burning napalm.

A hit squad strikes

A spy in de Gaulle's entourage told the OAS that the president was going to Colombey on September 8. The OAS also knew which of the four cars in the presidential convoy he would be traveling in.

At 9:35 P.M. de Gaulle reached the booby-trapped stretch of road. At the wheel of the Citroen Déesse was the president's usual driver, François Marroux; de Gaulle and his wife, Yvonne, were in the back. They were traveling at exactly 70 mph (113 kph) when the bomb went off. The force of the blast made the car veer to the left; the napalm threw a jet of fire across the road ahead. Urged on by de Gaulle, Marroux put his foot down, and the car went straight through the flames. The explosion had been mistimed. Only one headlight was damaged.

In April 1962, Degueldre and Salan were arrested. Salan was sentenced to life imprisonment; Degueldre was shot by a firing squad. In July, the month of Degueldre's execution, de Gaulle granted Algeria independence under an FLN government. The OAS had decisively lost the war—but there was still the possibility of vengeance.

Yet another plot

De Gaulle's vulnerable point remained his trips from Paris to Colombey. His enemies were able to obtain advance details from contacts in the presidential palace. On the evening of August 22, 1962, Colonel Jean Bastien-Thiry led 15 men in a plot.

The colonel was an air force officer, as well as as a scientist working on missile development. Two weeks earlier de Gaulle had awarded him the Légion d'Honneur. Now the colonel and his men positioned themselves on Avenue Petit-Clamart in the suburbs of Paris. He stood by a bus stop, while his colleagues waited in three cars down the road. One of the cars was supposed to block the road when Bastien-Thiry signaled de Gaulle's approach. The cars were packed with weapons.

De Gaulle was once more sitting in the back of his Citroen Déesse with his wife. Marroux was again the driver. Ahead of the car were two motorcycle outriders; behind it was a car carrying armed detectives.

Botched again

At 8:10 P.M. Bastien-Thiry saw the motorcycles and signaled, but none of his colleagues saw the sign. Taken by surprise, the assassins had no time to block the road. Instead, they fired at the passing car with machine guns. A front tire burst and the Citroen swerved, almost hitting another car. Marroux proved his skill as a driver once again, controlling the car while accelerating.

One of the assassination squad's cars gave chase. Georges Watin, an experienced Algerian terrorist, fired at and shattered the rear window of the Citroen. Shots passed through the vehicle at head height, yet missed de Gaulle. After a few moments jostling for road space with the motorcyclists and the escort vehicle, the assassins swerved off down a side road. The presidential car had been hit by six bullets, but the only injury was a cut on de Gaulle's hand, caused as he brushed broken glass off his lap.

Arrests soon followed. Nine men, including Bastien-Thiry, were tried by a military court. Despite their claims that they had intended only to kidnap, not kill de Gaulle, three were given death sentences. Two of these later had their sentences commuted to life imprisonment by the president, but for Bastien-Thiry there was no reprieve. He was executed by firing squad on March 11, 1963.

Charles de Gaulle died of a heart attack on November 9, 1970, while at home watching a soap opera on television.

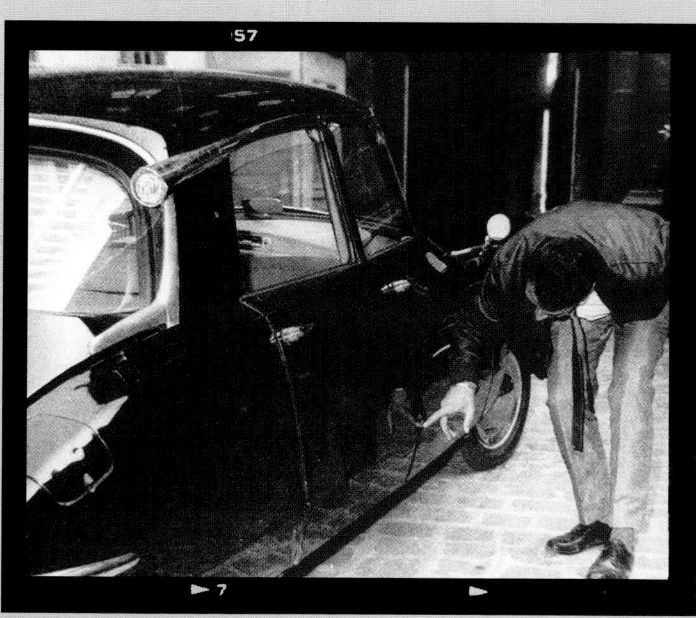

Luck escape *The Citroen in which de Gaulle was traveling on August 22, 1962, is riddled with bullets.*

VICTIM

Napoleón I

The attempts on President de Gaulle were reminiscent of an assassination attempt on a previous ruler of France, Napoleón I, or Napoleón Bonaparte. In December 1800, Napoleón was first consul of the French Republic. At around 8:00 P.M. on Christmas Eve, he left the Tuileries Palace in Paris. His carriage was preceded by a troop of mounted grenadiers.

As Napoleón's carriage turned into Rue Saint-Nicaise, a mare and cart partially blocked the way. Napoleón's coachman, César, would normally have slowed to pass this obstacle, but he was drunk that evening and sped through the narrow space. Moments later explosives hidden in a barrel on the cart exploded. Nine people were killed, including a girl the assassins had asked to hold the mare's bridle. Napoleón was unhurt.

The bomb was traced to Royalist conspirators trying to restore the French monarchy. Two of these men, François Carbon and Joseph Limoelan, were executed.

A CIA target

When Fidel Castro took power in Cuba at the beginning of 1959, the U.S. government gave the new regime a guarded welcome. However, within less than a year, Castro nationalized foreign businesses and sought close relations with the Soviet Union.

Discrediting the Cuban leader

In December 1959, a CIA internal memo asked that "thorough consideration be given to the elimination of Fidel Castro." This policy was endorsed by the Eisenhower administration, but whether "elimination" meant "assassination" was left vague.

The CIA's first plots against Castro were designed to discredit him. One plan was to give Castro a psychedelic drug just before he made a TV address to the Cuban people, either by spraying an aerosol into the studio or by smearing a chemical onto one of his cigars. Castro would then lose all credibility. Another idea was to put thallium powder, a strong depilatory, into his shoes to make his beard drop out, ruining his public image.

The CIA hires the Mafia

Such absurdities were abandoned in favor of an assassination plot. The killing was to be carried out by the Mafia, who hated Castro because their extensive business interests in Cuba had been almost wiped out under his regime. As a bonus, the assassination would be attributed to a Mafia hit, leaving the CIA and the U.S. government with clean hands.

The CIA offered $150,000 to Las Vegas–based Mafioso Johnny Roselli to

KEY DATES

1927 Born August 13 in Mayari, Cuba, son of a well-to-do sugarcane farmer
1950 Graduates from University of Havana with a doctorate in law
1953 Captured in revolt against General Fulgencio Batista and imprisoned
1954 Released in an amnesty; flees to Mexico
1956 Lands in Cuba by boat; begins a guerrilla campaign in the mountains
1959 Forces Batista to flee Cuba; takes power as prime minister
1961 Castro defeats invasion by CIA-backed Cuban exiles at the Bay of Pigs
1962 Cuban Missile Crisis ends as Soviet Union withdraws missiles from Cuba
1965 President Lyndon B. Johnson stops CIA assassination attempts against Castro
1976 Declares himself president of Cuba

organize the elimination. He involved Chicago Mafia boss Sam Giancana and Tampa Mafia chief Santos Trafficante. The CIA supplied botulinum toxin for their Mafia contacts to put in Castro's food or drink. They also provided a truckload of arms.

When the CIA–Mafia plot failed, the Mafia offered excuses. For example, Castro had stopped eating in the restaurant where a waiter planned to spike his food or drink. It is suspected that Trafficante may have passed details of the plots to Castro, hoping to gain more from him than from the CIA.

Waving the Cuban flag
On November 27, 2000, the revolutionary leader Fidel Castro leads a demonstration in Havana.

Secret agents plot

In 1963, CIA officer Desmond FitzGerald pursued new assassination plans. Once more, the CIA ideas were unrealistic. Their intention to plant a booby-trapped seashell on the sea bed where Castro went scuba diving and their attempt to put deadly bacilli in the breathing gear of his diving suit proved fruitless.

In September 1963, Cuban Army Major Rolando Cubela, a close associate of Castro, offered the CIA his services as an assassin. FitzGerald agreed to provide Cubela with rifles and explosives. The CIA also supplied a pen containing a hypodermic needle that could deliver poison.

Cubela may have been a double agent, trying to lure the CIA into an assassination plot that could then be revealed to the world. On the other hand, some believe Cubela did attempt to shoot Castro using U.S.-supplied sniper rifles but was foiled by Cuban security forces. Cubela was arrested and imprisoned by Castro in 1966.

Under Kennedy's successor, Lyndon B. Johnson, the covert offensive against Castro's regime was called off. Cuba's bearded leader has proved to be one of the great survivors.

LINKED KILLINGS

Many conspiracy theorists believe there is a link between the plots against Castro and the assassination of John F. Kennedy (see pp. 28–35). When Castro was told of Kennedy's death, he is reported to have said, "That is bad news." Yet, two months earlier, he allegedly threatened retaliation for attempts on his life: "United States leaders should think that if they assist in terrorist plans to eliminate Cuban leaders they themselves will not be safe." Add to this the fact that Kennedy's assassin, Lee Harvey Oswald, visited the Cuban Embassy in Mexico before the Kennedy assassination, and some find grounds for suspicion.

Alternatively, it has frequently been asserted that a plan to assassinate Kennedy originated among the CIA, Mafia, and Cuban exile groups. These groups were involved in plots to kill Castro and in other covert action to subvert the Cuban government. Again, nothing has been proven—but nothing has been disproven, either.

Paralyzed

In the spring of 1972, George Wallace, 52-year-old governor of Alabama, was campaigning for nomination as the Democratic candidate for the U.S. presidency. To say that Wallace was a controversial figure would be an understatement. In the 1960s, he had been outspoken about his opposition to racial integration, making him disliked by many, but admired by a small constituency.

KEY DATES

1919 Born on August 25, in Clio, Alabama

1947 Elected to the Alabama state legislature

1953 Becomes Alabama state judge

1963 Becomes governor of Alabama; resists racial integration imposed by federal government

1970 Elected governor of Alabama a second time

1972 Campaigns for nomination as Democratic candidate for the presidency; shot on May 15

1974 Reelected governor of Alabama

1982 Reelected governor of Alabama, winning black votes after abandoning segregationist views

1998 Dies on September 13 of respiratory failure

A man for the everyday American

In 1972, Wallace claimed to represent the average citizen on a raft of issues, from getting tough on crime to making the rich pay more tax. Yet, when campaigning in the Maryland primary on May 15, missiles—including a brick, tomatoes, and eggs—were thrown at him.

On the afternoon of that same day, the Wallace team set up his podium for a speech in a shopping center parking lot in Laurel, Maryland. Security was tight, with police and Secret Service agents scanning the crowd. Wallace delivered his speech from behind an armor-plated screen, but he did not wear his usual bullet-proof vest because it was too hot.

Working the crowd *On May 4, only days before being shot, Wallace greets his supporters.*

ARTHUR BREMER

Born in Milwaukee, Wisconsin, in 1950, Arthur Herman Bremer was the fourth of five children of a truck driver. Bremer grew up lonely, but he was not disruptive or rebellious. In late 1971, his first attempt at a dating relationship ended after his girlfriend was revolted by his crude behavior, which included showing her pornographic magazines. This rejection seems to have tipped him into a psychopathic state.

Beginning in January 1972, Bremer thought about suicide or mass murder, or both. He shaved his head and bought two guns, which he originally planned to use for a random killing spree in Milwaukee. Partly inspired by a book on Sirhan Sirhan, the assassin of Robert F. Kennedy (see pp. 106–9), he decided instead to assassinate a leading politician. At the end of his trial, Bremer said, "Looking back on my life I would have liked it if society had protected me from myself."

Leaving court *The alleged assassin Arthur Bremer is escorted from court after being held on charges of assaulting a federal officer.*

A lone stalker

Among those listening to the speech was 21-year-old Arthur Bremer. He had been stalking the governor all month, attending rallies in Maryland and Michigan. The previous March, Bremer had decided, as he wrote in a diary, "to kill by pistol either Richard Nixon [then U.S. president] or George Wallace." Over the following weeks, he also considered killing Wallace's rival, Democratic candidate George McGovern. Bremer finally decided that Wallace should "have the honor" of being his victim.

Wearing a Wallace button in his lapel, Bremer worked his way to the front of the crowd as Wallace concluded his speech. The reception had been more friendly than usual, and the governor decided to risk mingling with potential voters. He took off his jacket, rolled up his sleeves, and stepped down from the stage to shake a few hands.

Bremer pulled out a .38 revolver, thrust his arm forward to within 18 inches (45 cm) of Wallace's stomach, and fired several shots. Bystanders leaped on Bremer, who was badly beaten by the time police took him away.

Wallace lay on the ground, ashen and bleeding profusely from his right arm and through his shirt, with his wife, Cornelia, by his side. He had been hit by four, possibly five, bullets. Three other people were also wounded: a Secret Service agent, a journalist, and one of Wallace's personal bodyguards. All were hit by bullets that had probably passed through the governor's body.

Wallace was rushed to a hospital in Silver Spring, Maryland, where he underwent a five-hour operation. He had two bullets lodged in his body, one in his abdomen, and the other in his spine. Although his life was saved, the spinal injury left Wallace paralyzed from the waist down for the rest of his life.

Was it a conspiracy?

At his trial Bremer pleaded insanity, but the plea was rejected and he was found guilty and sentenced to 63 years in prison. However, conspiracy theories soon emerged claiming that Bremer had not been a lone assassin.

> **"Wallace lay on the ground, ashen and bleeding profusely...."**

They were based on confused ballistics evidence and hints of skulduggery by some of President Nixon's Watergate break-in team. Wallace later said, "I have no evidence, but I think my attempted assassination was part of a conspiracy." More than 30 years later, no one else has found any evidence either.

RONALD REAGAN·1981

Hit by a bullet

On March 30, 1981, 69-year-old U.S. President Ronald Reagan went to the Hilton Hotel in Washington, D.C., to give a speech to a labor union convention. It was a minor political occasion, but a small crowd of casual onlookers, press photographers, and TV news crews clustered on the sidewalk. John W. Hinckley Jr. stood unnoticed among them. He was carrying a .22 caliber revolver.

The president is shot

At 2:30 P.M., the president emerged from the hotel and headed for his limousine. He had almost reached the car door when Hinckley crouched down, holding his revolver with two hands, and opened fire. Secret Service agent Tim McCarthy blocked the line of fire between the gunman and the president with his body. Another agent, Jerry Parr, seized the president and threw him down on the back seat of the car. As Parr landed on top of him, Reagan realized he was in pain. He thought that he had been injured when Parr fell on top of him. The president's car drove off quickly, at first heading for the White House, but then to George Washington University Hospital as Reagan coughed up blood.

Mayhem at the hotel

Back on the sidewalk outside the hotel, there was chaos. Three men had been shot—McCarthy, police officer Tom Delahanty, and Reagan's press secretary, James S. Brady. As the noise

A wave for the crowd *Just moments before being shot, President Reagan cheerfully acknowledges the crowd.*

KEY DATES

1911 Born on February 6 in Tampico, Illinois
1937 Given his first Hollywood contract as a screen actor
1940 Marries Jane Wyman (divorced 1948)
1947 Becomes president of the Screen Actors' Guild
1952 Marries Nancy Davis
1966 Elected Republican governor of California
1980 Defeats incumbent Jimmy Carter to become president
1981 Survives assassination attempt on March 30
1984 Wins a landslide second presidential election victory
2004 Dies of pneumonia on June 5

Moments later *Press Secretary James Brady and police officer Tom Delahanty lie wounded on the ground as Secret Service agents apprehend the assailant.*

of screams and sirens filled the air, the three men were being given first aid on the ground. The injury to Brady was the most serious: A bullet had entered his head just above the left eye and was lodged in the right side of his brain. Meanwhile, Hinckley had been seized and disarmed by the president's bodyguards.

In the emergency room at the hospital, doctors established that the president himself had been shot. A bullet had entered his body near the left armpit and was embedded in the lower part of his left lung, about an inch (2.5 cm) from his heart. It had ricocheted off the armored limousine—traces of paint from the car were later found on the bullet.

Reagan displayed admirable courage and humor. He told his wife, Nancy, "Honey, I forgot to duck." And he remarked to one of the surgeons about to operate on him, "I hope you're a Republican." The doctors did a fine job on the president, and he made a full recovery from his injuries.

Lasting consequences

Less fortunate than the president, Press Secretary Brady suffered brain damage that permanently impaired his movement. He and his wife, Sarah, became passionate campaigners for gun control, and in 1994 they saw the Brady Act come into law. The act imposed background checks on gun purchasers.

Investigation of the crime failed to reveal a conspiracy. Hinckley was tried in 1982. There was a public outcry when he was found not guilty on grounds of insanity and was confined indefinitely to a mental institution.

Reagan was more forgiving than many of his fellow Americans. He said of Hinckley, "He was a mixed-up young man from a fine family. That day, I asked the Lord to heal him, and to this day, I still do."

Self-portrait *John W. Hinckley Jr. took his own photograph while holding a gun to his head. The picture is part of the court records from his trial.*

JOHN W. HINCKLEY JR.

The young man who shot President Reagan was the son of an oil executive—the Hinckleys knew the Bush family. John W. Hinckley Jr. never completed his education, and although he thought about being a songwriter, his plans came to nothing.

In 1976, Hinckley developed an obsession for film star Jodie Foster. By 1980, Hinckley was stalking her at Yale, where she was a student. He decided to attract her attention by killing a president. On October 9, 1980, he was arrested at the airport in Nashville, Tennessee, when guns were detected in his bag; President Jimmy Carter was in Nashville that day. Hinckley escaped with a fine.

John Lennon was killed the following December, giving Hinckley the model for his assassination attempt. By now, he was taking antidepressants and tranquilizers and seeing a psychiatrist. He was not sure whether to kill himself or someone else.

Hinckley arrived in Washington, D.C., on March 29 with three guns (he used only one of them when he shot at Reagan). He left a letter for Jodie Foster in his hotel room. He wrote, "By sacrificing my freedom and possibly my life, I hope to change your mind about me."

Vatican attack

On Wednesday, May 13, 1981, Pope John Paul II was conducting his weekly ritual of blessing the crowd in Rome's St. Peter's Square. Standing in the back of a white open-top vehicle, the pontiff drove slowly along a narrow path cleared through the thousands of people packing the square. Occasionally, he stopped and reached down to touch the hands of the faithful.

KEY DATES

1920 Born Karol Józef Wojtyla near Craków, Poland, May 18

1946 Ordained as a Catholic priest

1958 Appointed an auxiliary bishop of Craków

1963 Named archbishop of Craków

1967 Elevated to cardinal

1978 Elected pope

1979 Makes first visit to Poland since becoming pope

1981 Survives assassination attempt on May 13; Mehmet Ali Agca convicted of attempted murder

2000 Visits the shrine of Our Lady of Fatima, Portugal; Agca is freed by the Italian government and returned to Turkey to resume serving original murder sentence

Mingling with the crowd was a 23-year-old Turk, Mehmet Ali Agca, a convicted murderer who had escaped from a Turkish jail. When the pope arrived in front of him, Agca raised a Browning 9-mm pistol and quickly fired four shots. The pope collapsed, his white cassock stained with blood—he had been hit in the lower abdomen. Members of the crowd seized the assassin and handed him over to the police. The pope was rushed away for surgery, which saved his life.

Extreme motives

The motivation for the assassination attempt appeared to be Islamic extremism. Agca had become involved with a Turkish right-wing terrorist organization, the Grey Wolves. In 1979, he was arrested for the murder of Abdi Ipekci, the editor of a left-wing newspaper in Istanbul. However, one month after starting a life sentence, he walked out of a high-security prison disguised in an army uniform. In a note left in his prison cell, Agca threatened to kill the pope, denouncing him as the "Commander of the Crusades" against Islam and a representative of Western imperialism.

Conspiracy from behind the Iron Curtain?

Although Agca was convicted of the assassination attempt in 1981 and given a life sentence, some claimed that the whole story had not emerged. The election of the Polish Cardinal Karol Wojtyla as pope in 1978 represented a challenge to the Communist rulers of the Soviet Union and its satellite states in Eastern Europe. Pope John Paul's triumphant visit to Poland in 1979 shook the authority of the country's Communist government and led directly to the formation of the pro-Democracy Solidarity movement a year later. Had the Soviet KGB or any of its East European offshoots planned the assassination attempt?

Agca first claimed that he had acted alone, then that he was a member of a Palestinian terrorist group; but, in 1982,

Pope mobile *The Pope is riding in his open vehicle in St. Peter's Square moments before Mehmet Ali Agca pulled the trigger and shot him—the gun can be seen in the white circle.*

he stated that he was employed by the Bulgarian secret service. Allegedly, Bulgarian agents gave him the pistol and drove him to St. Peter's Square. In 1985, based on Agca's new testimony, the Italian authorities held a trial accusing three Bulgarians and four Turks of conspiracy to kill the pope. However, in court, Agca made such bizarre and contradictory statements that the case was abandoned for lack of evidence.

Interest in the Bulgarian angle was revived in 1999, when documents released from Czech secret archives showed that from 1979 forward the KGB and secret services of the Warsaw Pact countries had given priority to operations designed to discredit the pope and the Catholic Church. Individuals who worked in the Soviet system at the time, including former President Mikhail Gorbachev, denied these operations included attempting to assassinate the pope. For his part, on a visit to Bulgaria in 2002, Pope John Paul stated that he had never believed the Bulgarians were responsible for the shooting.

THE THIRD PROPHECY OF FATIMA

On May 13, 2000, on the anniversary of the assassination attempt, the pope visited the shrine of our Lady of Fatima, in Portugal. The shrine celebrates a series of visions three children had of the Virgin Mary, the first occurring on May 13, 1917. The pope believes that more than a coincidence of dates links the visions to the assassination attempt.

The children had recorded three prophecies. The content of the third prophecy was kept secret until the pope's visit to the Fatima in 2000. It was then revealed that it described "a bishop clothed in white" who "falls to the ground, apparently dead, under a burst of gunfire." According to the Vatican, the prophecy foretold the attempted assassination. The pope had the bullet that wounded him welded into the statue of the Virgin at Fatima.

Bombed

In the early hours of October 12, 1984, British Prime Minister Margaret Thatcher was working on the speech she was to deliver at the annual conference of the Conservative Party. Along with other party officials, she was staying at the Grand Hotel in Brighton, the seaside venue chosen for the conference. Security was strict, at least by British standards, with three Special Branch officers guarding the prime minister and other police on duty on the hotel landings. There had been a tip that the Irish Republican Army (IRA), which was then engaged in a terrorist campaign to drive the British out of Northern Ireland, was planning to strike.

KEY DATES

1925 Born October 13 as Margaret Roberts in Grantham, England

1959 Elected as a Conservative MP for Finchley, in London

1970 Appointed secretary of state for education and science

1975 Becomes leader of the Conservative Party

1979 Wins general election, becoming Britain's first woman prime minister

1982 Britain defeats Argentina in the Falklands War

1983 Wins general election again

1984 Survives IRA bombing on October 12

1987 Wins third general election

1990 Resigns as prime minister on November 22

The Iron Lady

Thatcher was possibly the most confrontational politician ever to run a British government. She had proved uncompromising in her approach to the Northern Ireland situation. In 1980, several IRA prisoners had gone on hunger strikes, wanting "special status"—to be treated as military prisoners, not common criminals. Thatcher refused their demand; 10 men starved to death. This earned her the particular hatred of Irish Republicans.

Advanced planning

About three weeks before the Conservative conference, a man using the name Roy Walsh checked into the Grand Hotel. His real name was Patrick Magee, and he was an explosives expert. In his room, he hid a bomb in a bathroom wall, with a timing device set for 24 days ahead.

The Grand Hotel *The facade of the hotel in Brighton shows the destruction caused by the IRA bomb.*

The Iron Lady *Thatcher speaks to the Conservative party only hours after the bombing.*

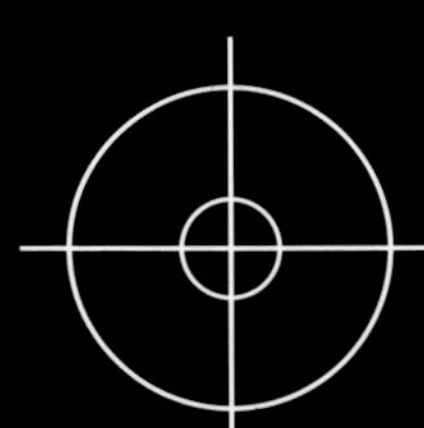

FAILURE OR CONSPIRACY

The 1984 Brighton bombing reminded many people of an earlier attempt to blow up an English government—the Gunpowder Plot of 1605. It was planned by Catholics angry at King James I for being an enemy of Catholicism. They decided to blow up the monarch and his Parliament on November 5, during the opening of Parliament.

The conspirators recruited Guy Fawkes, a Catholic and an explosives expert. They packed a cellar under the House of Lords with barrels of gunpowder. The plot was apparently discovered after one of the plotters warned a relative to stay away from the opening. The cellar was searched, the explosives found, and Fawkes arrested on the scene. Four conspirators were killed resisting arrest. Five others, including Fawkes, were hanged, drawn, and quartered.

At 2:54 A.M. on October 12, the bomb exploded. One side of the hotel collapsed. The bathroom in Thatcher's suite—which she had used only minutes before—was demolished, but the prime minister was unhurt. Others were not so lucky. Three women and two men were killed. Thirty-four people were injured.

The show must go on

Thatcher insisted that the conference go ahead as planned. She delivered a keynote speech in which she denounced the bombing as an attempt "to cripple our government."

Police traced 800 people who had stayed at the hotel. Only Roy Walsh could not be found. His identity was established, using a print left on a hotel registration card. The print matched one taken from Magee as a youth, when he had been arrested for a minor offense.

In June 1985, police caught Magee in a raid in Glasgow. He was tried and given eight life sentences. The judge recommended he should spend at least 35 years in prison. In 1999, Magee was released. He stated that he was glad Thatcher had not been killed because it might have made a political solution to the conflict harder to achieve.

Early release *Magee (left) was released from prison in 1999 as part of a bid to end the Northern Ireland conflict.*

Other notable killings

On the following pages, you'll find brief accounts of other killings that have not been included in the main section of the book but which deserve mention.

King Abdullah (1882–1951)
Abdullah bin Hussein played a leading role in the Arab revolt against Turkish rule during World War I and was rewarded by his British allies with the emirship of Transjordania in 1921. When Jordan became an independent country in 1946, he was its first king. Although King Abdullah joined other Arab countries in the war against the newly founded state of Israel in 1948–49, he offended many Arabs by seeking a separate peace with Israel after the conflict.

On July 20, 1951, while visiting the al-Aqsa mosque in Jerusalem, he was shot and killed by Palestinian militant Mustapha Shukri Usho, who was also killed at the scene. A Jordanian court later sentenced six other people to death for plotting the assassination, two in absentia.

Alcibiades (*c.* 450–404 B.C.)
Born in Athens, Greek military leader and politician Alcibiades fought in the Peloponnesian War between Athens and Sparta. In fact, he fought on both sides at different times. After disputes with both Greek city-states, he fled to the court of the Persian governor of Phrygia, Asia Minor, in 404 B.C. There the Persians assassinated Alcibiades at the Spartans' request.

King Alexander of Serbia (1876–1903)
Alexander Obrenovic succeeded to the throne of the Balkan kingdom of Serbia in 1889. In 1900, he married a widow, Draga Mashin, who had been a lady-in-waiting to his mother. It was an unpopular match. In April 1903, he suspended the country's liberal constitution, abolishing freedom of speech and the secret ballot. On the night of April 10, Serbian army officers attacked the royal palace. The king and queen were killed and their mutilated bodies thrown out of a window. Seventeen other people were killed, including the prime minister and minister of war.

The coup had been organized by Colonel Mashin, the brother of Queen Draga's first husband. Captain Dragutin Dimitrijevic, who later planned the assassination of the Archduke Franz Ferdinand (see pp. 22–27), played a prominent role in the massacre.

King Alexander I of Yugoslavia (1888–1934)
Alexander came to the throne of what was then the Kingdom of the Serbs, Croats, and Slovenes in 1921—the country was renamed Yugoslavia in 1929. The king was a Serb, and his authoritarian rule met with violent opposition from movements representing other nationalities in the kingdom, including the Croatian Ustashi and the Macedonian Revolutionary Movement.

On October 9, 1934, King Alexander landed at the port of Marseilles for a state visit to France. He was driving from the port when a Macedonian nationalist, Vlada Gheorghief, jumped on the running board of the car and shot him at point-blank range with a Mauser. King Alexander and French Foreign Minister Louis Narthou, who was sitting alongside him, were both killed. The assassin was also killed at the scene. Four accomplices, all members of the Croat Ustashi, were sentenced to life imprisonment. They were released when Hitler conquered France in 1940.

Pope Alexander VI (1431–1503)
Born in Spain, Rodrigo Borgia was made a cardinal through family influence at the age of 25 and assumed the papacy in 1492. He was notorious for his corrupt and licentious behavior, fathering seven children, including Cesare and Lucrezia Borgia.

The cause of Pope Alexander's death in August 1503 is not known for certain, but many authorities believe that he was poisoned. According to one version, he was the accidental victim of an assassination plot by his son Cesare. The intended victim was an enemy of the Borgias, Cardinal Adrian Corneto, whom Cesare tried to kill by giving him some wine spiked with poison. However, while dining with the cardinal, Pope Alexander drank the poisoned wine instead.

Benigno Aquino (1932–83)
Philippine politician Benigno Aquino was an opponent of the country's authoritarian president Ferdinand Marcos. Aquino was arrested in 1972 on false charges and later sentenced to death. Under pressure from the American government, in 1980 Marcos released Aquino to undergo medical treatment in the United States. He flew back to the Philippines on August 21, 1983, defying Marcos's efforts to keep him out of the country. At Manila International Airport, Aquino was taken from the plane by aviation security guards and was shot on the tarmac.

Philippine authorities blamed the killing on Ronaldo Galman, supposedly an airport worker, who was shot alongside Aquino. However, investigation confirmed suspicions of a conspiracy, probably reaching into the highest levels of the Marcos regime. Indignation at Aquino's death sparked the popular movement that overthrew the Marcos regime in 1986, bringing Aquino's widow, Corazon Aquino, to power. In 1990, 16 aviation security guards were convicted of the killing.

Solomon Bandaranaike (1899–1959)
Prime Minister Bandaranaike of Ceylon (now Sri Lanka) was a victim of his country's religious and ethnic divisions. He was at first supported by groups who wanted Buddhism to be recognized as Ceylon's main religion and Sinhalese as the sole official language. When he failed to deliver all they wanted, these groups turned against Bandaranaike. On September 25, 1959, he was shot in his own home by a Buddhist monk, Talduwe Somarama. The following year his wife, Sirimavo, became prime minister.

King Birendra Bikram (1945–2001)
Birendra succeeded to the throne of Nepal in 1972 and at first governed as an absolute ruler. However, from 1990 he accepted modernizing reforms that made him a constitutional monarch. On June 1, 2001, his eldest son, Crown Prince Dipendra, allegedly opened fire on his family with a submachine gun in the royal palace after a dispute over whom he should be allowed to marry. The king, his wife, Queen Aiswarya, and six other members of the Nepalese royal family were killed. Dipendra was also wounded and died three days later. There were suspicions that a political plot, rather than a personal grudge, may have been behind the assassination, but no evidence to support this theory has emerged.

Emperor Caracalla (A.D. 188–217)
On the death of their father, Emperor Septimus Severus, in A.D. 211, Caracalla and Geta became emperors jointly. Caracalla soon assassinated his brother and ruled alone, allegedly showing

great cruelty. In A.D. 217, a high official, Opilius Macrinus, who feared he was about to fall into disfavor, arranged to have the emperor killed. The assassination was carried out by a soldier, Martialis, who stabbed Caracalla while he was on his way from Edessa to the Temple of the Moon at Carrhae. Macrinus briefly took the imperial throne, but he was killed by Heliogabalus the following year during a mutiny by soldiers.

Admiral Carrero Blanco (1903–73)
Spanish Admiral Carrero Blanco was one of the leading figures in the regime of dictator General Francisco Franco. In June 1973, he was appointed prime minister, second only to Franco in the government hierarchy. On December 20, 1973, the car in which he was traveling was blown up by a bomb as he was driving back from attending Mass. It had been planted in a tunnel dug under the road. The vehicle was hurled over the roof of a church and landed on the second-floor balcony of an apartment building. Carrero Blanco was still alive when he was found in the wreckage but died shortly afterward. The bombing was carried out by the Basque terrorist group ETA, whose stated mission is to campaign for independence for the Basque region of northern Spain.

King Carlos of Portugal (1863–1908)
Carlos succeeded to the throne of Portugal in 1889. Faced with mounting social and political unrest, his rule became increasingly authoritarian. On February 1, 1908, as the king and members of his family drove through the Praça do Comercio in the center of Lisbon, they were attacked by armed assailants led by a cavalry sergeant in the Portuguese army. Both the king and his eldest son, Crown Prince Luiz Felipe, were killed. Because the prince took longer to expire, he was technically king for 20 minutes. Manuel II succeeded to the throne but was overthrown in a revolution in 1910, when Portugal was proclaimed a republic.

Sadi Carnot (1837–94)
French politician Sadi Carnot was elected president of the French Republic in 1887. On June 24, 1894, he visited the city of Lyons, which was holding an International Exhibition. As he drove through crowd-lined streets, a young man ran up to his carriage and fatally stabbed the president with a knife that he had concealed in a newspaper. As he did so, he shouted, *"Vive l'anarchie!"* (Long live anarchy!) The assassin was Santo Caserio, a baker's apprentice from Milan, Italy. He was arrested at the scene and later sentenced to death. He was killed by the guillotine.

Lord Frederick Cavendish (1836–82)
On May 6, 1882, British Liberal politician Lord Cavendish arrived in Dublin to fill the post of chief secretary to Ireland, then under British rule. That evening, as he walked in Dublin's Phoenix Park with the permanent undersecretary, Thomas Burke, they were attacked by nine Irish assailants with knives. Both men died of multiple stab wounds. The assassins were members of a group called the Invincibles, connected with the Irish nationalist Fenian movement. Eight of the men were later arrested for the crime; five were hanged and three sentenced to penal servitude.

Marcus Tullius Cicero (106–43 B.C.)
By the time Julius Caesar was assassinated in 44 B.C. (see pp. 42–43), distinguished Roman politician and author Cicero had retired from public life. However, the following year, he stepped forward to deliver a series of speeches denouncing Mark Antony (Marcus Antonius), who held supreme power in Italy after Caesar's demise. In the fall of 43 B.C., Mark Antony made an agreement with Octavian (the future Emperor Augustus) and Lepidus to form a "triumvirate" to rule Rome. As part of the deal, Mark Antony insisted that Cicero's name be put on a death list.

Word of the decision reached Cicero while he was at his country villa outside Rome. He fled to the coast, hoping to escape by ship. He was, however, an old man and had to come ashore to rest after only a short voyage along the Italian coast. The soldiers sent by Mark Antony found him on December 7, as he was being carried in a litter down to the sea to resume his journey. Steadfast in the face of death, Cicero submissively leaned his head out of the litter, allowing one of the assassins to cut it off with a single stroke of his sword.

Crazy Horse (1849–77)
Lakota Sioux warrior Crazy Horse (Tashunca-uitco) was a visionary leader of Native American resistance to settler encroachment. He took part in fighting against settlers and the U.S. Army from 1865 onward and played a decisive role in the annihilation of General George Custer's cavalry at Little Big Horn, Montana, in 1876.

After enduring a winter of declining food supplies and relentless harassment by U.S. military forces, Crazy Horse agreed to abandon resistance in 1877. U.S. General George Crook, however, suspected that Crazy Horse intended to mount a fresh rebellion. At the same time, Sioux who were hostile to Crazy Horse—many of them working for the U.S. Army as scouts—plotted against him. In September 1877, Crazy Horse was escorted by U.S. soldiers and Sioux scouts to Fort Robinson, Nebraska. He thought he was going to hold talks with General Crook about the treatment of Native Americans. However, once Crazy Horse was inside the fort, his arms were pinioned by a scout and a U.S. soldier, and another soldier ran him through with a bayonet.

Engelbert Dollfuss (1892–1934)
The leader of the Austrian Christian Socialist Party, Engelbert Dollfuss became chancellor of Austria in 1932. After Nazi leader Adolf Hitler became chancellor of Germany in January 1933, Dollfuss was put under intense pressure from the Austrian Nazi Party, which wanted Austria to be part of a greater Germany. Dollfuss was an uncompromising ruler who ruthlessly repressed all political opposition, including Nazis.

On July 25, 1934, Austrian Nazis attempted a coup. A group of Austrian SS men occupied the chancellery in Vienna. One of them, Otto Planetta, shot Dollfuss twice at point-blank range. Denied medical care, he died of his wounds hours later. The coup was suppressed by the Austrian army, and 13 of the SS men involved in the assassination were hanged, including Planetta. Austria eventually joined Nazi Germany without a fight in the Anschluss of March 1938.

Giovanni Falcone (1939–92)
Italian judge Giovanni Falcone achieved international fame in the 1980s for his crusade against the Sicilian Mafia. Between 1986 and 1987, he brought 475 alleged criminals to trial, although few of them received significant jail terms. He cooperated with legal authorities in the United States, including then New York judge Rudolph Giuliani, to attack the Mafia's international organization.

As Falcone's investigations increasingly pointed to links between the Mafia and major figures in Italian political life, he found government support for his work vanishing. On May 23, 1992, Falcone was driving from Sicily's Palermo International Airport into the city of Palermo when a large explosive charge concealed in an underpass blew up his car. He was killed, along with his wife and three police bodyguards. The shock of the assassination provoked a revival of official enthusiasm for a crackdown on the Mafia, leading to a significant number of arrests of prominent leaders over the following years.

King Faisal II of Iraq (1935–58)
Faisal succeeded his father as titular king of Iraq in 1939, but because he was only four years old, his uncle Emir Abd al-Illah ruled as regent. After being educated in Britain, Faisal took over from the regent in 1953. The king's hostility to the radical Arab nationalism of Egypt's Gamal Abdel Nasser led to his downfall.

On July 14, 1958, Nasserite Iraqi army officers led by Brigadier Abdul Karim Qassem staged a coup in Baghdad. Faisal was killed, along with Emir Abd al-Illah and his entire household. Brigadier Qassem took power but was himself assassinated in a coup that brought the Baath Party to power in Iraq in 1963.

King Faisal of Saudi Arabia (*c.* 1906–75)
Faisal ibn Abdul Aziz played a major role in running Saudi Arabia long before he succeeded to the throne in 1964, after his brother Saud's abdication. On March 25, 1975, the birthday of the Prophet Mohammed, the king's 27-year-old nephew Prince Faisal ibn Musad stood in a reception line in the royal palace at Riyadh. When it was his turn to be greeted by the king, Prince Faisal pulled out a gun and shot him in the face, killing him instantly. Opinions about the assassin's motives differ. Some believe he was merely insane, while others suggest that, influenced by a long stay in the United States, he wanted to end the religious conservatism of King Faisal's rule and introduce Western-style modernization. After trial by an Islamic religious court, Prince Faisal was publicly beheaded and his severed head exhibited on a stake.

Federico García Lorca (1899–1936)
Although Spanish poet and dramatist Garcia Lorca was not a political activist, he had Republican sympathies. When General Franco's Nationalists staged an armed insurrection against the Spanish Republic in 1936, Garcia Lorca knew his life was in danger. Details of his death are obscure, but it appears that on August 19, 1936, he was arrested by insurgent troops in Granada, Andalusia, beaten up, and shot. It has been suggested that he was assassinated because he was a homosexual.

Chris Hani (1942–93)
Hani was a prominent black South African anti-apartheid activist and, from 1991, secretary general of the South African Communist Party. On April 10, 1993, during the period of transition from white rule to democratic government, he was shot and killed in the driveway of his house in Johannesburg. Janusz Walus was arrested within hours of the shooting.

Walus was a right-wing extremist who had been born in Poland and emigrated to South Africa in 1981. A white politician, Clive Derby-Lewis, was also found guilty of Hani's murder—he had supplied Walus with the gun. Walus and Derby-Lewis were sentenced to death, but their sentences were commuted to life imprisonment when the death penalty was abolished after Nelson Mandela came to power in 1994.

Jean Jaurès (1859–1914)
The founder of the French Socialist Party, Jaurès was a major figure in left-wing politics in France. He was a dedicated internationalist, calling for all European Socialist parties to work together to prevent war. In the summer of 1914, during the crisis that followed the assassination of the Archduke Franz Ferdinand (see pp. 22–27), Jaurès campaigned relentlessly for peace. However, the belligerent right-wing nationalist press openly called for his assassination.

On July 31, a student, 19-year-old Raoul Villain, shot Jaurès twice in the head as he sat in a café in Paris. Four days later, France was at war with Germany. Villain was detained in prison throughout the war, but in 1919 a French court found him not guilty on the grounds of mental instability—a politically motivated decision that caused outrage among socialists. After his release, Villain went to live in Spain. When civil war broke out there in 1936, he was killed by Spanish Republicans to avenge Jaurès's death.

Laurent-Désiré Kabila (1939–2001)
Laurent Kabila was one of the leading figures in the political turmoil that racked the Congo from independence in 1960 into the 21st century. He spent much of his life as a rebel against the dictatorial government of Mobutu Sese Seko, financing his armed band through illegal diamond trading. In 1997, Mobutu's regime disintegrated and Kabila became president of the Democratic Republic of Congo. Kabila was both corrupt and incompetent, plunging the country into even worse civil bloodshed.

On January 16, 2001, he was shot and killed in the Marble Palace, Kinshasa. The killing is alleged to have been carried out by one of his guards, 18-year-old Rashidi Kasereka, who was killed at the scene. Later a mass trial was staged at which Eddy Kapend, a cousin and close adviser of Kabila, was accused of leading a conspiracy to kill the president. Kapend and 25 others were given death sentences.

Pierre Laporte (1921–70)
Laporte, a Liberal politician in the Canadian province of Quebec, was vice premier of Quebec and minister of labor in 1970. On October 10, he was kidnapped by the "Chenier cell" of the Front de Libération du Québec (FLQ), a terrorist movement seeking independence for the French-speaking province. In response to this and other terrorist acts by the FLQ, the Canadian government declared martial law. On October 17, Laporte was strangled and his body left in the trunk of a car. The members of the Chenier cell—Bernard Lortie, Francis Simard, and brothers Paul and Jacques Rose—were arrested. Although they were sentenced to life in prison, all had been released on parole by 1982.

Georgi Markov (1929–78)
Prominent in Bulgaria as an author and critic of the Bulgarian Communist government, Georgi Markov became well known to the rest of the world through the manner of his death. He was living in exile in London, when on September 7, 1978, he was stabbed in the leg while standing at a bus stop. The blow was delivered by the tip of an umbrella. The umbrella had been used to inject a metal capsule containing the poison ricin. Markov died in agony on September 11. The assassin, who was never found, is believed to have been a Bulgarian secret agent.

Ahmed Shah Massoud (1953–2001)
Afghan warlord Ahmed Shah Massoud, known as the Lion of Panjshir, came to prominence as a leading mujahideen fighter resisting the Soviet occupation of Afghanistan in the 1980s. By 2001, he was the head of the Northern Alliance, fighting against Afghanistan's Taliban government and its Al Qaeda allies.

On September 9, 2001, Massoud agreed to give an interview to two Moroccan television reporters. They were in fact Al Qaeda terrorists, and their video camera was packed with explosives. The explosion fatally wounded Massoud; both of his assassins also died. The timing of the assassination, two days before the attacks on the United States on September 11, was probably not a coincidence. Anticipating that the United States would respond by invading Afghanistan, Al Qaeda had eliminated the man who could have been the Americans' most valuable Afghan ally.

Giacomo Matteotti (1885–1924)
Italian politician Matteotti was a socialist member of the Italian chamber of deputies who opposed the rise of the Fascist movement headed by Benito Mussolini. In 1922, Mussolini became head of the Italian government. Leading up to the elections in April 1924, he unleashed his Fascist blackshirts to

terrorize his opponents. Matteotti led the way in denouncing the violence and fraud that allowed Fascists to win the elections.

On June 6, 1924, he was abducted from his home and beaten to death. His body was not found until later in the year. Faced with general outrage in Italy, Mussolini got rid of some of his entourage who were considered to be implicated. In January 1925, however, in a speech celebrating Fascist violence, Mussolini accepted moral responsibility for the assassination.

Thomas D'Arcy McGee (1825–68)

The Irish-born McGee settled permanently in Canada in 1857. He was a prominent author and politician and is credited with a major role in persuading various British North American colonies to unite as the Dominion of Canada in 1867. Although an active opponent of British rule in Ireland in his younger years, he became an outspoken critic of Irish Republican Fenians, especially after they mounted an attempted invasion of Canada from the United States in 1866.

On April 7, 1868, McGee was shot outside his rooming house in Ottawa. Fenians were immediately suspected, and an Irish tailor, Patrick James Whalen, was subsequently convicted of the killing and hanged. However, no evidence of a conspiracy was ever found.

Ross McWhirter (1925–75)

With his twin brother Norris, British fascinating-fact fanatic Ross McWhirter created the international best-seller, *The Guinness Book of Records*. He was also a political campaigner. In response to the IRA terrorist campaign in Britain in the 1970s, he called for the reintroduction of the death penalty and offered a cash reward for information leading to the arrest of terrorists.

On November 27, 1975, two IRA gunmen shot and killed McWhirter at the front door of his house in Enfield, Middlesex, England. Two weeks later, four members of the IRA cell who were believed to be responsible for the killing were arrested after a six-day police siege at an apartment in London. They were sentenced to life imprisonment, but in 1999 they were released under the terms of the Good Friday agreement—a bid to end the Northern Ireland conflict.

Chico Mendes (1944–88)

Born in a remote area of the Brazilian interior, Francisco Alves Mendes Filho—known as Chico Mendes—became famous for organizing the traditional inhabitants of the rain forest to defend their threatened environment and way of life. He took on cattle ranchers and logging companies, as well as the Brazilian government. In 1987, he was given the United Nations Global 500 Award for defense of the environment. Mendes and his followers accepted that they would inevitably face extreme violence from those wishing to open up the forest to economic exploitation. On December 22, 1988, Mendes was shot in the chest outside his home in Xapuri, Acre. A local landowner, Darli Alves da Silva, and his son Darcy Alves were convicted of the crime, but suspicions remain of a wider conspiracy.

Harvey Milk (1930–78)

New York–born Harvey Milk emerged as a prominent gay-rights campaigner in San Francisco in the 1970s. In 1977, he became the first openly gay person elected to the San Francisco Board of Supervisors (City Council)—indeed, to any major public office in the United States. On November 27, 1978, he was gunned down in San Francisco City Hall, along with Mayor George Moscone.

The assassin, Danny White, a former member of the Board of Supervisors, was a conservative opponent of gay rights. White was found guilty only of manslaughter—his defense counsel argued that he was depressed because he had been eating too much junk food. The verdict provoked rioting by gays in San Francisco.

Nadir Shah (1688–1747)

Nadir Qali, better known as Nadir Shah (King Nadir), was born into a Turkish tribe in Iran, then ruled by the Safavid dynasty. He was a superb military commander and rose to supreme power in the state through his prowess at war. In 1736, he deposed the last of the Safavids and took the throne himself. He conquered central Asia, Afghanistan, and northern India, sacking the Moghul capital, Delhi, in 1740.

The ruler was cruel and ruthless, responsible for thousands of arbitrary executions and mutilations. He attempted to impose the Sunni form of Islam on Shi'ite Iran, which was widely resented. On June 10, 1747, he was assassinated in his sleep by the captain of his guard. After his death, the empire he had conquered swiftly disintegrated.

Airey Neave (1917–79)

British Conservative politician Airey Neave won renown in his younger years as one of the few British prisoners of war to escape from the notorious German camp at Colditz. He was one of Margaret Thatcher's closest associates after she became leader of the Conservative Party in 1975. As her shadow secretary of state for Northern Ireland, he favored a hard-line policy to uphold British rule in the province.

On March 30, 1979, Neave's car was blown up as he drove out of the underground parking lot at the Houses of Parliament. The bomb was almost certainly planted by the Irish National Liberation Army (INLA), an Irish Republican splinter group that had broken away from the Irish Republican Army (IRA). The following May, Thatcher won her first general election.

Park Chung Hee (1917–79)

South Korean General Park Chung Hee seized power in a military coup in 1961. As president of South Korea, he stimulated economic growth but suppressed all opposition, and his regime was guilty of the systematic abuse of human rights. President Park survived an assassination attempt in 1974, when he was fired at by a student allegedly operating on behalf of the North Korean government. Park's wife, Yook Young Soo, was killed in this attack.

By October 1979, South Korea experienced widespread protests against Park's dictatorial rule. On October 16, the head of the Korean CIA, Kim Jae Kyu, shot and killed Park after inviting him to dinner at the KCIA headquarters. Some sources claim Kim wanted to end the political chaos brought about by Park's rule; others say Kim simply feared Park was going to get rid of him. Kim and four other members of the KCIA were hanged for the killing in May 1980.

Mujibur Rahman (1920–75)

Bangladeshi politician Mujibur Rahman (Sheikh Mujib) is known as the "Father of Bangladesh." In 1971, after an election victory for his Awami League, Sheikh Mujib declared Bangladesh independent of Pakistan. Pakistani forces were defeated, thanks to military intervention by India, and in 1972 Sheikh Mujib became Bangladesh's first prime minister. He attempted to create a secular, democratic state; however, within three years the country had been reduced to chaos by natural disasters and general lawlessness.

In 1975, in an effort to restore order, Mujib declared himself president with almost dictatorial powers. On August 15, he was assassinated by a group of army officers, along with his wife and three sons. Only his two daughters, who were abroad at the time, survived. After a long period of military rule, one of these daughters, Sheikh Hasina, became prime minister in 1996. Two years later, 15 officers were convicted of Mujib's assassination and sentenced to death, 12 of them in absentia.

Abdel-Aziz al-Rantassi (1947–2004)
A Palestinian Arab, al-Rantassi became a refugee when the state of Israel was created in 1948. In 1988, he was one of the founder members of the Hamas extremist movement dedicated to the destruction of the Israeli state. Al-Rantassi became the leader of Hamas on March 22, 2004, when his predecessor Sheikh Ahmed Yassin was assassinated. He survived for 25 days, sleeping in a different place each night and varying his daily routine. However, he was killed on April 17 when his car was struck by a missile from an Israeli helicopter, close to his home in Gaza City. His driver and bodyguard were also killed. Hamas decided to keep the identity of their next leader a secret.

Ernst vom Rath (1909–38)
Junior German diplomat Ernst vom Rath was not an important figure, but his assassination triggered the Kristallnacht pogrom, a key event in 20th-century history. On November 7, 1938, a 17-year-old Polish Jew, Herschel Grynszpan, went to the German embassy in Paris and shot vom Rath five times. The diplomat died two days later. The previous month Grynszpan's family had been expelled from Germany by the Nazi regime in a brutal mass deportation of Polish Jews. Protest against Nazi anti-Semitism seems certain to have been Grynszpan's main motive, although there is evidence that he had had a homosexual relationship with vom Rath.

Once vom Rath died, Nazi propaganda chief Josef Goebbels called for revenge against Jews in the Reich. Beginning on the night of November 9, hundreds of synagogues were burned, Jewish businesses and homes were attacked, and 30,000 Jews were taken to concentration camps. Grynszpan was in a French prison when Germany occupied France in 1940. He was sent to Sachsenshausen concentration camp and never seen again.

Walter Rathenau (1867–1922)
German industrialist Walter Rathenau became minister of reconstruction in the Weimar Republic in 1921, and he was given the task of rebuilding his country's economy after defeat in World War I. The following year he was appointed foreign minister. Rathenau was hated by German right-wing extremists because he argued that Germany must fulfill the terms of the Versailles Treaty imposed on Germany by the victorious allies at the end of the war. They also hated him for having signed the Rapallo Treaty, which established close relations between Germany and Bolshevik Russia. However, above all, they hated him because he was a Jew.

On June 24, 1922, he was assassinated by two right-wing extremists—former army officers—as he drove away from his house in a Berlin suburb in an open-topped car. His death led to mass demonstrations in favor of the Weimar Republic and against the anti-Semitic nationalists.

Raymond II, Count of Tripoli (1115–52)
Raymond II was a French knight who ruled one of the small Christian states established in the Levant after the invasion of Palestine by the Crusaders. He is famous only for his death—he was the first recorded Christian victim of the Muslim sect known as the Assassins (see p. 10).

Early in 1152, Raymond rode a short distance out of Tripoli to say farewell to his wife, Countess Hodierna, who was embarking on a journey to Jerusalem. As he reentered Tripoli through one of the gates in the city wall, he was ambushed by a band of Assassins who stabbed him to death, along with two knights who were accompanyimg him. The murderers escaped, so the Crusader knights massacred every Muslim they came across in the city.

Augusto Sandino (1895–1934)
In the 1920s, Nicaraguan rebel leader Augusto "César" Sandino formed a peasant army to fight against the U.S.-backed Conservative government. In 1933, American troops left Nicaragua, and Sandino agreed to a peace deal with President Juan Bautista Sacasa. In February 1934, Sandino went to Managua for talks with the president, demanding the dissolution of the National Guard, commanded by Anastasio Somoza García. On the evening of February 21, Sandino and three of his associates were seized by National Guardsmen as they left the presidential palace. They were taken to an airfield, shot, and buried in unmarked graves. Three years later, Somoza made himself dictator of Nicaragua, but he himself was later assassinated—by Nicaraguan poet Rigoberto Lopez Perez—in September 1956.

Hanns-Martin Schleyer (1915–77)
In 1977, German industrialist Schleyer was selected as a target by terrorists of the Red Army Faction (RAF), also known as the Baader-Meinhof gang. They kidnapped Schleyer in Cologne on September 5, 1977, shooting and killing three bodyguards and a chauffeur. The RAF hoped to use their hostages to negotiate freedom for their imprisoned colleagues.

On October 13, other terrorists hijacked an airliner to Mogadishu, Somalia, to reinforce this demand. The crisis ended in a welter of blood: The airliner was stormed by German and British special forces; Baader, Raspe, and Ensslin commited suicide in prison; Schleyer's dead body was found in the trunk of a car in Mulhouse, France, on October 19.

Although RAF activity never reached the same peak again, in 1979 the group made a failed attempt to assassinate Alexander Haig, then supreme commander of NATO forces in Europe.

Song Jiaoren (1882–1913)
Chinese politician Song Jiaoren was a young associate of revolutionary leader Sun Yat-Sen. After the fall of the Qing dynasty in China in 1911, the warlord General Yuan Shikai held power. However, Sun and his associates hoped to see the country become a Western-style democratic republic. Song formed the Guomindang (Nationalist Party) to run in China's first nationwide elections in January 1913.

The Guomindang won the largest share of the vote, and on March 20 Song traveled from Shanghai to Beijing in the expectation of becoming prime minister. As he waited for a train on the platform at Shanghai station, a man walked up to him and shot him twice at close range. He died in hospital two days later. General Yuan is generally believed to have ordered the assassination. He banned the Guomindang and made himself in effect military dictator of China. The country's best chance of becoming a democratic republic was lost.

Piotr Stolypin (1862–1911)
Russian statesman Piotr Stolypin was prime minister and minister of the interior under Czar Nicholas II from 1906. He repressed political opposition but was also a vigorous modernizer, attempting to turn Russian peasants into private landowners, farming for profit. On September 1, 1911, he attended an opera performance in Kiev, at which the czar was also present. During an intermission, he was shot at point-blank range by a young man in evening dress. He died of his wounds four days later.

The assassin, Dmitry Bogrov, was an anarchist but also a police informer. He had been given a ticket to the opera by the secret police, allegedly so he could help prevent an attack on the czar. Whether he killed Stolypin as a revolutionary gesture or on the orders of reactionary elements in the secret police has never been established.

Rafael Trujillo (1891–1961)
Generalissimo Rafael Trujillo Molina ruled the Dominican Republic with an iron fist for 31 years. His ruthless police force exercised a reign of terror by murdering and torturing political

opponents. By the 1960s, the United States had decided that Trujillo should, if possible, be overthrown. In 1961, the CIA encouraged anti-Trujillo elements in the Dominican Republic to assassinate the dictator.

On May 30, Trujillo's chauffeur-driven sedan was ambushed on a road outside Ciudad Trujillo (now Santo Domingo) by seven assassins in three cars. In an exchange of fire, the dictator was killed, although two of the assassins, Pedro Livio Cedeño and Lieutenant Amado Garcia, were also wounded. Unwisely, the conspirators failed to take the initiative and immediately seize power. Trujillo's family remained in power for the next six months, enough time to torture and murder hundreds of opponents of the regime, including most of the conspirators involved in the assassination plot.

Gianni Versace (1946–97)

Born in poverty in Calabria, Italy, clothing designer Gianni Versace built up one of the world's most profitable fashion empires. His flamboyant, outrageous creations clothed the rich and famous, many of whom he numbered among his friends. On July 15, 1997, Versace was shot twice in the back of the head as he stood outside the gates of Casa Casuarina, his mansion in South Beach, Miami.

Rumors immediately circulated that he had been killed by a Mafia hit man. However, the FBI believed that Versace had been shot by gay serial killer Andrew Cunanan, who was on their "Ten Most Wanted" list as a suspect in four other murders of gay men. On July 24, Cunanan was traced to a houseboat at Miami Beach. When police stormed the boat, they found a dead Cunanan. He had apparently committed suicide by shooting himself. No clear motive for his alleged killing of Versace has been established.

Hendrik Verwoerd (1901–66)

South African politician Verwoerd was one of the principal architects of the racial segregationist apartheid system in South Africa. He was South African prime minister from 1958, ruling at the time of the notorious Sharpeville massacre of antiapartheid protesters in 1960 and the imprisonment of Nelson Mandela in 1964.

Verwoerd survived an assassination attempt in 1960 when he was shot by a white farmer. On September 6, 1966, he died after being stabbed in the chest while sitting in the South African House of Assembly. His assassin was a parliamentary messenger, Demetrio Tsafendas, of mixed Greek and black African parentage. No motive for Tsafendas's action was established. He was declared insane and unfit to stand trial.

George Villiers, 1st duke of Buckingham (1592–1628)

In 1614, George Villiers was introduced to England's King James I. He became the king's favorite and enjoyed a startlingly swift rise to power and fortune. By the time of James's death in 1625, Buckingham was a duke, the head of the government and the navy, and a rich man. He was also much hated for his greed and corruption, his at times flagrant incompetence, and his leanings toward Roman Catholicism.

An unsuccessful army officer, John Felton, shared the general loathing of Buckingham and also had personal motives for resentment—the duke had brusquely turned down his demands for promotion. On August 23, 1628, Felton mingled with petitioners at Buckingham's lodgings in Portsmouth, on England's south coast, and seized the opportunity to stab the duke to death. The assassin was imprisoned in the Tower of London and was hanged on November 28.

Albrecht von Wallenstein (1583–1634)

Austrian general Wallenstein, Duke of Friedland and Mecklenburg, was the foremost military commander on the side of the Catholic Holy Roman Emperor during the early phases of the Thirty Years' War (1618–48). By 1634, however, Wallenstein had fallen from favor and was accused of treason by Emperor Ferdinand II.

On February 25, at the town of Eger, Hungary, he was killed by Wild Geese—Irish mercenary soldiers—who were among his followers. The fatal blow was struck by Captain Devereux. Although no order for the assassination had apparently been given, the assassins received a handsome reward from the emperor.

King William II (*c.* 1056–1100)

The second surviving son of William the Conqueror, William "Rufus" became king of England on his father's death in 1087. He held on to the throne despite a rebellion in favor of his elder brother, Robert, duke of Normandy. A huntsman, William was chasing deer in the New Forest on August 2, 1100, when he was killed by an arrow, apparently fired by a knight named Walter Tirel. William's death may have been accidental, but it is widely believed that he was deliberately assassinated on the orders of his younger brother Henry, who was crowned king—in unseemly haste—only three days later.

William I, the Silent (1533–84)

William of Nassau, Prince of Orange—known as "the Silent"—was the military and diplomatic leader of the Protestant side in the Dutch Revolt, helping the United Provinces (now the Netherlands) to win independence from Catholic Spain. Spanish King Philip II offered a reward to anyone who would kill William.

On July 10, 1584, Balthazar Gerards, a French Catholic, gained access to William's house in Delft and shot him. The assassin was tortured, then publicly executed—he was disembowelled, dismembered, and decapitated. His family was rewarded by the Spanish king.

Sheikh Ahmed Yassin (1936–2004)

Like many thousands of Palestinian Arabs, Islamic fundamentalist leader Sheikh Yassin became a refugee when the state of Israel was created in 1948. At around the same time, while still a child, he suffered an injury to his spine that left him partially paralyzed for life.

In 1988, Sheikh Yassin founded Hamas ("Zeal"), a terrorist movement dedicated to the destruction of the state of Israel. In 1989, he was arrested by the Israelis and sentenced to life imprisonment but was released in a prisoner swap in 1997. By then, half blind as well as paralyzed, he continued to act as an inspiration to Hamas suicide bombers attacking Israel.

On March 22, 2004, as he left morning prayers at his local mosque in Gaza in his wheelchair, Sheikh Yassin was targeted by missiles fired from an Israeli helicopter. The attack, personally ordered by Israeli Prime Minister Ariel Sharon, also killed seven other people, including two of Sheikh Yassin's sons.

Rehavam Zeevi (1926–2001)

A former military man, Rehavam Zeevi was a prominent, if controversial, Israeli politician. He was known for his extreme views regarding the conflict between Israel and the Palestinian Arabs. His Moledet (Homeland) party advocated the removal of more than 3 million Arabs from the West Bank and Gaza.

As minister of tourism in 2001, Zeevi supported the policy of assassinating leaders of militant Palestinian organizations. On August 27, 2001, Mustafa Ali Zibri, leader of the Popular Front for the Liberation of Palestine (PFLP), was killed when his office in the West Bank town of Ramallah was destroyed by missiles fired from an Israeli aircraft. The PFLP vowed revenge.

On October 17, Zeevi was staying at a hotel in east Jerusalem. He had just resigned from the Sharon government on the grounds that it was not taking a tough enough stance toward the Arabs. As Zeevi returned to his room after breakfast, he was shot in the head and neck by PFLP gunmen at close range. He was taken to hospital but declared dead on arrival.

Index

Note: Page references in *italic* indicate a photograph or illustration.

A

Abdullah bin Hussein, King, 184
assassin: Usho, Mustapha Shukri, 184
African National Congress (ANC), 139, 150, 151
Alcibiades, 184
Alexander I of Russia, Czar, 39, 51
Alexander I of Yugoslavia, King, 184
assassin: Gheorghief, Vlada, 184
Alexander II, Czar 59, 62–63, *62, 63*
assassins: Grinevitsky, Ignatai, 63; Karakosov, Dmitri, 62; Khalturin, Stephen, 62; Kibalchich, N.I, 63; Mikhailov, Alexander, 63; Perovskaya, Sophia, 62, 63; Rysakov, Nikolai, 63; Solovev, Alexander, 62; Zhelyabov, Andrei, 62, 63
People's Will, The, 62–63
Alexander III, Czar, 63
Alexander III (the Great), 38, 41, *41*. *See also* Philip II of Macedon
Alexander VI, Pope, 184
Alexander of Serbia, King, 184
assassin: Mashin, Colonel, 184
Alexandra, Czarina, 53, 146, 147, 149
Alexis, Czarevich, 53, *53*, 146, 147, 149
Allende, Salvador, 121, 125
Al Qaeda, 113, 186
American Civil War, 14, 16, 18
Grant, General Ulysses S., 16
Lee, General Robert E., 16
anarchy and terrorists, 59
anticapitalists, 59
Antony, Mark, 43, 185
Aquino, Benigno, 184
assassin: Galman, Ronaldo, 184
Arafat, Yasser, 116
Arkan (Zeljko Raznatovic), 129
assassination, definition and derivation of, 10
Assassins, the (Shi'ite Muslim sect), 10, 188

B

Baader-Meinhof gang (Germany), 59, 188
Baath Party (Iraq), 186
Bakunin, Mikhael, 59
Bandaranaike, Solomon, 184
assassin: Thero, Talduwe Somarama, 184
Becket, Thomas, 39, 46–47
Ben-Gurion, Prime Minister David, 105
Bernadotte, Count Folke, 100, 104–5, *104*
as United Nations mediator, 104
assassins: Cohen, Yehoshua, 105; Zeitler, Yehoshua, 105
Lehi, Israeli terrorist group, 104–5
Biko, Stephen, 144, 150–51, *150–51*
assassins: Nieuwoudt, Gideon, 150; Siebert, Daniel, 150; Snyman, Harold, 150
Black Consciousness movement, 150
bin Laden, Osama, 113
Birendra Bikram, King, 184
assassin: Dipendra, Crown Prince, 184
Black Consciousness movement, 150
Black Hand (Serbia), 27
Blanco, Admiral Carrero, 184–85
Bolsheviks. *See* Russia
Bonaparte, Napoléon. *See* Napoléon I
Booth, John Wilkes, 16–21, *18*
as Confederate agent, 17, 18
assassination of Lincoln, 17, *17*
death of, 19
Borgia, Rodrigo. *See* Alexander VI, Pope
Borgias, the, 184
Brady, Hon. James. S., 9, *9*, 178–79, *179*
assailant: Hinckley Jr., John W., 145, 178–79, *179*
Brady Center to Prevent Gun Violence, 9
Burke, Thomas, 185
assassins: Invincibles (Irish Nationalists), 185

C

Caesar, Julius 9, 38, *38*, 42–43, *42, 43*, 61, 185
assassins: Casca, 43; Longinus, Cassius, 42; Brutus, Decimus, 42; Brutus, Marcus, 42–43, 61; Cimber, Tillius, 43
Ides of March, the, 43
Plutarch, 43
Suetonius, 43
Caligula (Emperor Gaius), 44–45
assassins: Chaerea, Cassius, 44; Sabinus, Cornelius, 44
gladiators, 45, *45*
murder of Caesonia and Drusilla, 45
Caracalla, Emperor, 185
assassin: Macrinus, Opilius, 185
Carlos of Portugal, King, 185
Carnot, Sadi, 185
assassin: Caserio, Santo, 185
Castro, Fidel, 33, 121, 157, 174–75, *174–75*
CIA and Mafia, 174–75
Cubela, Rolando, 175
linked killings, 175
secret agents, 175
Catherine the Great of Russia, Empress, 39, 50–51, *51*
Cavendish, Lord Frederick, 185
Central Intelligence Agency (CIA), 33, 35, 77, 95, 97, 121, 124–25, 126–27, 157, 174–75, 189
Conein, Colonel Lucien E., 126–27
Devlin, Lawrence, 125
Dulles, Allen, 124
Fitzgerald, Desmond, 175
Gottlieb, Sidney, 125
Cicero, Marcus Tullius, 185
civil rights, 80–81, 90–91, *91*
Collins, Michael, 68–69, *68, 69*
Irish independence struggle, 68–69
Combat Organization (Russia), 59
Asev, Yevno, 59
Communist bloc assassins, 120
Confederate Secret Service (Canada), 18
Corday, Charlotte, 58, 60–61
Crazy Horse, 185
Crusader knights, 10, 188

D

Dando, Jill, 129, *129*
assassin: George, Barry, 129
Darnley, Lord, 39, 48–49, *48, 49*. *See also* Rizzio, David
Bothwell, Earl of, 48–49
Moray, Earl of, and Protestant lords' assassination plot, 48–49
De Gaulle, Charles, 157, 170–73, *170–71, 172, 173*
Algerian problems, 171–73
assailants: Bastien-Thiry, Colonel Jean, 173; Degueldre, Lt. Roger, 172; Salan, General Raoul, 171–72
bungled attempts, 170, 173
Organisation Armée Secrète (OAS), 172–73
Djindjic, Zoran, 128–29, *128, 129*
suspected assassin: Lukovic, Milorad, 129
Red Berets, 129
Dollfuss, Engelbert, 185
assassin: Planetta, Otto, 185

E

Elizabeth, Empress of Austria, 24, *24*, 59
assassin: Luccheni, Luigi, 24
Elizabeth, Empress of Russia, 50–51
ETA (Basque terrorist group), 185
ethnic conflicts, 101
Evers, Medgar, 81, 86–87, *86, 87*
assassin: de la Beckwith, Byron, 87, *87*

F

Faisal II of Iraq, King, 186
assassin: Qassem, Brigadier Abdul Karim, 186
Faisal of Saudi Arabia, King, 186
assassin: Musad, Prince Faisal, 186
Falcone, Giovanni, 185
Fascist movement (Italy), 186–87
Fawkes, Guy, 183
Federal Bureau of Investigation (FBI), 33–34, 95, 189
Ferdinand, Archduke Franz, 9, 14, 22–27, *22, 23, 25, 27*, 184, 186
assassins: Dimitrijevic, Colonel Dragutin, 27; Cabrinovic, Nedjilko, 24; Princip, Gavrilo, 25–26
Black Hand, 27
Chotek, Sophie, 22–27, *22, 23, 25, 27*
failed assassination attempt, 24
fatal shooting 25–26, *25, 26*
political resentment, 23–24
Potoriek, General, 25–26
World War I, 27
First, Ruth, 139, 151
assassins: Raven, Roger, 151; Williamson, Craig, 139, 151
Ford, President Gerald, 157, 169
assailants: Fromme, Squeaky, 157, 169; Moore, Sara Jane, 169
Fortuyn, Pim, 133, 141
assassin: Graaf, Volkert van der, 141
Franco, General Francisco, 184, 186
Franz Joseph of Austria, Emperor, 22, 24, 145
assassination of Empress Elizabeth, 24, *24*

G

Gandhi, Indira, 101, 114–15, *114, 115*
assassins: Singh, Beant, 115; Singh, Satwant, 115
Golden Temple desecration, 114
Gandhi, Mahatma, 80, 82–85, *82, 84, 85*
assassins: Godse, Nathuram, 84–85, *85;* Savarkar, Vinayak Damodar, 85
conspirators: Apte, Narayan, 84–85, *85;* Karkare, Vishnu, 84
Hindu and Muslim violence, 82–83, *83*
satyagraha, 80
Gandhi, Rajiv, 115, *115*
assassins: Tamil Tigers, 115
Garcia Lorca, Federico, 186
Garfield, James Abram, 132, 134–35, *135*, 156
assassin: Guiteau, Charles, 132, 135, *135*
Gettysburg Address, 14
Goebbels, Joseph, 167, 188
Gorbachev, Mikhail, 181
Grey Wolves (Islamic terrorist organization), 180

H

Hamas (Israeli extremist movement), 188, 189
Hani, Chris, 186
assassins: Derby-Lewis, Clive, 186; Walus, Janusz, 186
Hapsburgs, the, 22–27, 145
Henri IV, King, 101
Henry II, King, 39
Heydrich, Reinhard, 121, 122–23, *122*
assassins: Gabcik, Josef, 123; Kubis, Jan, 123; Valcik, Jan, 123
Hinckley Jr., John W., 9, 145
Hitler, Adolf, 14, 58, *71*, 156, 164–67, *165, 166, 167*, 185
conspirators and assassins: Beck, General Ludwig 164, 167; Elser, George, 167; Haeften, Lt. Werner von, 164, 166–67; Stauffenberg, Colonel Claus Schenk von, 164, 166–67, *167;* Tresckow, Major General Henning von, 167
failed bombing, 167
Gestapo, 167
Munich bombing, 167
Operation Valkyrie, 167
People's Court, 167
Holocaust, the, 14, 165
Hoover, Herbert, 163
Hoover, J. Edgar, 31, 33–34, 95

I

Inukai, Tsuyoshi, 103
assassins: Blood Brotherhood, 103
Irish mercenaries (Wild Geese), 189
Irish nationalist organizations
Fenians, 185, 187
Invincibles, 185
Irish National Liberation Army (INLA), 187
Irish Republican Army (IRA), 68, 101, 110–11, 156, 182, 187
Islamic Jihad, 112–13
Ito, Prince, 102–3, *102, 103*
assassin: Joong-Gun, An, 103
Korean nationalist resistance, 102–3

J

Jackson, Reverend Jesse, *93*, 95
Japanese prime ministers as victims, 103
Jaurès, Jean, 186
assassin: Villain, Raoul, 186
Jewish deportations, 188

John Paul II, Pope, 120, 156, 180–81, *180–81*
assassin: Ali Agca, Mehmet, 180–81, *181*
conspiracy theory, 180–81
extreme motives, 180
third prophecy of Fatima, 181
Johnson, Lyndon B., 15, 32, *32*, 33, 175
Julius Caesar. *See* Caesar, Julius

K

Kabila, Laurent-Désiré, 186
assassins: Kapend, Eddy, 186; Kasereka, Rashidi, 186
Kennedy, Jacqueline, *13*, 15, 28–30, *28, 31*, 32, *32, 34*, 35
Kennedy, John F., 9, *9*, 11, *13*, 15, 28–35, *28, 29, 31*, 94, 120, 121, 144, 175. *See also* Oswald, Lee Harvey
Connally, Governor and Mrs., 28, 30, 34
conspiracy theories, 34–35
Dallas motorcade, 28–30
fatal shots, 30
House Select Committee, 34–35
hunt for killer, 32, *33*
individual reactions, 31
Ruby, Jack, 32, *33*, 35
Warren Commission, 32–34
Kennedy, Robert F., 15, 34, 94, 106–9, *107, 108, 109*, 121, 132
assassin: Sirhan, Sirhan, 108–9, *109*, 132, 133
Californian victory, 106, *108*
investigation, 108
rumors and conspiracy theories, 109
the Kennedy curse, 109
King Jr., Martin Luther, 9, 15, 31, 34, 80–81, 90–95, *90, 91, 93, 94, 95*, 106, 121, 144
assassin: Ray, James Earl, 94–95, *94, 95*
attempted murder, 92
conspiracy theories, 95
Memphis visit, 90–91
response to assassination, 93, Kennedy, Robert F. 94
search for killer, 93–94
Kirov, Sergei, 120
assassin: Nikolaev, Leonid, 120
Kristallnacht, 188
Kurdish Workers' Party, 139

L

Laporte, Pierre, 186
Chenier cell, Front de Libération du Québec, 186
Lehi, Israeli terrorist group 104–5
Lenin, Vladimir Ilyich, 59, 63, *73*, 147, 160–61, *160, 161*
assassin: Kaplan, Fanya, 59, 161, *161*
Lennon, John, 9, *142*, 145, 148, 152–53, *152, 153*, 156
assassin: Chapman, Mark David, 152–53, *153*
Lidice, destruction of, 123, *123*
Lincoln, Abraham, 11, 14–15, *14*, 16–21, *17, 18, 19, 20*. *See also* Booth, John Wilkes
arrest of assassins, 18–19, *19*
conspiracy theory, 17, 20–21
conspirators, sentencing and execution of, 19–20, *19*
Ford's Theatre, 16, *16*, 17
Stanton, Edwin M., 17, 18
Stanton theory, the, 21
wounding and death of, 17–18
Lindh, Anna, *132*, 133, 140–41, *140, 141*, 145
assassin: Mijailovic, Mijailo, 140–41
Lodge, Henry Cabot, 126, 127
Lorca, Federico Garcia. *See* Garcia Lorca, Federico
Long, Huey, 133, 136–37, *136, 137*
assassin: Weiss, Dr. Carl, 133, 137, *137*
Share Our Wealth Society, 136
Luiz Felipe of Portugal, Crown Prince, 185
Lumumba, Patrice, 121, 124–25, *124, 125*, 144

M

Mafia, 33–34, 35, 163, 174–75
and CIA, 174–75
Giancana, Sam, 35, 175
Marcello, Carlos, 35
Nitti, Frank, 163
Roselli, Johnny, 174–75
Sicilian, 185
Trafficante, Santos, 175
Malcolm X, 31, 81, 88–89, *88, 89*
assassins: Butler, Norman, 89; Hayer, Talmadge, 88–89, 89; Johnson, Thomas, 89
conspiracy theory, 89
Nation of Islam, 89
Mandela, Nelson, 150, 186, 189
Marat, Jean-Paul, 58, 60–61, *60, 61*
assassin: Corday, Charlotte, 60–61, *61*
Jacobins and Girondins, 60–61
Markov, Georgi, 186
Mary, Queen of Scots, 39, 48–49, *48, 49*
Massoud, Ahmed Shah, 186
assassins: Al Qaeda, 186
Masaryk, Jan, 120
Matteotti, Giacomo, 186–87
Maximilian of Mexico, Emperor, 144, 145
McGee, Thomas D'Arcy, 187
assassin: Whalen, Patrick James, 187
Irish Republican Fenians, 187
McKinley, William, 11, 59, 64–65, *64, 65*, 156
assassin: Czolgosz, Leon, 11, 64–65, *65*
McWhirter, Ross, 187
assassins: Irish Republican Army, 187
Mendes, Chico, 187
assassins: Alves da Silva, Darli, 187; Alves, Darcy, 187
Mexican leaders as victims, 67
Carrenza, Venustiano, 67
Madero, Francisco 67
Milk, Harvey, 187
assassin: White, Danny, 187
Milosevic, Slobodan, 120, 128–29
Moro, Aldo, 59, 76–77, *76, 77*
assassin: Moretti, Mario, 77
conspiracy rumors, 77
execution, 77, *77*
kidnapping, 76–77
Red Brigades, *76, 77*
Moscone, George, 187
Mountbatten, Lord Louis, 81, 101, 110–11, *110, 111*
assassins: McGirl, Francis, 111; McMahon, Tommy, 111
family members, 110–11
IRA retaliation, 110
Moyne, Lord, 100, 105
assassins: Beit-Tzuri, Eliyahu, 105; Hakim, Eliyahu, 105
Mussolini, Benito, *166*, 167, 186–87

N

Nadir Shah (King Nadir), 187
Napoléon I,173, *173*
assailants: Carbon, François, 173; Limoelan, Joseph, 173;
Narthou, Louis, 184
Nasser, Gamal Abdul, 112, 113
Nation of Islam, 89
Nazi party/regime, 70, 188
Austrian, 185
Neave, Airey, 187
Nehru, Jawaharlal, 82
Ngo Dinh Diem, 121, 126–27, *127*
CIA involvement, 126–27
Kennedy and Diem, 127
Ngo Dinh Nhu, 126–27
Nicholas II, Czar of Russia, 53, 144, 146–49, *146*, 188. *See also* Rasputin *and* Romanovs, the
Night of the Long Knives, 71
Nixon, Richard, 15, 127

O

Obregón, Álvaro (Mexico), 67
assassin: de León Toral, José, 67
Okhrana (Russia), 59
opposition, attackers of 58–59
Organisation Armée Secrète (OAS), 172
Oswald, Lee Harvey, 32–35, *33, 35*, 120, 133, 175
assassination weapon, *35*
links with Russia, 33
motives, 33
murder of Tippet, J. D., 32
shooting by Ruby, Jack, 32, *33*, 35
Ottoman Empire, Turkish, 39
Mustafa, Grand Vizier Kara, 39

P

Palme, Olaf, 133, 138–39, *138, 139*
assassin: Pettersson, Gustav Christer, 133
South African angle, 139
suspects, 139
Park Chung Hee, General, 187
assassin: Kim Jae Kyu, 187
Paul I, Czar of Russia, 51
assassins: Pahlen, Count Peter von, Zubov, Count Platon, 51
Perceval, Spencer, 133
assassin: Bellingham, John, 133
Peter III, Czar of Russia, 39, 50–51, *50*. *See also* Romanovs, the
assassins: Orlov, Count Alexei, 51; Orlov, Count Grigorii, 51
foreign policy, 51
Philip II of Macedon, 38, 40–41, *40*
Aristotle's account, 41
assassin: Pausanias, 41
Pinochet, General, 125
Pompey, General, 42–43, *43*

Q

Al Qaeda, 113, 186

R

Rabin, Yitzhak, 101, 116–17, *116, 117*
assassins: Amir, Yigal, 116–17, *117;* Raviv, Avishal, 117
compromise with Palestinians, 116
conspiracy theory, 117
peace process rally, 116–17
Rahman, Sheikh Mujibur, 187
al-Rantissi, Abed el-Aziz, 188
Rapallo Treaty, 188
Rasputin, 39, 52–55, *52, 54*, 148
assassins: Lazovert, Dr. Stanislaus, 55; Mikhailovich, Grand Duke Nikolai, 55; Pavlovich, Count Dmitri, 53, 55; Purishkevich, Vladimir, 55; Yusupov, Prince Felix, 53, 55, *55;*
Czarina, power over, 53
favoritism and political power, 53
murder of, 53, 55
prophecy, 148
Spala miracle, 53
Rath, Ernst vom, 188
assassin: Grynszpan, Herschel, 188
Rathenau, Walter, 188
Raymond II, Count of Tripoli, 188
Reagan, Ronald, 9, 145, 178–79, *178–79*
assailant: Hinckley Jr., John W., 145, 178–79, *179*
Red Berets (Serbia), 129
Lukovic, Milorad, 129
Red Brigades (Italy), 59, *76*, 77
religious conflicts, 101
Rizzio, David, 39, 49, *49*
Darnley's jealousy, 49, *49*
Protestant murder plot, 49
Röhm, Ernst, 58–59, 70–71, *70*
creation of SA (Stormtroopers), 70–71
Munich SA demonstration, 71
Night of the Long Knives, 71
Roman emperors, assassinations of 38–39
Romanovs, the, 144, *144*, 146–49, *146, 147, 148, 149*
alleged survivors, 149
assassin: Yurovsky, Yakov, 147–49
Botkin, Dr., 147, 148
final burial, 149
and Rasputin, 52–53, 55, 148
saints and martyrs, 149
Romero, Archbishop, 81, 96–97, *96, 97*
investigation, 97
massacre at funeral, 97
motive for murder, 96–97
suspected assassins: D'Aubisson, Major Roberto; 97; Linares, Oscar Perez, 97
Roosevelt, Franklin D., 156, 162–63, *162, 163*
assailants: Cermak, Anton, 163; Zangara, Giuseppe 163, *163*
Roosevelt, Theodore, 163
assailant: Schrank, John 163
Rush to Judgment, 34
Russia, 188. *See also* Rasputin *and* Romanovs, the
1917 Bolshevik Revolution, 14, 53, 58, 59, 146–47
Bolsheviks, 59, 144, 147–48
Cheka (Bolshevik Secret Police), 160–61
Combat Organization, 59
Communist rulers, 39
czarist regime, 39
NKVD, 120

OGPU, 75
Okhrana, the, 59
The People's Will *(Narodnya Volya),* 59, 62–63
Red Army, 58, *58*
Socialist Revolutionary (SR) Party, 59, 160–61
Soviet KGB, 33
Soviet Secret Service, 120
Soviet Union, 32, 33

S

Al-Sadat, Anwar, 112–13, *113*
assassins: Faraj, Abdel Salem, 113; Faraj, Sheikh Omar Abdel, 113; Islambouli, Lt. Khaled Ahmed, 112
Sandino, Augusto, 188
assassin: Somoza Garcia, Anastasio, 188
Sarajevo, 14, 23–26, *23,* 27
Schleyer, Hanns-Martin, 188
Serbia, 23, 25, 27
Sergei, Grand Duke, 59
assassin: Combat Organization, 59
Shi'ite Muslim(s), 10, 187
Hasan as-Sabah, Grand Master, 10
Shin Bet (Israeli Secret Service), 117
Sikh separatists, 114–15
Somoza Garcia, Anastasio, 188
assassin: Lopez Perez, Rigoberto, 188
Song Jiaoren, 188
assassin: General Yuan Shikai, 188
Sun Yat-Sen, 188
South African Secret Police, 139
de Kock, Euguene, 139
Special Operations Executive, British (SOE), 120–21, 122
Stalin, Josef, 58, 72–73, *73,* 156
Stern Gang (*Lehi,* Israeli terrorist group), 104–5
Stolypin, Piotr, 188
assassin: Bogrov, D.G., 188
Strategic Services, American Office of (OSS), 120–21
Sunni Muslim(s), 10, 187

T

Tamil Tigers 115
terrorism, 100–1, 104–5
Thatcher, Margaret, 156, 182–83, 187
assailant: Magee, Patrick, 182
Irish Republican Army, 182
Trotsky, Leon, 58, 59, 72–75, *72–73, 75,* 147
assassins: Mornard, Jacson, 74–75; Siqueiros, David Alfaro, 74
in Mexico, 72–73
machine-gun attack, 73–74
Sheldon Harte, Bob, 73, 74
Trotsky, Natalia, 73–74
Trujillo, Rafael, 188–89
Truman, Harry S, 157, 168–69, *169*
assailants: Collazo, Oscar, 168–69, *169;* Torresola, Griselio, 168–69
Coffelt, Private Leslie, 169
Puerto Rican Nationalists, 168
Truth and Reconciliation Commission (TRC), 151

U

Umberto of Italy, King, 59, 65, *65*
assassin: Bresci, Gaetano, 65

V

Versace, Gianni, 189
assassin: Cunanan, Andrew, 189
Versailles, Treaty of, 188
Verwoerd, Hendrik, 189
assassin: Tsafendas, Demetrio, 189
Victoria, Queen, 158–59, *158, 159*
assailants: Maclean, Roderick, 158–59; Oxford, Edward 159;
Vietnam War, 15
Villiers, George, 1st duke of Buckingham, 189
assassin: Felton, John, 189

W

Wallace, George, 156, 176–77, *176, 177*
assassin: Bremer, Arthur, 177, *177*
conspiracy theory, 177
Wallenstein, Albrecht von, 189
assassin: Devereux, Captain, 189
Wild Geese Irish mercenaries, 189
Warhol, Andy, 157, *157*
assailant: Valerie Solanas, 157
William II, King, 189
assassin: Tyrell, Walter, 189
William the Silent, 189
assassins: Gerards, Balthazar, 189; Philip II, King of Spain, 189
Wilson, Sir Henry, 69, *69*
assassins: Dunne, Reggie, 69; O'Sullivan, Joseph, 69
World War I, 14, 27, 188
World War II, 14, 104, 105, 156

Y

Yassin, Sheikh Ahmad, 188, 189
Sharon, Prime Minister Ariel, 189

Z

Zapata, Emiliano, 58, 66–67, *66, 67*
as national figure, 66–67
assassins:
Gonzalez, General Pablo, 67
Guajardo, Colonel Jesus, 67
Plan of Ayala, 66–67
trapped, 67
Zapatistas (Mexico), 66–67
Zeevi, Rehavam, 189
assassins: Popular Front for the Liberation of Palestine (PFLP), 189
Zibri, Mustafa Ali, 189

Picture credits

2–3 Corbis. Pages 8–9 Rex Features/Sipa Press, L; Brady Campaign to Prevent Gun Violence. 12 Corbis/Ron Watts. 14–15 Corbis/Bettmann. 16–17 Corbis. 17 National Parks Service. 18–19 Corbis, TL; Corbis/Bettmann, B. 20 Corbis/Bettmann. 21 Corbis. 22–23 Corbis/Bettmann. 23 Corbis/Hulton-Deutsch Collection. 24 Bridgeman Art Library/Kunsthistorisches Museum, Vienna. 24–25 Corbis/Bettmann. 25 Bridgeman Art Library/Archives Charmet. 26 Corbis/Bettmann. 27 Corbis/Hulton-Deutsch Collection, TR; Corbis, B. 28 Corbis/Brooks Kraft. 28–29 Corbis. 30 Topham/Picturepoint. 30–31 Corbis/Bettmann. 30–31 John Frost Newspapers, M. 32–34 Corbis. 35 Corbis/Sygma. 36–37 Bridgeman Art Library/Guildhall Art Gallery/Corporation of London. 38 Bridgeman Art Library/Vatican Museums and Galleries. 40 akg-images/Bibliothèque Nationale, Paris. 41 Corbis/Archivo Iconografico, S.A. 42–43 Bridgeman Art Library/Museo e Gallerie Nazionale di Capodimonte, Naples. 43 Bridgeman Art Library/Giraudon, T; Corbis/Archivo Iconografico, S.A., B. 44 Corbis/Archivo Iconografico, S.A. 45 Corbis/Alinari Archives. 46 Corbis/Hulton-Deutsch Collection. 47 Corbis/Stapleton Collection. 48–49 Corbis/Bettmann. 49 Bridgeman Art Library/Private Collection, T; Bridgeman Art Library/Victoria & Albert Museum, London, B. 50–51 Corbis/Archivo Iconografico, S.A. 52 akg-images. 53 Corbis/Hulton-Deutsch Collection. 54 Corbis/Hulton-Deutsch Collection. 55 Bridgeman Art Library/State Russian Museum, St Petersburg. 56–57 Corbis/Hulton-Deutsch Collection. 58 Art Archive/Musée des Deux Guerres Mondiales, Paris/Dagli Orti. 60 Bridgeman Art Library/Musée de la Ville de Paris/Musée Carnavalet/Giraudon. 61 Bridgeman Art Library/Giraudon/Musée Bonnat, Bayonne, L; Bridgeman Art Library/Musées Royaux des Beaux-Arts de Belgique, Brussels, T. 62 Corbis, T; Corbis/Hulton-Deutsch Collection, B. 62–63 Corbis/Photo Collection Alexander Alland, Sr. 64 Corbis (background); Corbis/Bettmann, BL. 65 Corbis, TL; Corbis/Bettmann, TR, BR. 66–67 Corbis/Bettmann. 68 Corbis/Hulton-Deutsch Collection. 69 Hulton Getty, T; Corbis, B. 70 Corbis/Austrian Archives. 71 Bridgeman Art Library/Archives Charmet. 72–73 Bridgeman Art Library/Illustrated London News Picture Library. 73 Bridgeman Art Library/Collection Kharbine-Tapabor, Paris. 74 Hulton Getty. 75 Corbis/Hulton-Deutsch Collection. 76 Corbis/Bettmann. 77 Corbis/Bettmann. 78–79 Corbis/Hulton Deutsch Collection. 80–81 Corbis. 82 Hulton Getty. 83 Corbis/Hulton-Deutsch Collection, T; Hulton Getty, B. 84 Corbis/Hulton-Deutsch Collection. 85 Corbis/Hulton-Deutsch Collection, T; Corbis/Bettmann, B. 86 Associated Press (background). 87 Associated Press, T; B. 88–89 Corbis/Bettmann. 90 Corbis/Flip Schulke. 91 Corbis/Bettmann. 92 Corbis/Flip Schulke. 93 Associated Press, T; Hulton Getty, B. 94–95 Corbis/Bettmann. 96–97 Corbis/Bettmann. 98–99 Katz Pictures/Gamma/Mohamad Ismail/UPI. 100 Corbis /Araldo de Luca. 102–103 Corbis. 104 Corbis/Hulton-Deutsch Collection. 105 Corbis/Bettmann. 106–107 Corbis/Bettmann. 108–109 Corbis/Bettmann. 110 Corbis/Norman Parkinson Limited/Fiona Cowan. 111 Associated Press. 112 Corbis/Bettmann (background). 113 Associated Press, B; Corbis/Kevin Fleming, M. 114–115 Corbis/Bettmann. 115 Corbis/Hulton-Deutsch Collection, T; Corbis/Peter Turnley, B. 116 Associated Press/Doug Mills, T; Associated Press/Giulio Broglio. 117 Corbis, T; Associated Press, B. 118–119 Hulton Getty/AFP. 122 Corbis. 123 Corbis/Hulton-Deutsch Collection. 124 Corbis/Hulton-Deutsch Collection. 125 Associated Press (background). 127 Associated Press. 128 Corbis/Sygma/Lorenc Ivo. 129 Hulton Getty, T; Corbis, B.130–131 Getty Images/AFP. 132 Associated Press/Swedish Police. 134 Corbis/Bettmann (background). 135 Corbis, T, B. 136 Corbis/Bettmann. 137 Corbis/Bettmann, T; B. 138–139 Corbis/Bettmann. 139 John Frost Newspapers (background); Hulton Getty/AFP, T. 140–141 Corbis. 141 Hulton Getty/AFP, T; B. 142–143 Corbis/Sygma/Goldberg Diego. 144 Katz Pictures/Gamma/Shone. 146 Corbis/Sygma. 147 Corbis. 148 akg-images, T; Corbis/Sygma/AgenceNo 7, B. 149 Corbis/RPG/V.Velengurin. 150–151 Corbis/Sygma/Selwyn Tait. 152 Associated Press. 153 Rex Features (background); Associated Press, T; B. 152–153 Corbis/Bettmann (background). 154–155 Corbis/Bettmann. 156 Associated Press. 157 Corbis/Robert Lewis. 158 Corbis/Bettmann. 159 Photography John Meek. 160–161 Hulton Getty. 161 Corbis/Bettmann. 162–163 Corbis/Bettmann; John Frost Newspapers (background). 163 Corbis/Bettmann. 165 Hulton Getty. 166 Corbis/Hulton-Deutsch Collection. 167 Hulton Getty. 168 Corbis. 169 Corbis/Bettmann, T; B. 170–171 Corbis/KIPA. 171 Corbis/Bettmann. 172 Corbis/Bettmann. 173 Corbis/Archivo Iconografico, S.A., T; HarperCollins/Harvill from *De Gaulle the Ruler* by Jean Lacoutre/Photography John Meek, B. 174–175 Associated Press/Cristobal Herrera; Associated Press/Arnulfo Franco (background). 176 Corbis/Bettmann. 177 Corbis/Bettmann, T; B. 178 Corbis/Bettmann. 179 Corbis/Bettmann, T; Associated Press, R. 180 Corbis/Bettmann. 180–181 Katz Pictures/Gamma. 182 Corbis/Bettmann. 182–183 Corbis/Bettmann. 183 Associated Press/Peter Morrison.